Preventing Stress in Organizations

D1227645

Preventing Stress in Organizations

How to Develop Positive Managers

Emma Donaldson-Feilder,
Joanna Yarker and Rachel Lewis

WILEY-BLACKWELL

A John Wiley & Sons, Ltd., Publication

This edition first published 2011
©2011 John Wiley & Sons Ltd.

Wiley-Blackwell is an imprint of John Wiley & Sons, formed by the merger of Wiley's global
Scientific, Technical, and Medical business with Blackwell Publishing.

Registered Office
John Wiley & Sons Ltd, The Atrium, Southern Gate, Chichester, West Sussex,
PO19 8SQ, UK

Editorial Offices
The Atrium, Southern Gate, Chichester, West Sussex, PO19 8SQ, UK
9600 Garsington Road, Oxford, OX4 2DQ, UK
350 Main Street, Malden, MA 02148-5020, USA

For details of our global editorial offices, for customer services, and for information about how
to apply for permission to reuse the copyright material in this book please see our website at
www.wiley.com/wiley-blackwell.

The right of Emma Donaldson-Feilder, Joanna Yarker and Rachel Lewis to be identified as the
author of this work has been asserted in accordance with the UK Copyright, Designs and
Patents Act 1988.

All rights reserved. No part of this publication may be reproduced, stored in a retrieval system,
or transmitted, in any form or by any means, electronic, mechanical, photocopying, recording
or otherwise, except as permitted by the UK Copyright, Designs and Patents
Act 1988, without the prior permission of the publisher.

Wiley also publishes its books in a variety of electronic formats. Some content that appears in
print may not be available in electronic books.

Designations used by companies to distinguish their products are often claimed as
trademarks. All brand names and product names used in this book are trade names, service
marks, trademarks or registered trademarks of their respective owners. The publisher is not
associated with any product or vendor mentioned in this book. This publication is designed to
provide accurate and authoritative information in regard to the subject matter covered. It is
sold on the understanding that the publisher is not engaged in rendering professional services.
If professional advice or other expert assistance is required, the services of a competent
professional should be sought.

Library of Congress Cataloging-in-Publication Data

Donaldson-Feilder, Emma.
  Preventing stress in organizations : how to develop positive managers /
Emma Donaldson-Feilder, Joanna Yarker, and Rachel Lewis.
      p. cm.
  Includes bibliographical references and index.
  ISBN 978-0-470-66552-7 (cloth) – ISBN 978-0-470-66553-4 (pbk.)
  1. Job stress. 2. Job stress–Prevention. 3. Executive ability. 4. Management.
I. Yarker, Joanna. II. Lewis, Rachel, 1973- III. Title.
  HF5548.85.D66 2011
  658.4'095–dc22

                                                                            2010036011

A catalogue record for this book is available from the British Library.

Set in 10/12pt and Helvetica by Thomson Digital, Noida, India
Printed in Singapore by Ho Printing Singapore Pte Ltd

1   2011

Contents

1

Introduction

Work-related stress is a major challenge facing organizations. While there are numerous books focusing on work stress, few consider the vital role line managers take in preventing, managing and reducing stress at work. This book aims to be a resource to support line managers in the challenging task of managing stress in others. Moreover, our approach focuses on *Positive Manager Behaviour* and through this we aim to enhance the portfolio of behaviours managers can use to manage work-related stress and develop a positive team and working environment.

This book draws from 5 years worth of research conducted by the authors and many more years worth of consultancy working with organizations, line managers and employees in the area of stress, health and performance. Here, we have distilled the relevant theory and research literature and combined it with practical learning and case studies developed from our work.

Chapters 1 to 4 introduce work-related stress, how stress can be managed and the line manager's role in effective stress management. These initial chapters aim to provide those new to the area with a backdrop to the chapters that follow, while also providing some quick-view material for those already familiar with the area of work-related stress. This information can be used when developing training or awareness materials for use in your organization.

Preventing Stress in Organizations: How to Develop Positive Managers,
Emma Donaldson-Feilder, Joanna Yarker and Rachel Lewis.
© 2011 John Wiley & Sons, Ltd. Published 2011 by John Wiley & Sons, Ltd.

Chapters 5 to 8 introduce the *Positive Manager Behaviours* and provide detailed case studies, exercises and discussion about those behaviours we have identified as core to managing stress and promoting a positive workplace.

Chapters 9 to 12 consider the barriers and facilitators to showing positive manager behaviours and provide suggestions and illustrative case studies to show how these behaviours can be put into practice and embedded within the organization.

What is Stress?

The term 'stress' has been widely debated and there have been many different definitions of stress over the years. With over a hundred years worth of research to draw from, there is now reasonable consensus that stress can be defined as 'the adverse reaction people have to excessive pressures or other types of demands placed upon them'. It is, therefore, the reaction people have when the pressures or demands placed upon them are not matched by their ability to cope, or by any other available resource.

Stress is..

the adverse reaction people have to excessive pressures or other types of demand.

a situation where demands on a person exceed that person's resources or ability to cope.
(Health and Safety Executive, 2004)

One of the things that makes stress such a tricky business is that we all experience stress differently. Stress can be caused by different factors (as we all experience different demands and have different resources available to us to cope with these demands) and it can give rise to a range of different symptoms that can present themselves in isolation or combination.

Although stress is experienced in lots of different ways, there are a number of recognized common symptoms, particularly in reaction to severe stress. These symptoms can include impaired concentration, exhaustion, insomnia, changeable moods, changes in health-related behaviours such as increased alcohol or drug taking behaviours, among many others. The range of symptoms of work-related stress is considered further in a discussion of the individual costs of stress (see Chapter 2). These symptoms often present themselves in combination making stress difficult to diagnose. Rather, in cases of work-related stress the diagnosis is often vague and noted as exhaustion, or non-specific anxiety or depression. Stress itself is not a clinical diagnosis.

What Stress is Not: Common Misperceptions

Stress is often misunderstood. All too often in the workplace we hear statements that are misinformed. These comments, most likely to come from people who have been lucky enough not to have experienced stress, do little to help combat stress and can on occasion do harm to others, particularly those who are experiencing stress. Here, we unpick some of the common misperceptions of stress:

- '*A little bit of stress is good for you*': It is important to make a distinction between stress and pressure. Pressure can be good. We are all aware of times we have been under pressure and most people will say that this motivates them and helps them to perform at their best. But, when the pressure becomes unmanageable and the individual no longer has the resources available to cope with the demands, the pressure becomes stress. Stress is never a good thing.
- '*Stress wasn't a problem in my day...*': For many of its critics 'stress' does not exist. Research would suggest otherwise. However, when considering whether stress is real or not, or poses a real problem for people and for business, it is useful to take a historical view. Only as far back as 50 years ago, the challenges that many people faced at work were very different. A greater majority were engaged in manufacturing work, where concerns for physical health were at the forefront of ones mind – 'Is the machinery I am working with safe?', 'Am I going to slip, trip, fall etc?'. Since the shift into the service sector, the pressures are not necessarily greater but they are different. In parallel to this industry shift, there has been a shift in the demographic profile of our workforce. More people are juggling work with caring responsibilities for children and elderly relatives; more women are in employment; more people work over the weekend; two-income families and sole parents face challenges in balancing home and work responsibilities. This increase in the psychological demands placed on individuals has lead to an increase in the psychological problems experienced by people, and therefore an increase in the prevalence of stress.
- '*People who suffer from stress are weak or lazy...*': Another common misconception is that people who suffer from stress are weak as they

are unable to cope with the demands of the job, or lazy and just use stress as an opt-out. While there may be a small minority of cases where stress is used erroneously, for those who experience genuine stress this is a truly unpleasant and sometimes debilitating experience characterized by a range of physical and psychological symptoms. Therefore suggesting that stress is an easy opt-out is misconceived.

- *'He was signed off with stress...'*: Stress is not a clinical condition however there has been a history of General Practitioners citing stress on certificates to avoid stigma on the employees' behalf. Diagnoses such as anxiety, depression or other mental health problems may be signs of stress and the GP may cite the causes of this anxiety or depression as stress or work-related.

Common Causes of Stress

There is a vast body of research that has identified the common causes of stress at work. There is now reasonable consensus that the following aspects of work give rise to, or are associated with, the experience of stress. The most common causes of stress include:

- *Demands*: aspects of work to which people have to respond, such as workload, work patterns and the work environment;
- *Control*: the extent to which people have a say in the way they do their work;
- *Support*: the encouragement, sponsorship, and resources provided by the organization, line management and colleagues;
- *Relationships*: promoting positive working to avoid conflict and dealing with unacceptable behaviour such as bullying;
- *Role*: the extent to which individuals understand their role within the organization, and the degree to which roles are conflicting;
- *Change*: the extent to which organizational change (large or small) is effectively managed and communicated within the organization;
- *Career development*: the extent to which the organization provides opportunities for promotion, skills development and job security; and
- *Work–home interface*: the extent to which individuals are able to balance the demands of work and home, particularly in the context of dependent care and dual-earning families

Research in the last 20 years has identified the aspects of work that can give rise to, or are associated with, the experience of stress. Links have been made between these aspects of work, and various unfavourable employee and organizational outcomes, such as mental and physical ill-health, job dissatisfaction, turnover and sickness absence.

Work-Related Stress and the Line Manager

Throughout this book we examine the line manager's role in the management of stress and the promotion of a positive work environment. Research has consistently identified the line manager as playing a pivotal role in the stress equation. The relevant research is condensed in this section to provide an overview of the important role line managers take in determining how an organization manages stress.

The line manager can influence employee stress by:

- causing (or preventing) stress by the way they behave towards their staff;
- influencing the impact of the work environment (demands, control etc) on their staff;
- identifying, monitoring and working to reduce work-related stress through the uptake of risk assessments; and
- supporting the design and implementation of stress management solutions.

Line manager as manager of the causes of stress

The line manager is cited by employees as one of the most significant sources of stress (Hogan, Curphy and Hogan, 1994; Tepper, 2000). To understand why this might be the case, researchers have looked to the dominant academic theories of leadership for answers. Three dominant theories of leadership have offered some explanation:

Task- and relationship-focused behaviour
This theory of leadership makes a distinction between *task-focused behaviour* where managers focus on achieving goals, planning, assigning tasks, communicating information and monitoring performance; and *relationship-focused behaviour* where managers focus on supporting employees, showing respect for others' ideas, mentoring, managing conflict and team-building.

Overall, research based on task- and relationship-focused theories suggest that high levels of task-focused behaviour can have a detrimental impact on employee well-being, but that its effect can be minimized where line managers also demonstrate a range of relationship-focused behaviours.

Transactional and transformational leadership behaviour
This theory of leadership is possibly the most endorsed leadership framework. *Transformational leadership* is characterized by leaders that generate and drive forward a vision, who create opportunities for employee development and set high expectations for performance. *Transactional leadership* is characterized by leaders that develop a straightforward exchange with their employees, whereby expectations for performance are communicated and good performance is rewarded appropriately.

Overall, research shows there is a positive relationship between transformational leadership and job performance, job satisfaction and organizational commitment.

Leader-member exchange (LMX)
This theory of leadership places a focus on the quality of the relationship (or the exchange) between the leader (manager) and the member (employee). Central to this theory is the idea that a leader is likely to develop close or high quality relationships with a proportion of their team. Subsequently, those employees with high quality relationships are more likely to report greater trust, support and liking than those employees who experience lower quality relationships with their manager.

Overall, the research shows that employees reporting better quality LMX also report higher levels of job performance, job satisfaction, and well-being, and lower levels of strain.

Line managers influencing the impact of the work environment (demands, control etc.) on their staff

The line manager has been found to play a significant role in buffering, or exacerbating, the impact of the work environment. The line manager is the person directly responsible for much of the day-to-day communication with the employee, and, therefore, it is not surprising that line manager behaviour can influence the way in which employees perceives their work environment, and subsequently, influence the impact of the work environment on their staff (see Figure 1.1). For example:

- There is a wealth of research that demonstrates the value of social support in reducing employees' stress. While there is some debate over the extent to which line manager support buffers the effect of the wider work environment, it is generally accepted that line manager support plays an important role. Studies have found that job-related social support, followed by non-job related social support can reduce employee stress (Fenalson and Beehr, 1994). Furthermore, employees who perceive their manager to be supportive are likely to report higher job satisfaction, lower turnover and lower levels of depression (Rooney and Gottleib, 2007).

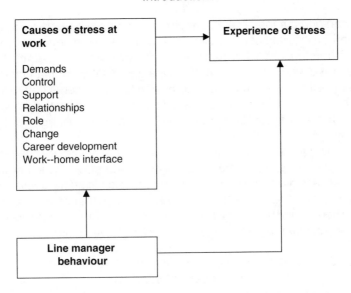

Figure 1.1   Causes of stress and the role of the line manager

- Research has shown that the relationship between transformational leadership and well-being may be both direct and indirect, via its influence on the work environment. One study has shown that transformational leadership influences the way in which employees experience meaningful work, role clarity and opportunities for development. These in turn, where rated positively by employees, lead to increased and maintained levels of well-being over time (Nielsen, Randall, Yarker and Brenner, 2008).
- High quality LMX or manager-employee relationships have been found to buffer the effects of a negative work environment (Harris and Kacmar, 2005; Van Dyne, Jehn and Cummings, 2002).
- Manager behaviour has been found to reduce role ambiguity, a recognized source of work-related stress. For example, O'Driscoll and Beehr (1994) found that when managers were reported to communicate effectively and set goals, their employees experienced less ambiguity and subsequently, lower levels of psychological strain.

Identifying, monitoring and working to reduce work-related stress through the uptake of risk assessments

As the line manager typically has the most direct contact with their staff, it is often their responsibility to monitor the employees' well-being. For example:

- In carrying out their line management responsibilities, managers are often best positioned to notice any changes in employee behaviour and therefore are at the front line to identify signs and signals of stress.
- As part of team meetings and routine appraisals, line managers are well positioned to identify individual and team concerns that relate to aspects of their work environment (for example, the level of workload, the resources available, working hours, how change is being received).
- Increasingly, line managers are also being asked to conduct or champion risk assessments for work-related stress, whether these risk assessments are conducted via discussion or staff surveys. Here, the line manager has a key role in encouraging their team to be open and honest and unless the line manager is on board with the process, it is unlikely that the risk assessment will achieve its aim.

Supporting the design and implementation of stress management solutions

There is a vast body of research that highlights the important role line managers play in achieving organizational change. This research can be applied to the management of work-related stress and the change it requires to reduce and prevent stress. For example:

- Line managers have been found to hold the key to work redesign initiatives, whereby line manager support and engagement is essential to the success of the implementation of change. This has been found to be the case in the redesign of work to reduce work-related stress following risk assessments: line managers have the insight into the nature of the job and therefore inform the new ways of working; they play an intermediatory role between the employees and senior management and therefore their behaviour and skill at communicating vertically within the organization can secure (or compromise) resources required to better manage work-related stress within their team; and finally, the way in which the line manager communicates any resulting changes can have a direct impact on the intervention's effectiveness (Saksvik, Nytro, Dahl-Jorgensen and Mikkelsen, 2002; Thomson, Rick and Neathey, 2004).
- Line managers also play a significant role in managing stress at the individual level. Their behaviour cannot only affect the disclosure of work-related stress by team members, but also the uptake of stress management solutions (e.g., counselling) and subsequently the effectiveness of these approaches. Here line managers can provide opportunities for employees to seek help, and work flexibly to accommodate their needs, while also encouraging others within the team to be supportive.

In sum, there is a significant body of research that demonstrates the pivotal role line managers play in the management of work-related stress. That said, much of the research shows that those behaviours important to managing well-being are also important for managing performance. A key message to line managers, and one that the remainder of this book aims to embed, is that effective stress management does not have to be a separate activity: stress management is a part of normal general management activities.

Summary

This chapter serves as an introduction to work-related stress and provides a back-drop to the following chapters that place a focus on the line-manager's role in managing stress and promoting a positive work environment.

The definitions and theories of work-related stress were introduced, and the causes of work-related stress outlined. It is important that line managers are aware of what stress is, and how it can be caused. As such, managers will then be in a position to identify stress in others and be more aware of the types of issues that cause stress in the workplace.

References

Fenalson, K.J. and Beehr, T.A. (1994). Social support and occupational stress. Effects of talking to others. *Journal of Organizational Behaviour*, 15, 157–175.

Harris, K.J. and Kacmar, K.M. (2005). Easing the strain: The buffer role of supervisors in the perceptions of politics-strain relationship. *Journal of Occupational and Organizational Psychology*, 78, 337–354.

Health and Safety Executive (2004). Managing the causes of work related stress – A step-by-step approach using the Management Standards. Health and Safety Executive. HMSO. Norwich.

Hogan, R., Curphy, G.J. and Hogan, J. (1994). What we know about leadership. *American Psychologist*, 49, 493–504.

Nielsen, K., Randall, R., Yarker, J. and Brenner, S.-O. (2008). The effects of transformational leadership on followers' perceived work characteristics and well-being: A longitudinal study. *Work and Stress*, 22, 16–32.

O'Driscoll, M.P. and Beehr, T.A. (1994). Supervisors' behaviours, role stressors and uncertainty as predictors of personal outcomes for subordinates. *Journal of Organizational Behaviour*, 15, 141–155.

Rooney, J.A. and Gottlieb, B.H. (2007). Development and initial validation of a measure of supportive and unsupportive managerial behaviours. *Journal of Vocational Behaviour*, 71, 186–203.

Saksvik, P.O., Nytro, K., Dahl-Jorgensen, C. and Mikkelsen, A. (2002). A process evaluation of individual and organisational occupational stress and health interventions. *Work and Stress*, 16, 37–57.

Tepper, B.J. (2000). Consequences of abusive supervision. *Academy of Management Journal*, 43, 178–190.

Thomson, L., Rick, J. and Neathey, F. (2003). *Best Practice in Rehabilitating Employees Following Absence Due to Work Related Stress*. Health and Safety Executive, HMSO, Norwich.

Van Dyne, L., Jehn, K.A. and Cummings, A. (2002). Differential effects of strain on two forms of work performance: Individual employee sales and creativity. *Journal of Organizational Behaviour*, 23, 57–74.

2

Why managing stress is important: The business and legal reasons

There is no need to convince some people that managing stress is important – looking after your people makes business sense. However, before putting in place strategies to manage stress at work, it is necessary to convince others that there is a need to manage stress, and importantly that there is need for a budget to help manage stress. This chapter presents the business and legal reasons for managing stress. We have included a number of case studies and simple formulae that can be used to work out the true cost of stress in your organization.

The Business Case

Stress is costly for businesses. Recent estimates suggest that over half a million people are affected by work-related stress at any one time. Stress is thought to account for one-third of all new instances of sickness absence (CBI, ONS), with approximately 13.5 million working days lost to stress, depression and anxiety each year. The UK Health and Safety Executive have estimated that stress costs the UK industry an estimated £9.6 billion every year (HSE, 2006).

Preventing Stress in Organizations: How to Develop Positive Managers,
Emma Donaldson-Feilder, Joanna Yarker and Rachel Lewis.
© 2011 John Wiley & Sons, Ltd. Published 2011 by John Wiley & Sons, Ltd.

European figures suggest that approximately 41 million people in Europe (nearly one in three workers) are affected by stress, costing European member states more than 20 billion Euros every year. (Paoli and Merllie, 2000).

The picture is no better in the United States, with an estimated 297 million working days lost to stress, costing the US economy $150 billion every year (Whatson Wyatt Worldwide, 2001)

The Costs of Work-Related Stress

The cost of work-related stress

- One-third of new absences are stress-related.
- Nearly one in three workers are affected by stress.
- 13.5 million working days lost per year in the UK.
- £9.6 bn per year to UK economy, 20 bn Euros to European economy and $150 billion to the US economy.

These are significant figures but what do they mean for you and your organization? In this section, we outline the many costs to your employees and your organization, provide tools to help you calculate the costs incurred in your organization, and suggest ways in which you can report and monitor the costs of stress within your organization.

The costs of work-related stress

Costs to the individual

- Physical health
- Psychological health
- Health behaviours
- Social and relational health
- Work-related health

Costs to the organization

- Absence
- Presenteeism
- Turnover
- Accidents and injury

Hidden or indirect costs

- PR
- Employee relations disputes
- Insurance premiums
- Salaries for replacement staff/overtime
- Training for replacement staff
- Reduced productivity
- Deterioration in work atmosphere/climate

Distant costs

- Statutory sickness pay
- Incapacity benefits
- NHS and other healthcare costs

The costs to the individual

The impact of stress on an individual can be wide reaching and there are many different responses an individual can have. The individual responses to stress are typically clustered into the following (also see Table 2.1):

- *Physical health*: including increased headaches, migraines, risk of cardiovascular disease, digestive system disorders (e.g., ulcers or irritable bowl syndrome), musculoskeletal pain, exhaustion, hyper tension.
- *Psychological health*: including increased risk for common mental health problems such as anxiety, depression, reduced concentration, forgetfulness, moodiness, loss of sense of humour, tearfulness, reduced self-esteem and confidence.
- *Social and relational health*: including a lowered desire for social interaction, snappiness and irritability, all of which can lead to a decline in relationships with others.
- *Health behaviours*: increased drug taking, alcohol intake, eating disorders, sexual disorders.
- *Working health*: impact on the psychological contract i.e., the relationship between the employee and the employer, feelings of unfair treatment, decreased morale, engagement and commitment.

These individual level responses to stress may cost the individual dearly, but they are also likely to have a knock on effect to the team, colleagues, clients and therefore the organization.

Table 2.1. Cost of work-related stress to the individual

Physical health	Psychological health	Social health	Health behaviours	Working health
Exhaustion	Depression	Isolation	Drug taking	Disinterest
Headaches	Anxiety	Irritability	Alcohol dependency	Motivation
Musculoskeletal pain	Boredom	Superficial relationships	Eating disorders	Psychological contract
Allergies	Memory loss	Conflict at work	Sexual disorders	Morale
Digestive disorders	Impaired concentration	Impaired relationships with friends and family		Creativity
Increased blood pressure				Engagement
Migraines				Commitment
Sleep disturbance				

What should we be doing?

Over the following chapters of this book there are a number of suggestions, exercises and approaches to help you prevent and reduce stress in your workforce. However, the first thing that you can do is identify stress in individuals before it becomes a problem.

- Increase awareness of signs and symptoms of stress within your organization using fact sheets, briefings, or training programmes.
- Put in place processes to monitor signs and symptoms of stress. This could include regular work planning sessions, appraisals, informal chats, team meetings.
- Ensure your managers are aware of what stress is and what it can look like in others.

The costs to the organization

The impact of stress on an organization can be significant and can be measured in many ways including:

1. Absence
2. Presenteeism
3. Turnover
4. Accidents and injury
5. Hidden costs (including negative PR, employee relations disputes, insurance premiums)

1. Absence
Sickness absence is one of the most significant costs of work-related stress, and one of the most tangible to calculate.

- *Sickness absence due to stress*: Employees may be off work as their doctor has signed them off with anxiety or depression, or both. This may be stress-related
- *Sickness absence exacerbated by stress*: Stress has been found to exacerbate a range of chronic illnesses including asthma, allergies, diabetes, menstrual difficulties, migraine, arthritis, and skin disorders among others.
- *Absence as work avoidance*: removing themselves from a difficult situation, for example, an employee being 'ill' every second Wednesday when they know a particular supervisor will be on shift etc.

Recording sickness absence is one of the quickest ways to capture information about the sickness absence patterns of your workforce. However, these costs are often masked by poorly collected or stored records and data, or simply because people don't have time to review all the organizational data simultaneously. Sickness absence management is a challenging task and for a number of reasons many organizations struggle to keep accurate and efficient records. First, many organizations find it difficult to capture detailed information, or where information is held it may be poorly classified – for example, where depression has been reported, it is often difficult to recall whether this is work-related or not. Second, where an organization may have a good absence management system in place, many find that managers and employees do not always follow the correct procedures – for example, line managers may let one-off absences go unrecorded or may fail to forward information to central resources, particularly when they know that another absence for the employee may have ramifications such as a disciplinary hearing. Finally, the stigma attached to mental health problems is well recognized and many employees give alternative reasons for being off work when they are suffering from stress for fear of reprisals – for example, they may say they have a cold or back pain in place of reporting stress. For many smaller organizations the challenges are emphasized as they do not have the resources expendable to manage absence. Help is at hand however and a number of government agencies (e.g., Health and Safety Executive), professional bodies (e.g., Chartered Institute of Personnel Development) and consultancies now offer a wealth of advice on absence management.

2. Presenteeism

One of the less obvious costs of work-related stress is presenteeism. The Sainsbury Centre for Mental Health suggest that when considering the cost of stress to business, absence figures only give half of the picture. It is increasingly recognized that many people suffering from ill-health (not just stress, but many other illnesses) come in to work when they are feeling unwell as they are worried about taking too many days off sick. Research has shown that people come into work despite feeling unwell for a number of reasons. It may be that they are concerned about the losses to their salary, letting the team down, not wanting to miss out on future career opportunities and so on. Coming into work when you are not 100 per cent can have a number of implications. When people are feeling unwell, it is often the case that they have lower concentration levels, are more exhausted and may be more distracted than usual. This is likely to mean that they will struggle to meet performance levels when they are at work, and this may also impact along the business chain leading to mistakes, accidents, impact on colleagues or clients, and reduced effort in non-core business tasks.

Research on presenteeism is still in its infancy; however what is known is that many organizations inadvertently encourage presentee-ism through the use of punitive absence management systems. For example, many employees come to work feeling unwell as they know that if they do not meet attendance targets then they will not receive their salary or sickness benefits, or worse still may face a disciplinary which will only further add to the stress of being unwell. Tackling presenteeism is something that needs to be done in conjunction with a review of the management of health and well-being as a whole within the organization.

3. Staff turnover

Research has found a strong link between causes of stress and employees' intention to leave the organization. The costs of stress-related turnover are significant. These costs may include temporary replacement cover and the costs incurred in recruiting new staff including advertising, selection process, induction and training.

Understanding why employees are leaving the organization is key to addressing the source of the problem. Where employees are under pressure and are unable to manage the demands placed upon them, they are likely to do one of three things: try to carry on and seek out additional training, support or resources to help readdress the balance of demands and resources thereby alleviating the stress; try to carry on without additional training, support or resources and find they start to experience work-related stress; or they look to remove themselves from the situation – in other words they start looking for another job. When this happens not only does it mean that the organization is going to loose a valuable resource in that person, but it is likely to have a knock on effect within the organization on the team and department ('if they can find something better, then maybe I can too..') and potentially to the organizations competitors ('This is Jane, she *left xxx* as they didn't look after her').

There are a number of ways to investigate the causes of turnover. One option is to identify the problem before it occurs by asking employees about their intention to leave in anonymous staff surveys, that way organizations can identify teams or departments that may be suffering from work-related stress and put in place actions to address the problem. Another option is to conduct exit interviews with employees, preferably with an impartial person (either someone within Human Resources, or someone other than a direct line manager or colleague) to ascertain information about why the person was driven to look elsewhere for employment.

4. Accidents and injury

There is a strong link between stress and accidents and injury. Lapses in concentration, fatigue and reduced motivation are all common symptoms of stress and can lead an individual to make a mistake leading to an accident or injury. Furthermore, a study by Kerr and colleagues (Kerr, McHugh and McCrory, 2009) shows significant links between the HSE Management Standards for work-related stress and work errors and near misses. For those working in safety critical environments, with machinery or in health care for example these lapses can cause a serious accident or injure the person experiencing stress or others around them.

A paper in the *Harvard Business Review* showed that claims for stress related industrial accidents cost businesses and insurers twice as much as non-stress related claims (Perkins, 1994). The American Institute for Stress estimate that between 60 and 80 per cent of accidences are stress-related.

Organizations with good safety checks and accident reporting systems are likely to experience fewer accidents and be better able to monitor any patterns in accident and injury data. In addition to this, the importance of embedding a safety culture, in other words, ensuring that employees within the organization take safety seriously and adhere to processes or ways of working, is key to minimizing accidents and injury.

5. Hidden costs
Not only are the costs of stress difficult to calculate, but there are many hidden costs. These can include:

- *Impact on public relations and reputation*: Where organizations fail to manage stress effectively, and word gets out, this can have a disastrous impact on how they are perceived publically.
- *Recruitment*: Where an organization has a poor public image, the ability for them to recruit high calibre staff will be compromised.
- *Investor relations*: Investors increasingly consider the corporate responsibility elements within their portfolios. Where organizations have a poor history of looking after their main resource, investors are likely to be put off.
- *Insurance premiums*: Employer liability insurance premiums may increase in line with the rise in sickness absence claims. Many insurers are now offering incentives for organizations that run stress management and health promotion programmes.
- *Salaries for replacement staff/overtime*: The work doesn't go away simply because the employee is off work. Replacing staff or asking existing staff to cover the additional workload can have costs. These maybe financial, but for the colleague who has to work additional hours these may also be personal costs to health.
- *Training for replacement staff*: Training replacement staff costs money and often places additional pressure on the team and manager who are helping the new member of staff navigate the organization, taking time out of their day to answer questions and show them how to do elements of their job.
- *Reduced productivity*: Research has shown that when employees are under pressure they are less able to perform at their best.

- *Deterioration in work atmosphere/climate*: Where an individual is experiencing stress this is likely to have a knock on effect to the rest of the team. Similarly where a team is consistently under pressure and unable to cope with the demands the organization or manager is placing on them, the atmosphere is likely to deteriorate. This in turn is likely to start a cycle of increased turnover, absence and poor morale.

The distant costs

There are a number of other distant costs that we often don't think of but are costs to the economy all the same:

- Statutory sickpay;
- Incapacity benefits; and
- NHS and healthcare costs including clinician time, medicines and therapy.

Calculating the Cost of Stress to Your Business

When it comes to managing stress, one of the first barriers to implementing any work-related stress intervention is cost. By calculating the cost of stress to your business you will be able to see just how much money is lost due to stress. It will also give you a solid platform on which to form a case for a budget to develop a programme to making changes or investing in training and development to help reduce work-related stress.

How much does stress cost your business?

Absence + Presenteeism + Turnover + Accidents and injury = £££?
Plus the hidden costs.

To calculate the costs of work-related stress to your business, you can:

- Use the estimates provided below
- Use sector-specific estimates. These can be found from a range of sources including your professional bodies, unions, or sources such as the CIPD absence survey report.
- Use your own figures. For example, if your organization has good absence management data, you can use the average cost of sickness absence and the estimated percentage of absence due to stress in your company.

Using your own company figures will give you the most accurate information, but if you don't have the time or resources using the estimates are a useful starting point.

1. The cost of stress-related absence

The CIPD 2008a estimate that the average cost of sickness absence per employee per year is £666. For exact costs, you would need to take into account salary, sickpay costs, cost of covering the employee's workload, administration costs and lost performance and productivity costs.

Calculating the cost of absence

   No. of employees x £666 (ave sickness absence cost) x 40% (estimate of absence due to stress)

For example:

   For a business with 2500 employees the cost of stress could be estimated at £666,000 (2500 × £666 × 40%)
   For a department with 50 employees the cost of stress could be estimated at £13,320 (50 × £666 × 40%)

---

2. The cost of stress-related presenteeism

The Sainsbury Centre for Mental Health estimate that the average cost of presenteeism per employee per year is £605. For the exact costs, you would need to take into account losses in performance where an individual is suffering from fatigue, loss of concentration, the difficulties experienced when communicating with colleagues and clients, and the lower self-motivation and engagement experienced.

Calculating the cost of presenteeism

   No. of employees × £605 (ave presenteeism cost)

For example:

   For a business with 2,500 employees the cost of stress could be estimated at £1,512,500 (2500 × £605)
   For a department with 50 employees the cost of stress could be estimated at £30,250 (50 × £605)

---

3. The cost of stress-related turnover

Recent research shows that approximately 19 per cent of employees cite stress of the job as a key reason for leaving their employment, with a further 19 per cent citing workload, 14 per cent citing lack of line manager support and 14 per cent citing long working hours (CIPD, 2008b). It is likely that a reasonable proportion of those citing workload, manager support and long working hours may also be associated with stress. Therefore 20 per cent would be a reasonable estimate of the percentage of turnover attributable to stress.

The average cost of turnover is £5,800* and the turnover rate within the average UK business is 17 per cent. (*Note*: * Turnover costs will vary significantly between roles and industry sectors. The turnover costs for a senior manager may be in excess of £20,000 while the costs for replacing a manual labourer may be £2,750.)

Calculating the cost of turnover

No. of employees leaving the organization each year × 20% (the percentage of turnover attributable to work-related stress) × £5800 (ave turnover cost)

For example:

For a business with 2,500 employees, approximately 425 employees would leave the business each year and the cost of stress could be estimated at £493,000 (425 × 20% × £5800)
For a department with 50 employees, approximately 8–9 employees would leave the department or business each year and the cost of stress could be estimated at £9860 (8.5 × 20% × £5800)

---

4. The cost of stress-related accidents and injury

Accidents can be classified into three categories: those leading to injury causing absence from work, those leading to injury requiring first aid, or those leading to damage only. The costs of these accidents vary across different sectors and occupations, however, the 2000/2001 Labour Force Survey (UK) shows that over a half of injuries result in absence of one or more days, and nearly a quarter result in absences lasting over a week. Estimates used by the UK Health and Safety Executive suggest that accidents causing absence cost an estimated £2,234, those leading to injury requiring first aid cost an estimated £35 and those resulting in damage only costing an estimated £151. Further research has found that costs for a serious or major injury typically cost £17–19,000.

These costs may include damaged machinery/equipment, lost productivity, payouts to the individual and others affected by the incident, as well as other opportunity costs such as where machinery is left running idle or other staff are waiting to work at an idle machine.

Calculating the cost of accidents

As the nature and frequency of accidents differ so significantly between sectors, it is difficult to provide a reasonable generic estimate. However, using your accident and injury records, you could use the following calculation:

(No. of accidents causing absence × £2234)
  + (No. of accidents requiring first aid × £35)
  + (No. of accidents resulting in damage only × £151)
  /60% (the percentage of accidents attributable to work-related stress)

For example:

For a business that recorded six accidents that lead to employee absence, 25 accidents that lead to machine or property damage and 30 accidents that required first aid the cost of stress could be estimated at £10,937.40 ((6 × 2234) + (30 × 35) + (25 × 151)/60%

Calculate the cost of stress to your business

Exercise: Take the opportunity to review the cost of stress to your business.

- Gather together all of the organizational records you have centrally stored.
- Do they give you sufficient information to track the key indicators of stress?
- What further information do you need/could you put in place to be able to gain a full understanding of the costs of stress to your business.
- Using the information you have about your business, or estimates relating to the UK or to your organizations sector, calculate the cost of stress to your business.
- Consider how these costs relate to the expenditure required to make meaningful and significant changes to the way you manage stress within your organization.

What Should We Be Doing to Monitor these Costs?

All organizations gather and store records in different ways. However large or small your organization we would encourage you to consider the following four elements.

1. Keep good sickness absence records

- Put in place a simple, clear and usable system to collect sickness absence information.
- Make sure everyone (particularly line management) knows the system is there, how it should be used and what the benefits are.
- Explore patterns of sickness absence, including individual patterns, team or department 'hot spots', identify work-related causes.
- Use this information to plan and undertake work adjustments and interventions.

2. Understand presenteeism in your organization

- Are employees coming to work when they feel unwell? Consider your work culture and approach to managing sickness absence.
- When employees do come to work feeling unwell, what are the consequences to your business? Do they make mistakes? Are they disengaged when speaking to clients? Do you have patterns of recurrent absence?

3. Understand how much of your organization's turnover is related to stress

- Conduct exit interviews to understand the reasons people are leaving your organization.
- For those working in large organizations, cross-department communication is key – are there regular meetings and discussions between Human Resources and Occupational Health?
- For those working in businesses with high turnover statistics, have you conducted employee consultations to identify the source of the turnover?

4. Keep good accident and injury records

- Capture information about the context of the accident or injury. Not only when and where it happened, but how and why.

The Legal Case

Employers have a legal duty of care to their employees. The legal context is complex and there are a number of areas of legislation that relate to stress at work. It is fortunate that only a few cases of work-related stress have reached the courts in the UK. However those that have are both high profile and costly, and there has been a gradual increase in the number of cases settled out of court. It is, therefore, important that organizations, and their managers, are aware of the legal responsibilities.

This section includes an overview of the legislation relating to stress at work; a basic introduction to the various pathways to legislation that an employee may take when pursuing a claim for work-related stress; and case studies of recent cases of work-related stress.

The legislation

There are a number of areas of legislation that relate to stress at work. These include:

- The Health and Safety at Work Act 1974;
- Disability Discrimination Act 1995;
- Human Rights Act 1998; and
- Management of Health and Safety at Work Regulations 1999.

The health and safety at work act 1974
The HASWA states that all employers have a duty to 'ensure, so far as is reasonably practical, the health, safety and welfare at work of all employees'. This act was the first step towards ensuring that not only physical health was considered under health and safety law, but also mental health.

The HASWA requires employer to:

- consider the impact of work on their employees' mental health as well as their physical health; and
- take reasonable and practical action to reduce the exposure of employees to aspects of work that may harm mental health.

Disability Discrimination Act 1995
In the DDA, disability is defined as 'an impairment, mental or physical, which has a substantial long-term adverse effect on a person's ability to

carry out normal day-to-day activities'. Therefore a person may have a disability, even if it is not obvious. This is relevant to stress as among the core symptoms of work-related stress are anxiety and depression, both of which are often hidden to the eye.

The DDA requires employers to do two things:

1. a duty to make reasonable adjustments; and
2. a duty not to treat employees with disabilities less favourably than others unless this is justified.

Management of Health and Safety at Work Regulations 1999
These regulations highlight the role of risk assessment and state that employers must make suitable and sufficient risk assessment of *all* risks to health.

The HASAW regulations impose:

- a duty on employers to make suitable and sufficient assessments of the risks to health and safety of employees and others affected by their work;
- a duty to take reasonable and practical action to prevent an employee's exposure to stress; and
- the *Management Standards for Stress* provide guidance and a framework within which to manage work-related stress, and set out a framework for assessing and managing stress at work. (See Chapter 2 for further information about the HSE Management Standards.)

Legal Cases of Work-Related Stress

Stress cases are complex and are often very difficult for both the claimant and the employer. The three landmark cases are described below: these include cases brought by Walker against Northumberland County Council, Barber against Somerset County Council and Sutherland against Hatton.

Walker v Northumberland County Council (1995)

Mr Walker, a social worker, suffered a nervous breakdown following a period of steadily increasing workload. His psychiatrist attributed the pressure at work for the breakdown and advised that he should not return to work with the same level of responsibility. On his return, he was supposed to be assisted by another social worker. This did not happen and in the following months he had a second breakdown and was diagnosed with stress-related anxiety. The council had failed to take reasonable steps to avoid exposing Mr Walker to a health endangering workload, and Mr Walker was awarded £175,000 in damages.

Barber v Somerset County Council (2002)

Mr Barber, a teacher who was head of maths and involved in marketing the school, complained of overwork. He was working between 61 and 70 hours a week during term time over an academic year. He went off sick for three weeks with a sickness certificate stating stress and depression. On his return, there was no change to his job and when he raised his complaints to the headmistress and deputy headmistress, his complaints were not treated sympathetically. While making a further complaint to the deputy headmaster, he was advised to prioritize his workload. Mr Barber then lost control of a classroom the term later and went off sick. He did not return to work. He was awarded £101,042. The case was taken to the Court of Appeal, where considered with four other cases, it was noted that Mr Barber was not the only teacher to have an increased workload, and he had not informed the school of his depressive symptoms. It was decided that the school did not breach its duty of case and the original award was revoked.

Sutherland v Hatton

Mrs Hatton was a teacher who developed depression and took a number of spells of long-term absence over a period of a couple of years, for both personal and family reasons. While she was seeing a stress counsellor, she did not report her symptoms of depression to either the counsellor or anyone in her organization. Within the year, she went on sick-leave with depression and did not return to work.

The Court of Appeal upheld the County court's view that Mrs Hatton's condition was not *reasonably foreseeable*. There was nothing about the nature of her work, her workload or the reasons for previous absences that could have highlighted to the organization the need to take action.

Stress cases are likely to take one of four forms:

1. Personal injury or negligence claim for damages in the Courts
2. Constructive dismissal claim at an employee tribunal
3. Disability discrimination claim at an employee tribunal
4. Bullying or harassment claim at an employee tribunal

Personal injury or negligence claim for damages in the Courts

The first notable case in the Courts was Walker v Northumberland County Council (1995). This landmark case, together with two other cases can be seen as the most significant in defining the outcome of a work-related stress case: Hatton v Sutherland (2002) and Barber v Somerset County Council (2002). In these latter cases, the prepositions shifted to place an emphasis on the employee reporting work-related stress and proving that the employer knew that they were likely to become ill, and demonstrating the employers' breach in duty of care.

In summary, where employees have not yet had a period of sickness absence due to a stress-related illness, and they have not raised any issues for concern, their case is likely to fail. Even where the stress is foreseeable (i.e., previous absence or complaint) there is need for the employee to prove causation of injury, breach of duty and the association between them.

Constructive dismissal claim at an employee tribunal

Employees can make a constructive dismissal claim involving occupational stress via an Employment Tribunal. In these cases employees must: prove there has been a breach of contract, prove that this breach is serious enough to justify their resignation, resign in response to the breech and must not wait too long before resigning otherwise the contract may be judged to be affirmed (there is a three month time limit to bringing cases to a tribunal).

Cases of work-related stress are most likely to focus on breech of terms where the employer has failed to ensure a safe place of work, breech of reasonable hours, or breech of trust and confidence.

The maximum claim for constructive dismissal is £60,100 (Employment Rights Act).

Disability discrimination claim at an employee tribunal

Employees can make a disability discrimination claim involving occupational stress via an Employment Tribunal. In these cases employees must: be disabled, prove that they are being treated less favourably because of their disability, consider whether there are any reasonable adjustments that can be made to accommodate the employee, and whether the proposed course of action is justifiable. Again, any claim must be brought within three months of the alleged discrimination.

The revised DDA (2005) covers mental impairments, which given the nature of work-related stress, enables claimants of work-related stress to cite disability discrimination.

There is no maximum claim for disability discrimination.

Bullying or harassment claim at an employee tribunal

Employees can make a bullying or harassment claim involving occupational stress via an Employment Tribunal. In these cases employees must: demonstrate harassment (which is defined as 'if a person in possession of the same information would think the course of conduct amounted to harassment of the other'), and that the harassment occurred on at least two occasions.

What Should We Be Doing to Comply with Legislation?

As noted above, all employers have a legal responsibility to ensure the health and safety of their employees while at work. This includes preventing or minimizing the exposure to stress at work. Please note that the law may be subject to change and therefore it is important to keep up to date with any changes that may affect your business.

Directors, Human Resource and Occupational Health professionals need to:

- monitor the key indices of work-related stress (e.g., absence, turnover, conflict, performance);
- ensure the health and safety policy addresses work-related stress;
- ensure that risk assessments for work-related stress have been carried out;
- ensure that where risks to health and well-being or stressors have been identified, recommendations to minimize the risk have been implemented;

- ensure that where no action has been taken to address risks to health and welfare, document why no action has been taken; and
- ensure that line managers and employees are aware of, and have access to, the policies and procedures necessary to monitor and take action to manage work-related stress.

The role of the line manager will differ from organization to organization. While some companies may prefer line managers to conduct regular risk assessments, others may prefer line managers to play a facilitative but not leading role in the process.

Line managers should:

- be made aware of the organization's approach to stress and stress management;
- be made aware of who to approach in the organization for further help and guidance in the area of work-related stress (e.g., Human Resources);
- be cognizant of the legal position;
- support the employee in making reasonable adjustments to their work where appropriate; and
- report any concerns as appropriate (to Human Resources, Occupational Health, Director).

Summary

This chapter presents the business and legal cases for managing work-related stress. The case is compelling – stress costs. It can cost the individual experiencing it their health, their relationships and their ability to work. The business can incur substantial losses through absence, presenteeism, turn over and accidents and injury. And finally, where organizations fail to take action to combat stress at work, they are open to legal action either from the Health and Safety Executive or from the individual employee.

References

Chartered Institute of Personnel Development (2008a). *Absence Management Survey 2008*. CIPD, London.

Chartered Institute of Personnel Development (2008b). *Recruitment, Retention and Turnover Survey 2008*. CIPD, London.

Health and Safety Executive (2006). *Self-Reported Work Related-Illness and Workplace Injuries in 2005/06 (SW105/0)* Health and Safety Executive, Caerphilly.

Kerr, R., McHugh, M. and McCrory, M. (2009). HSE management standards and stress-related outcomes. *Occupational Medicine*, 59, 574–579.

Paoli, P. and Merllie, D. (2000). *Third European Study on Conditions at Work.* European Foundation for the Improvement for Living and Working Conditions, Dublin.

Perkins, A. (1994). Saving money by reducing stress. *Harvard Business Review.* 72 (6), 12.

Sainsbury Centre for Mental Health (2007). *Mental Health at Work: Developing the Business Case.* Policy Paper 8. Sainsbury Institute for Mental Health, London.

Whatson Wyatt Worldwide (2001). *Staying at Work 2000/2001 The Dollars and Sense of Effective Disability Management. W-377.* Vancouver: Watson Wyatt Worldwide.

3

How to manage work-related stress

This chapter introduces the approaches you can take to manage work-related stress. You will find below a number of different approaches that can be adopted by the organization, the manager or the individual employee.

The line manager plays a vital role in all attempts to manage work-related stress. Without the endorsement and engagement of line managers any intervention is likely to fall short. For example, an evaluation of the risks posed to the team is unlikely to be taken seriously unless the line manager encourages it to be so; uptake for training events is likely to be low unless the line manager encourages the team to attend; and an employee is unlikely to have access to counselling unless the manager is supportive of the employee through this process.

In addition to traditional approaches to stress management, which typically place a focus on 'stress', our approach suggests that line-manager development should sit at the core of stress management interventions and furthermore, stress management should be a vital part of leadership development. The line manager's role in managing work-related stress is discussed in this chapter.

Preventing Stress in Organizations: How to Develop Positive Managers,
Emma Donaldson-Feilder, Joanna Yarker and Rachel Lewis.
© 2011 John Wiley & Sons, Ltd. Published 2011 by John Wiley & Sons, Ltd.

There are numerous ways stress can be managed in an organization and the most effective approaches will combine prevention, training and support.

- *Prevention* (Primary interventions) – action is taken to identify and address stressors, thereby preventing work-related stress.
- *Training and development* (Secondary intervention) – training and development interventions are provided for individuals or groups of employees to improve their technical skills or coping skills, thereby improving their ability to cope with the work.
- *Support* (Tertiary interventions) – assistance in the form of counselling or therapy is provided to an individual who is experiencing stress to help cure their symptoms.

Prevention

Preventative approaches for work-related stress refer to those where action is taken to identify and address stressors and therefore aim to prevent stress from occurring in the first place. Prevention is the strategy increasingly preferred by experts and organizations and the arguments for adopting a preventative approach are compelling: there is sufficient evidence to advise employers which factors in the workplace may cause stress and, therefore, which ones to look out for; stress when it does occur is very costly; and Health and Safety legislation requires all organizations to assess all risks to health, including those posed by stress at work.

A preventative approach to work stress involves four key elements (see Figure 3.1):

- the identification of sources of stress;
- the identification of reasonable and practicable interventions to remove or limit the source of stress;
- the implementation of an intervention; and
- a review of the intervention to monitor its effectiveness.

Possible methods for identifying sources of stress can include:

- Existing information such as absenteeism, turnover and performance records, and staff surveys can be reviewed to identify any 'at risk' groups. Use this information to target your resources.
- Surveys or audits can be used to assess employees' perceptions of their work. The UK Health and Safety Executive have developed an easy to use, 35 item Indicator tool for work-stress available on their

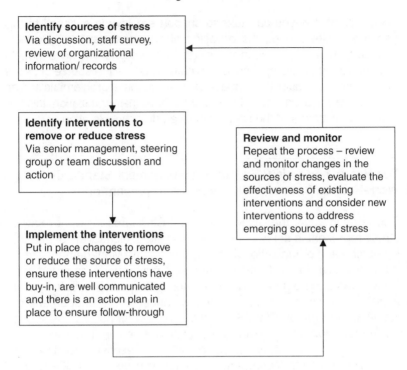

Identify sources of stress
Via discussion, staff survey, review of organizational information/ records

Identify interventions to remove or reduce stress
Via senior management, steering group or team discussion and action

Implement the interventions
Put in place changes to remove or reduce the source of stress, ensure these interventions have buy-in, are well communicated and there is an action plan in place to ensure follow-through

Review and monitor
Repeat the process – review and monitor changes in the sources of stress, evaluate the effectiveness of existing interventions and consider new interventions to address emerging sources of stress

Figure 3.1 A preventative approach to work-related stress

website; alternatively a bespoke survey can be used to assess employees' perceptions of their work.
- Focus groups or one-to-one meetings can be used where discussions are structured around the main causes of work-related stress.

Once the sources of stress have been identified it is necessary for you to:

- Consider how the source of stress can be removed or reduced through redesigning the way the work is done. This is often done in one of three ways: by senior management discussion/action; through the formation of a steering group involving representatives from different parts and levels of the organization; or through a team discussion or workshop. It is important at this stage to recognize those that can be changed and improved, and accept those things that can not. It is often the case that employees raise one particular issue that causes stress that can not be changed – rather than focusing discussion on how frustrating this is, resources are better spent focusing on what can be done to make work better.
- Where it is not possible to remove or reduce the source of stress, i) state why this is the case and keep documentation of your discussion and ii)

consider actions you can take to support employees exposed to this source of stress (e.g., the provision of additional training, guidance, support). This step is important as first, it ensures that you have thought through the possible options to eliminate or reduce the source of stress and second, should this aspect of work become problematic for an employee and a legal case be brought against the organization, this trail will demonstrate that the issue was given due consideration.

The Health and Safety Executive Management Standards for Work-Related Stress: A UK approach to prevention

Published in 2004, the UK Management Standards for work-related stress represent 'a set of conditions that reflect high levels of health, well-being and organizational performance'. The Management Standards cover six areas of work design that, if not properly managed, are likely to result in poor health and well-being, reduced productivity and increased sickness absence. By law, under the Management of Health and Safety at Work Regulations (see www.hse.gov.uk/stress for further information), every organization is required to assess all risks to health and safety, including the risk of exposure to stress at work. Therefore the Management Standards propose a risk assessment approach, whereby exposure to the main causes of stress (demands, control, support, role, relationships and change, see Chapter 1 for further information) is assessed and managed.

This guidance aims to provide information and support to businesses rather than impose additional legal responsibilities.

The HSE propose a five-step process that includes the identification of the risk factors, the consideration and assessment of the risks, the implementation of action plans, and the monitoring and continuous reviewing of the situation. There is no one best way or prescribed process to assess performance against the Management Standards as each organization is different, and has different needs and priorities. However, a multi-method approach that incorporates staff consultation is recommended and has been found to be key to its success. This can include using exiting records (e.g., absenteeism, staff surveys), conducting a risk assessment for work stress or running focus groups and consultations with staff.

The facilitators to the success of this type of intervention have been found to include: a company stress policy, adequate time and budget allocated to the intervention, senior management commitment, line manager buy-in, good data collection and a generally supportive and open environment.

Examples of situations where a preventative approach have been taken:

- A National Health Service trust was concerned about the level of absence reported. For many reasons, but largely due to the unique issues experienced by the staff in the different departments, the trust commissioned a bespoke risk assessment. Focus groups were conducted within each department to identify the key sources of stress within the department. This was followed by the development of a targeted questionnaire to capture the issues of concern. The analysis of the questionnaire data provided a clear indication of the primary causes of absence and work-related stress, which the trust could then use to develop specific department-based actions.
- A medium-sized manufacturing organization keen to understand the prevalence of work-related stress in their organization, and aiming to enhance management practice, looked to the HSE Management Standards approach. The company used the risk assessment tool available on the HSE web, asking employees to complete the questionnaire during their working hours, and used the generated report to identify areas of strength and development. On the basis of the report the organization held a series of employee forums to explore changes to production processes.
- A department within a university was focused on improving its management processes. Due to the size of the department (32 members of staff) and the lack of any overt problems related to absence or turnover, the department chose to run a half-day workshop during which sub-groups discussed the sources of stress, before bringing these together to identify overall themes/issues. Once consensus on the top five issues was gained, discussions were then held to identify and agree appropriate action to reduce the sources of stress.

Training and Development

Training and development interventions can be used to improve the technical skills or coping skills of individuals or teams, thereby improving their ability to cope with the work.

Returning to our definition of stress, stress can be defined as 'the adverse reaction people have to excessive pressures or other types of demand' (HSE, 2005). Training and development can help people manage the pressures on them in one of two ways:

- *Technical skills training*: improving their ability to do the core tasks of the job, therefore reducing the effort required to do the job with the aim of reducing the stress placed on the employee.

- *Stress management skills training*: improving their ability to cope with the demands placed on them by giving them tools and techniques to cope with the pressure.

Technical skills training

Technical skills training can focus on building the employee's skills and confidence in key areas of their job. These skills may be determined by a stress risk assessment or audit, a performance appraisal or a one-to-one conversation between the employee and manager.

Examples of situations where technical skills training can improve an individual's or team's ability to cope with the work include:

- Jane, a newly promoted manager in a retail bank, was coping with many of the demands of her new role. While she felt comfortable discussing performance issues with her team, she was growing increasingly anxious at the end of each month when she had to attend the regional managers' meeting. During the meeting she was required to do a presentation of her branch performance and face challenges from the Regional Director. A discussion with her Human Resources department helped her to identify that she was anxious about presenting in front of groups and experienced difficulties in managing upwards. As a result she attended a presentations skills course and received coaching to build her confidence in communicating her team's needs to senior management.
- Following a risk assessment conducted in a large engineering organization it was clear that two teams were reporting high incidences of work-related stress and job dissatisfaction. On investigation of the risk assessment data, a clear relationship was found between the new expenses and project management systems and the teams' stress and dissatisfaction. Focus groups with the teams highlighted that they had never received training in any of the new IT systems implemented by the business as the teams' members were frequently travelling internationally. Training on IT software had always been a low priority on the rare opportunities that the teams had all been in one place. Training was put in place for the teams' members and this enabled them to navigate the systems quickly and with less frustration.

Stress management skills

Stress management skills training can focus on fostering awareness of stressors and well-being, or on teaching stress reduction skills. This type of training is often used to bridge the gap between the demands placed on the individual and their ability or resources available to cope with them. The three most common types of stress management training are:

- multimodal (incorporating elements of raising awareness of what stress is, the signs and signals of stress; skill development and encouraging the acquisition of coping skills);
- relaxation-based (focusing on physical or mental relaxation to help cope with the consequences of stress); and
- cognitive behavioural therapy training (focusing on making the individual think and behave differently towards the source of stress).

All three types of training have been found to be effective. A recent review has shown that cognitive behavioural therapy training is more effective than relaxation-based training, and often more effective than multimodal training (Van der Klink, Blonk, Schene and van Dijk, 2004). However, the effectiveness of the training has much to do with the expertise and style of the trainer so this is a key consideration in the implementation of any training programme. Further, other reviews have shown the effectiveness of relaxation-based training and multimodal training suggesting that it is better to so something than do nothing.

Examples of situations where stress management skills training can improve an individual's or team's ability to cope with the work include:

- A senior school head master was concerned about the level of well-being of his staff. As the school had not done any work in well-being and work stress, it was decided that an introductory one-day programme that focused on awareness would be most appropriate. The course included an introduction to what stress is, what it is not, and the causes of stress. The afternoon session provided people with the opportunity to consider the stressors they experienced, and as a group consider how to eliminate or manage these more effectively.
- A central government department decided to provide their employees with an opportunity to develop their resources to deal with stress. This workshop trained senior managers in a range of stress management techniques, such as relaxation and acceptance, with a view that they could draw on these to protect their health but also pass these learnings on to their team.

Support

Supportive interventions offer assistance in the form of counselling or therapy to those individuals who are already experiencing stress, in other words for those who have fallen through the net of prevention and training and development. These interventions aim to help cure the symptoms of stress and often take the form of one-to-one counselling or coaching, or other medicalized treatment.

Examples of situations where supportive interventions can improve how individuals' cope with and recover from work-stress are highlighted below:

- A manager at a regional bank had been under pressure at work. He had not wanted to approach his line manager (believing that not being able to cope with the workload was a sign of failure on his part). He finally decided to contact an anonymous helpline sponsored by the organization. Through this he was put in touch with a counsellor and offered six sessions of specialist counselling. These helped him to rationalize some of his concerns and develop tools to manage the stress he experienced.
- A sales telephonist had been struggling to balance his work and home life and felt that the targets at work were becoming unrealistic. After trying to juggle this pressure for eight months, he went to the doctor for advice. At this point, he was diagnosed with clinical anxiety, prescribed medical treatment and referred to a clinical psychologist for counselling.

Organizational, Manager and Team, and Individual Level Interventions

Stress can be managed at different levels within the organization. In addition to thinking about whether a preventative, training or supportive approach is appropriate for your organization, it is necessary to consider where to target your resources: at the organizational level, the manager level, the team level or the individual level.

The organizational level

Organizational interventions take into account those aspects of work that impact across the organization. They tend to take the form of prevention, using surveys or existing data and focus groups to identify issues that affect employees throughout the organization or within 'hot spots' or groups of staff, either in particular job roles or specific teams or departments.

An organizational level intervention: Case study from an engineering company

One organization we worked with used a bespoke risk assessment survey to identify their employees' risks to stress. We found that the majority of staff across their 12 business units were dissatisfied with the performance appraisal system and believed that the system was poorly designed and lead to unfair performance management decisions. Those who responded that they system was unfair were also significantly more likely to also report poor general well-being and greater intention to leave the organization. This led to an organizational intervention whereby the performance appraisal system was reviewed, redesigned and a consultation process was used to ensure that the new system addressed the employees concerns. As part of the roll-out of the new system, managers were invited to training workshops and briefings to ensure that the system was being used fairly across the different departments.

The manager level

Manager-based interventions often take the form of training and development activities and can focus on stress management awareness training, or as this book proposes, behaviour-based skills training. These interventions may include upward feedback, self-reflection, coaching and/or training in specific behaviours to improve the managers' people management skills.

A manager level intervention: Case study from a bank

A UK bank experiencing moderate levels of work-related stress encouraged their line managers to sign up to a training course to develop their skills in managing and reducing work-related stress. Prior to the workshop, line managers were asked to complete a 360 degree feedback questionnaire and asked to invite team members to rate their behaviour. Line managers received a written feedback report incorporating their self-perceptions and those of their team. This was followed by a one-to-one feedback session with a consultant. Line managers then attended a one day workshop that incorporated stress management awareness and skills-based training. Following the course, line managers were encouraged to put their learnings into practice and a follow-up questionnaire enabled them to track their development.

The team level

Team-based interventions often take the form of training and development activities and can include the involvement of the whole team, with or without the manager present. These interventions may include a team-based risk assessment incorporating focus groups to identify the sources of stress within the organization; stress awareness training for the team so that the team can be better positioned to notice and respond to stress when it occurs; or skills-based training to address skills gaps within the team.

A team level intervention: Case study from a public sector organization

A public sector organization with a problem with stress-related absence commissioned us to run a series of stress awareness training sessions. As many of the issues raised in the scoping discussions were focused on the communication between senior management and staff, it was decided that separate workshops would be held for managers and employees. This gave teams an opportunity to discuss issues in a safe environment while also making sure that the managers and employees received the same information about the nature of stress and what can be done to address it. A series of team-based workshops incorporating aspects of stress awareness and stress management techniques were offered on a voluntary basis to all teams.

The individual level

These interventions focus on the individual and are need-driven. They may include training and development activities, such as technical skills based training or they may be focused on developing coping or resilience skills. Alternatively, individual interventions are also appropriate for those who are already experiencing stress and may include coaching, counselling or other rehabilitation techniques.

An individual level intervention: Coaching incorporating multimodal stress management training

A middle manager in a professional services organization was referred for coaching following a poor performance appraisal. The initial meeting aimed to scope out the needs of the client. At this stage it was evident that the client was experiencing difficulty managing two members of his team that did not get on, and this conflict was affecting the team's performance and ability to meet project deadlines. This constant challenge, plus the pressure from above to deliver results,

was making the client increasingly anxious and reducing his confidence in his ability to do his job. The coaching focused on two things:
addressing the issue of conflict and how to resolve the problems within
the team and developing a number of stress management techniques
to alleviate the anxiety when it arose.

Traditionally, stress management activity has largely focused on the
supportive, individual level with more recent attempts to drive a preventative organization-based approach. This book addresses one of the key
gaps in our understanding of stress management intervention: the role of
the line manager.

What Should Our Organization Be Doing?

Stress policy

It is useful for organizations to have a policy document that sets out their
aims and strategy for managing work-related stress. This may sit within a
wider policy document for health and well-being, occupational health or
organizational efficiency. Wherever the stress policy statement sites, it is
important to clearly outline the responsibilities of all parties including
senior management, line management, employees and departments
such as Human Resources and Occupational Health, what activities will
be undertaken on a regular basis, how these are to be recorded and what
interventions will be supported. Further, it is useful to also outline what
services and supports are available to employees should they experience work-related stress.

Stress prevention

As outlined in Chapter 2, employers have a legal obligation to identify
risks to health, and take reasonable and practical action to reduce any
stressors identified. This identification of stressors could take the form of
a risk assessment, review of existing documentation or employee consultation. Documented evidence of the findings, and importantly, what
actions are taken as a result, are required by law.

Training and development for employees

Training in stress awareness and key skills associated with the technical
aspects of the job and stress management will provide employees with
opportunities to protect themselves from sources of stress.

Training and development for managers

Training in stress awareness, and development in the skills necessary for people management will provide managers with the necessary level of competence to manage their teams effectively and in a way that will reduce and prevent work-related stress. The following chapters provide a range of exercises that can support this training.

Support services

Should employees experience stress it is important that organizations have services at hand to support them. Employees will be able to go to their General Practitioner and are likely to be offered either medication or counselling to help towards their rehabilitation. However waiting lists are often long and in some instances, counselling from an occupational health counsellor may have more benefits for the employees where the stress is work-related. Many employee assistance programmes offer a range of services and it is well worth organizations investing in such support providers so that action can be taken quickly and responsibly.

Return to work and rehabilitation

The difficulties involved in rehabilitating someone back from anxiety or depression, the most common symptoms of work-related stress are well-recognized. Where employees have been off work due to work-related stress it is of vital importance that a return to work programme is agreed between the employee, manager and if appropriate Occupational Health or Human Resource departments. Regular communication with the employee about their rehabilitation and the provision of work adjustments and additional counselling or other supports may also be beneficial. Together, these steps will help to reduce the experience of stress by employees and offer a comprehensive approach to stress management.

Where Does the Line Manager Fit In?

The line manager plays a vital role in the management of stress at work. A line manager's support is necessary to drive forward any stress management approach, be it preventative, training or supportive. Table 3.1 describes some of the roles and responsibilities that the line manager can take in supporting the approaches to stress management.

Table 3.1 The line manager's role in stress management

Stress management approach	Line manager's role
Prevention	• To support a stress risk assessment or audit in their team (gaining buy-in from team to complete the survey/give open honest feedback) • To work with their team, and Occupational Health or Human Resources, to identify appropriate interventions and adjustments to work to eliminate or reduce workplace stressors • To be the champion of changes that aim to reduce the source of stress within their teams
Training and Development	• To be aware of, and identify, signs and symptoms of stress and identify appropriate training courses to reduce individual stress • To provide team members with opportunities to identify and attend appropriate courses • To be supportive of team based training interventions that are designed to equip team members with skills to better cope with their work • To ensure that they act in a way that reduces and prevents work-related stress – Do they use appropriate behaviours when managing their team or is additional training required?
Support	• To be aware of, and identify, signs and signals of stress and to identify appropriate sources of support for the individual (e.g.., Occupational Health, employee assistance programme) • To provide opportunities for the employee to attend counselling or medical appointments during working hours • To work with the employee to identify work adjustments that will reduce the employees exposure to work-related stress • To work with the employee to help them decide how best to communicate (or not) with the team about their stress

Note: The Line Managers' behaviour has a significant impact on how the manager engages and carries out their responsibilities in each of these three areas of stress management practice.

Summary

In Chapter 1, we learnt that the line manager can play a significant role in causing or reducing the sources of stress. In this chapter, we have reviewed the various approaches to stress management and learnt that the line manager can play a significant role in driving forward stress management approaches. Line managers can, therefore, work to identify, monitor, reduce, remove and review the sources of stress exerted on their team.

Importantly, the way a line manager behaves on a day-to-day basis has a significant impact on the employees' experience of work and subsequently, their experience of stress. In the following chapters we demonstrate how line manager behaviour can impact on employee health and well-being, and turn our focus to the *Positive Manager Behaviours* necessary for promoting a healthy and productive work environment.

Reference

van der Klink, J.J., Blonk, R.W., Schene, A.H.and van Dijk, F.J. (2001). The benefits of interventions for work-related stress. *American Journal of Public Health*, 91, 270–276.

4

Developing a framework to promote positive manager behaviour

This chapter introduces the framework developed to promote Positive Manager Behaviour. This framework has been developed over five years of research, working with dozens of organizations, involving hundreds of managers and employees, across many different sectors. Throughout this research we have worked to balance the practical outputs with research rigour to ensure that the end result is both embedded in sound foundations and easy and meaningful to use in organizations.

In the pages that follow, we aim to do four things:

- present the rationale and need for a stress management approach focusing on Positive Manager Behaviour;
- explain why we took a competency-based approach;
- introduce the research we conducted to develop the Positive Manager Behaviour framework and approach; and
- provide evidence to support the Positive Manager Behaviour approach.

Preventing Stress in Organizations: How to Develop Positive Managers,
Emma Donaldson-Feilder, Joanna Yarker and Rachel Lewis.
© 2011 John Wiley & Sons, Ltd. Published 2011 by John Wiley & Sons, Ltd.

Rationale: The Need for a Stress Management Approach Focusing on Positive Manager Behaviour

As described in Chapter 1, line managers play a significant role in the management of stress at work. While their role in causing stress and their responsibilities to manage stress were recognized by many, little was known about *how* line managers caused stress or indeed how they could work to prevent and reduce work-related stress in their employees. Before embarking on research to develop the framework for Positive Manager Behaviour, we conducted a comprehensive review of the academic and practitioner literature and combined this knowledge with our experience of working with organizations to tackle work-related stress and promote positive, high performing organizations. Four arguments emerged highlighting the need for a stress management approach focusing on Positive Manager Behaviour.

The need for an approach focusing on positive manager behaviour

1. Line managers have a significant impact on the way employees experience work-related stress.
2. Line managers receive limited stress management training and guidance.
3. There is only a limited amount of research focusing on line manager interventions to improve employee well-being or reduce the effects of stress.
4. Line managers express concerns that stress management is yet another to-do in an expanding management portfolio.

Line managers have a significant impact on the way employees experience work-related stress

The influence line managers have over employees' experience of work-related stress was discussed, with supporting evidence from the literature, in Chapter 1. There are four main ways line managers can influence work-related stress within their team:

1. Causing (or preventing) stress by the way they behave towards their staff.

2. Influencing the impact of the work environment (demands, control etc.) on their staff.
3. Identifying, monitoring and working to reduce work-related stress through the uptake of risk assessments.
4. Supporting the design and implementation of stress management solutions.

Taken together, this body of evidence highlights line managers as a vital component to the management of work-related stress. However, in practice, our experience has been that on the whole, line managers receive very limited training in stress management. This brings us to our second argument for a new approach to stress management.

Line managers receive limited stress management training and guidance

Training in the area of work-related stress and available guidance has typically been focused at two levels: systems or policy level; and individual level. At the systems or policy level, there are a growing number of resources available to support organizations in the roll-out of risk assessments, outlining the policies and procedures organizations should have in place to better manage work-related stress. At the individual level, there are growing resources to raise the awareness of what stress is, what it might look like and what counselling or support services are offered by organizations. Where line managers are offered stress management training, the focus is typically placed on fostering an awareness of what stress is, signs and signals of stress; stress management techniques such as relaxation; and in some cases stress management prevention such as working to reduce the sources of stress prevalent at work (e.g., demands, workload, change).

The reasons for this narrow approach to stress management training is likely to stem from two things: first, there is a limited understanding of what works with regard to line manager training due to the paucity of evaluation research; and second, many organizations find it difficult to gain management buy-in to stress management training as it is seen as an extra to-do on an ever expanding to-do list.

The reason for this narrow approach aside, providing managers with an awareness of what stress is and/or what causes it only offers a partial solution to managing work-related stress. It has a missing 'so what do I do now?' ingredient: what should managers keep doing, and what should managers do differently to help prevent and reduce work-related stress?

There is only a limited amount of research focusing on line manager interventions to improve employee well-being or reduce the effects of stress

There are a small number of studies that demonstrate the effectiveness of line manager training. Evidence suggests that line manager-focused programmes can influence both the way employees experience their work environment (e.g., demands, support) and employee well-being. While these studies are rigorous and show significant and encouraging results, they do not provide a definitive picture as to the best approach for an organization to adopt.

Examples of this research include:

- Line managers in a Swedish insurance company received bi-weekly training sessions spread over a one-year period. The training incorporated information on: raising awareness of individual functioning; social psychology of groups; initiating practical changes; and how to initiate improvements to the work environment. Line managers were encouraged to share and discuss their learnings from the course with their team. At the end of the one-year period, employees working for line managers who had attended the training programme showed significantly reduced levels of the stress hormone cortisol, and reported increased decision authority or control over their work, as compared to employees working for managers who had not received the training who showed no changes in levels of stress hormone and reported decreased decision authority over their work (Theorell et al. 2001).
- Line managers in a Japanese office-based organization were invited to attend a single half-day training session incorporating lectures, case studies and discussion. An evaluation of employee well-being three months after the training session indicated that the training had a significant impact on levels of employee strain, but only where there was a critical mass of manager attendance. No reduction in employee strain was found for those employees working in departments where fewer than 30 per cent of managers attended the course (Tsutsumi et al. 2005)

Line managers express concerns that stress management is yet another to-do in an expanding management portfolio

It is well recognized that the role of the line manager is challenging. As organizations bring in ever more changes and new policies and practices, line managers are required to complete more paperwork, attend more meetings, take responsibility for more management issues – and all of this on top of doing the job itself. It is not surprising that line managers are sometimes reluctant to engage in stress management initiatives. The phrase 'I'll tell you what makes me stressed, it is things like this. . .' has all too often been heard when managers are asked to attend a stress management training course or a risk assessment focus group.

Our experience is that while line managers recognize the importance of employee well-being and stress management, and want to be good at stress management, they do not want to add to their ever expanding management to-do list.

This perception that stress management is separate from general good management is a myth and a key argument for a new approach to stress management. In fact, good managers are likely to be good *stress* managers. However, prior to our research programme, what we didn't know was: what is it about good management that prevents and reduces stress, and at the same time promotes a positive work environment? This is why our research was needed.

Why We Took a Competency-Based Approach

A review of the literature and our experience highlighted three things:

- first, a need to improve the way organizations engaged line managers in stress management;
- second, a need for an approach that both specified what line managers needed to do in order identify, reduce and prevent stress in their teams and leant itself to the development of interventions, so that these skills and behaviours could be measured, trained and developed; and
- finally, a need to be cognizant that line managers often feel overburdened and therefore any new approach should be integrated into what was already being asked of them.

A competency-based approach offered a solution.

Competencies refer to a complete collection of skills and behaviours required by the individual to do their job. (Boyatzis, 1982)

Competencies offered a way to:

- articulate the outcomes expected of the individual and the way in which these activities should be carried out;
- provide clear specification of *how* managers should behave to reduce stress and promote a positive work environment;

- develop behaviour-based interventions to ensure that managers have the skills, abilities and behaviours necessary to manage stress effectively;
- translate stress management into a language that organizations and line managers understand; and
- integrate stress management activity with other people management activities already in place within an organization (e.g., appraisal, job descriptions, training).

Competencies are used by many organizations to drive employee performance. Rankin (2004) found that 76 out of 100 organizations he reviewed used competency frameworks in some way. While these frameworks often differ in their content, their level of detail and the level within the organization at which they are targeted (e.g., employee, manager, director etc), they are typically used to guide selection and assessment, training and development and performance management. Using such a foundation for a stress-management approach offers many opportunities for integrating stress management into ongoing management practices. For example:

- *Selection and assessment:* Competencies often form the basis for job descriptions and person specifications. Through identifying the competencies associated with work-related stress, it is possible to identify and select those managers better able to manage work-related stress.
- *Training and development:* Competencies can be used to identify managers' development needs and for many organizations form the basis of the training or learning and development programmes offered. Through identifying the competencies associated with managing work-related stress, it is possible to design training interventions to develop the relevant skills, abilities and behaviours in managers.
- *Performance management:* Competencies are often used to form the basis of performance appraisals and other performance management processes. Through identifying the competencies associated with work-related stress, it is possible to appraise, and monitor, managers' stress management competence, thereby embedding stress management into general management practice.

Furthermore, in recent years a number of professional bodies and national initiatives, in the UK, Europe and America, have used competency frameworks as their foundation. A competency-based approach to stress management allows for the integration of stress management into these existing and widely promulgated resources. For example:

- General Management Standards: for example, Management Standards Centre, Chartered Management Institute, UK;

- Professional frameworks: for example, Investing in People and DTI Inspirational Leadership Framework, UK;
- Sector specific initiatives: for example, National Probation Service Living Leadership Framework, and the National Health Service Knowledge Skills Framework, UK; and
- International job description databases: for example, O*Net, United States.

The Research Underlying the Positive Manager Behaviour Framework and Approach

The framework for Positive Manager Behaviour was developed and tested over a three-phase research programme. Figure 4.1 shows the phases of research that have been carried out.

In the initial phases of the research the framework was entitled 'Management competencies for preventing and reducing stress at work'. However, as the research progressed, the framework was re-named

Phase 1	Data collected in Phase 1 resulted in the emergent 'Management competencies for preventing and reducing stress at work' framework, consisting of 19 competencies. Participants: 216 employees, 166 line managers and 54 HR professionals.
Phase 2	Data collected in Phase 2 resulted in: a refined version of the 'Management competencies for preventing and reducing stress at work' framework, consisting of 4 competencies and 12 sub-competencies; and a 66 item 'Stress management competency indicator tool' to measure the relevant competencies. Participants: 313 participants to initially test the tool. 22 organizations, 152 managers and 656 direct reports then used the tool as an upward feedback measure.
Phase 3	In Phase 3, an intervention was designed to develop managers' Positive Manager Behaviour. Data collected in Phase 3 provided both qualitative and quantitative evidence for the efficacy of this intervention approach. Participants: 207 managers and 594 employees participated in the intervention study.

Figure 4.1 The three-phase research methodology. Source Adapted from Donaldson-Feilder, Lewis and Yarker (2009) © Crown Copyright 2009

'Positive Manager Behaviour'. There are three reasons for this: first, the evidence suggests that the behaviours identified in the framework do more than prevent and reduce stress, rather they can work to foster a positive work environment. Second, many organizations avoid using the term 'stress' and prefer to use terms such as well-being, positive working, enhancing health and performance: feedback shows that a number of users have re-branded the framework to eliminate the term stress. Third, there has been a general movement in the last five years to focus on the positive end of the health continuum.

Phase 1: Identifying the manager behaviours and building a competency framework for preventing and reducing stress at work

Method
A qualitative, interview-based approach was used to identify the behaviours associated with the management of stress in employees. A 'critical incident technique' (Flanagan, 1954) was used whereby managers and employees were asked about the specific behaviours they (managers), or their manager (employees), had elicited under times of pressure.

Findings
The framework that emerged from the data included 19 competencies, or clusters of behaviour, reported to be relevant for the prevention and reduction of work-related stress, each with effective and ineffective examples.

Key implications
- There were no significant differences between sectors in the behaviours identified, however line managers reported fewer negative behaviours and employees fewer positive behaviours. The framework therefore seems to identify behaviours that are relevant for the prevention and reduction of stress at work across different organizations.
- When we compared the emerging framework to other general management frameworks, we found that all competencies were included in at least one of the general frameworks, but no general framework covered all of the competencies. This suggests that whatever management framework an organization is currently using, the likelihood is that it will not cover all the behaviours that are important for the prevention and reduction of stress at work.
- Feedback from participants and stakeholders indicated that this approach enabled people to talk about stress management in the context of people management and therefore offered a platform for professionals from different disciplines to meet on common ground.

For further details on the Phase One please refer to Yarker, Donaldson-Feilder, Lewis and Flaxman (2007).

Phase 2: Refining the manager behaviour framework and developing a measurement tool/questionnaire

Method
The competency framework was refined and the stress management competency indicator tool developed in three stages:

1. Statements were drawn from the Phase One interview data to develop questions relevant to each of the 19 competencies. This first draft was reviewed by experts and stakeholders for clarity, ambiguity and relevance.
2. The resulting questionnaire was distributed to employees who were asked to rate their manager's behaviour. The data collected were analysed and those questions that did not measure line management behaviour appropriately were eliminated.
3. The tool was then distributed within 22 organizations, using an upward feedback approach where employees were asked to rate their line manager's behaviour, and managers were asked to rate their own behaviour.

In addition, usability interviews were conducted with managers who had been through the process. Questions focused on the relevancy of the competencies to their role, the ease of use of the questionnaire and the resultant information provided, and the perceived accuracy of the questionnaire in identifying development areas. Interviews with stakeholders and workshops with experts focused on usability of the approach in relation to its integration with existing Human Resource and Occupational Health policies and practices.

Findings
Analysis of the questionnaire data revealed four clusters of behaviour relevant to stress management. These were:

- Respectful and responsible: managing emotions and having integrity;
- Managing and communicating existing and future work;
- Reasoning/managing difficult situations; and
- Managing the individual within the team.

These competencies are discussed in detail in the later section 'The Positive Manager Behaviour framework'.
The usability analysis suggested the approach could be readily used in organizations, through integration into existing people management and

health and safety practices. In particular, the approach could be used to inform stress management action plans at the organizational level, and dovetail into leadership or management training and development programmes. Line managers found the questions easy to answer and also found that the tool was accurate in identifying development needs. The majority of line managers reported that a 360 degree or upward feedback approach was the best format for the tool as it provided the most valuable information to inform development and change.

Key implications
- By taking a competency-based approach, the prevention and reduction of stress can be readily integrated into existing people management processes.
- A competency-based approach to stress management (or Positive Manager Behaviour) is well-received by line managers.
- Interventions based on the competency framework emerging from the research are needed to develop managers' ability to prevent and reduce stress at work and engender a positive work environment.

For further details on Phase Two please refer to Yarker, Donaldson-Feilder and Lewis (2008).

Phase 3: Creating and evaluating learning and development interventions to help managers demonstrate Positive Manager Behaviour

Method
An intervention was developed that was designed to help managers demonstrate Positive Manager Behaviour. It was made up of two elements:

- *Upward feedback*: Managers and their employees' (direct reports') were asked to complete the stress management competency indicator tool (questionnaire) to rate the degree to which the manager showed the behaviours set out in the Positive Manager Behaviour framework that emerged from phase 2. Provided a manager had responses from at least three employees, he or she was provided with a report that collated their self-report and an average employee score.
- *Half-day workshop*: Managers were invited to attend a workshop that aimed to introduce the importance of Positive Manager Behaviour, increase self-awareness, and develop skills to enhance or develop their stress management competence. The workshop provided an opportunity for managers to explore their feedback report further, with the aim of developing an understanding of Positive Manager

Behaviour. The interactive design included discussion, case studies, vignettes, debate and analysis.

To evaluate the impact of the intervention workshops, managers and employees were invited to complete questionnaires at two time points, one before the workshop and one three months after the workshop.

Findings
The findings from this phase of research are described in detail in the later section 'Evidence to support a Positive Manager Behaviour approach'. Overall, the upward feedback report was well received and those managers who initially scored themselves, or were scored by their employees, as not showing Positive Manager Behaviour saw the most significant change in their behaviour.

Key implications
- Raising awareness of manager behaviour through upward feedback is an important part of helping managers to change their behaviour.
- A half-day workshop, combined with upward feedback to managers, can achieve meaningful change and provides a steer as to where best to target management development resources.
- Line managers need support and opportunities to seek advice and guidance if they are to develop their skills in preventing stress in their team.

For further details of Phase Three please refer to Donaldson-Feilder, Lewis and Yarker (2009).

The Positive Manager Behaviour Framework

The research revealed four broad themes of behaviour that are important for managers to show in order to minimize stress in their staff.

1. *Respectful and responsible: managing emotions and having integrity.* This is about treating staff with respect, including acting with integrity, managing emotions and being considerate. For example, managers must act calmly in pressured situations and take a consistent approach, as opposed to panicking or exhibiting mood swings. Ensuring deadlines are realistic, giving more positive than negative feedback and showing consideration for staff's work-life balance are other key elements.
2. *Managing and communicating existing and future work:* This includes proactive work management, for example, communicating job objectives clearly and monitoring workloads, developing action plans and

prioritizing. Dealing rationally with problems and being decisive are key elements. Managers also need to keep staff informed and encourage their participation, for example through team meetings and individual discussions: however, they need to judge when to consult staff versus when to make a decision without doing so. Helping staff develop and acting as a mentor are also important.

3. *Managing the individual in the team*: This requires speaking to people personally rather than using email, providing regular opportunities for staff to speak one-to-one and being available to talk when needed. It may be as simple as being willing to have a laugh and socialize with staff. It is vital to recognize that every individual is different, so managers need to see others' point of view and understand what motivates them, regularly ask staff how they are and treat everyone with equal importance.

4. *Reasoning and managing difficult situations*: This involves dealing objectively with conflicts and acting as a mediator, then following up conflicts after resolution – seeking advice from others where necessary and supporting staff through incidents of abuse and bullying. Managers must make it clear they will take ultimate responsibility when things go wrong.

To improve usability, each of these four themes was grouped into three sub-clusters, providing a refined competency framework of four competencies and 12 sub-competencies. The competency framework is shown in Table 4.1.

Evidence to Support a Positive Manager Behaviour Approach

Using the Positive Manager Behaviour framework, it is possible to take a Positive Manager Behaviour approach in organizations: for example, through implementing interventions to increase levels of Positive Manager Behaviour. As explained in the research section earlier, Phase Three of the research programme aimed to evaluate a Positive Manager Behaviour approach that involved a learning and development intervention (upward feedback and a workshop) designed to help managers demonstrate Positive Manager Behaviour. Evidence to support this approach was gathered at three levels:

1. Manager behaviour change
2. Manager perspectives of the Positive Manager Behaviour approach
3. Practitioner perspectives of the Positive Manager Behaviour approach

Table 4.1. Management competencies for promoting Positive Manager Behaviour

Competency	Sub-competency	Do (✓)/ Don't (✗)	Examples of manager behaviour
Managing emotions and having integrity: Respectful and responsible	Integrity	✓	■ Is a good role model ■ Treats team members with respect ■ Is honest
		✗	■ Says one thing, then does something different
	Managing emotions	✓	■ Acts calmly in pressured situations ■ Takes a consistent approach to managing
		✗	■ Is unpredictable in mood ■ Passes on stress to employees ■ Panics about deadlines ■ Takes suggestions for improvement as a personal criticism
	Considerate approach	✗	■ Makes short term demands rather than allowing planning ■ Creates unrealistic deadlines ■ Gives more negative than positive feedback ■ Relies on others to deal with problems ■ Imposes 'my way is the only way' ■ Shows a lack of consideration for work–life balance

(continued)

Table 4.1 (*Continued*)

Competency	Sub-competency	Do (✓)/ Don't (✗)	Examples of manager behaviour
Managing and communicating existing and future work	Proactive work management	✓	■ Clearly communicates employee job objectives ■ Develops action plans ■ Monitors team workload on an ongoing basis ■ Stops additional work being taken on when necessary ■ Works proactively ■ Sees projects/tasks through to delivery ■ Reviews processes for improvements ■ Prioritizes future workloads
	Problem solving	✓	■ Deals rationally with problems ■ Follows up problems on team's behalf ■ Deals with problems as soon as they arise
		✗	■ Is indecisive at decision making
	Participative/empowering	✓	■ Gives employees the right level of responsibility ■ Correctly judges when to consult and when to make a decision ■ Keeps employees informed of what is happening in the organization ■ Acts as a mentor ■ Delegates work equally ■ Helps team members develop in their role ■ Encourages team participation ■ Provides regular team meetings
		✗	■ Gives too little direction to employees

Table 4.1 (*Continued*)

Competency	Sub-competency	Do (✓)/ Don't (✗)	Examples of manager behaviour
Reasoning/Managing difficult situations	Managing conflict	✓	■ Acts as mediator in conflict situations ■ Deals with squabbles before they become arguments ■ Deals objectively with conflicts ■ Deals with conflicts head on
		✗	■ Acts to keep the peace rather than resolve issues
	Use of organisational resources	✓	■ Seeks advice from other managers when necessary ■ Uses HR as a resource to help deal with problems ■ Seeks help from occupational health when necessary
	Taking responsibility for resolving issues	✓	■ Follows up conflicts after resolution ■ Supports employees through incidents of abuse ■ Makes it clear they will take ultimate responsibility if things go wrong
		✗	■ Doesn't address bullying

(*continued*)

Table 4.1 (*Continued*)

Competency	Sub-competency	Do (✓)/ Don't (✗)	Examples of manager behaviour
Managing the individual within the team	Personally accessible	✓	■ Speaks personally rather than uses email ■ Provides regular opportunities to speak one to one ■ Returns calls/emails promptly ■ Is available to talk to when needed
	Sociable	✓	■ Brings in treats ■ Socializes with the team ■ Is willing to have a laugh at work
	Empathetic engagement	✓	■ Encourages employee input in discussions ■ Listens when employees ask for help ■ Makes an effort to find out what motivates employees at work ■ Tries to see team member's point of view ■ Takes an interest in team's life outside work ■ Regularly asks 'how are you?' ■ Treats all team members with equal importance
		✗	■ Assumes rather than checks employees are OK

Source: Adapted from Donaldson-Feilder, Lewis and Yarker 2009 © Crown Copyright 2009

1. Manager behaviour change

Manager behaviour change was measured by comparing manager and employee responses to the two questionnaires: one before the workshop and the other three months following the workshop. Comparisons between managers who had received feedback and/or had attended the workshop were then made with those managers in the control group who had received no feedback or workshop.

The feedback and workshop were found to have a different impact depending on the extent to which the managers already showed Positive Manager Behaviour.

Managers who initially showed low levels of positive manager behaviour

- Managers who rated themselves as 'ineffective' (i.e., demonstrating low levels of Positive Manager Behaviour) reported improvements in their behaviour whether they had received feedback and/or attended the workshop, or not.
- Employees' perceptions of these 'ineffective' managers' suggest that their behaviour changed over time only if they received feedback with or without a workshop. Where managers received no feedback, ratings of their behaviour showed little or no change over time; whereas, where managers received feedback, employees ratings suggested that their manager's behaviour had significantly improved (i.e., they were showing more Positive Manager Behaviour) three months later.

Managers who showed average levels of positive manager behaviour

- Managers who rated themselves as 'average' at the start of the process typically reported that their behaviour remained unchanged over the three months.
- Employees' perceptions of these managers' effectiveness changed in the intervention group, but in unexpected ways. Where managers had received no feedback, or received feedback but no workshop, employees' ratings suggested that their behaviour remained largely unchanged. Where managers had received feedback and attended a workshop, employees' ratings suggested that the manager was perceived as less effective at time two.

Managers who initially showed high levels of positive manager behaviour

- Managers who rated themselves as 'effective' (i.e., demonstrating high levels of Positive Manager Behaviour) at the start of the process

but received no feedback or workshop rated themselves significantly less effective on all four competencies at the second time point.
- Employees who initially rated their manager as 'effective', rated their manager as less 'effective' at time two (i.e., demonstrating lower levels of Positive Manager Behaviour), regardless of whether the manager had received feedback, attended a workshop or received neither intervention.

What do these findings mean? While the managers indicated that the intervention increased their level of self-awareness, the findings suggest that this increase in self-awareness did not necessarily translate into improved behaviour if the manager was already showing high levels of Positive Manager Behaviour. A number of explanations can be offered:

- Completing the questionnaire for the first time may have heightened managers' and employees' awareness of the specific stress management behaviours and in doing so, made both parties more acutely aware of when the behaviours were being used, and when they were not.
- For those managers already perceived as average or effective, it is unlikely that they started doing anything wrong or behaving in a less effective way, but self- and employee expectations may have been raised simply by going through the process of responding to the questionnaire.
- For the employees of managers who received no feedback or workshop, the absence of change or development may have felt frustrating given the investment in completing the questionnaire.
- Managers attending the workshops were encouraged to share their reports with their team. This may have lead to increased expectations or may have been interpreted by the employees as the manager suggesting that their current behaviour is the ideal state, and thereby leading to frustration.

2. Manager perspectives of the positive manager behaviour approach

Following the workshop, managers were asked to provide feedback on their reactions and learning. 112 managers responded:

- 85 per cent of managers who received feedback reported they understood the importance of positive manager behaviour.
- 87 per cent of managers who received feedback reported that they had increased their awareness of their own behaviour.

- 82 per cent of managers who received feedback reported that they could go on to apply their learning and improve their behaviour.
- 57 per ent of managers reported that understanding the views of their team through the feedback report was the most useful element of the intervention, followed by the case studies and scenarios explored in the workshop.

Three months after the intervention, and after completion of the second upward feedback reports, managers were asked to provide feedback on their experience of the whole process – 40 managers responded:

- Managers typically discussed their feedback with both their manager and their direct reports.
- 75 per cent of managers reported that they had been able to make changes to their behaviour following the workshop.
- 88 per cent of managers felt that they had learnt something about themselves.
- While the majority of managers felt their manager had been positive about the process, only 56 per cent reported that they felt the organization had been supportive of them taking action following the workshop.

3. Practitioner perspectives of the positive manager behaviour approach

Stakeholder discussions were held to evaluate how the Positive Manager Behaviour approach impacted on the organization. The following themes were identified as differentiating successful and challenging experiences from a stakeholder or Human Resource/Occupational Health perspective:

- *Steering group*: Practitioners recommended setting up a steering group, preferably involving a diverse membership, for example, managers, Occupational Health, Human Resources, senior management and employee representatives.
- *United front*: Rather than presenting the project as an initiative from Human Resources or Occupational Health, projects are seen to have more weight if they are driven by the organization.
- *Branding*: Different approaches suit different organizations and investing time in getting the branding right is worthwhile. Is the programme part of a leadership programme or a workplace well-being programme? Stress or positive management? Compulsory or voluntary? The right branding will increase engagement and participation.

- *Integration*: Embedding the intervention within a wider programme or workplace initiative strengthens the buy-in and helps to ensure the longevity of the intervention. For example, including the process in the organization's stress management or employee well-being programme; making the intervention part of the management training programme or linking it to performance management and development plans.

Key Points from the evaluation of a Positive Manager Behaviour approach

- Managers who initially see themselves, or are perceived by their team, as not showing Positive Manager Behaviour benefit most from the process.
- Following the upward feedback and workshop, line managers reported they were more self-aware, were committed to make changes to their behaviour and felt that they would be able to go on to apply their learning.
- Developing a steering group, integrating the process into existing HR/OH initiatives and policies, and branding the process appropriately are vital to the success of the intervention.

Useful Resources

The research reports can be downloaded from the HSE and CIPD websites as follows:

- Phase 1: www.hse.gov.uk/research/rrhtm/rr553.htm
- Phase 2: www.hse.gov.uk/research/rrhtm/rr633.htm
- Phase 3: www.cipd.co.uk/subjects/health/stress/_preventing_stress

Short guidance leaflets can be downloaded from the CIPD website:

- www.cipd.co.uk/subjects/health/stress/_Instrswrk.htm?IsSrchRes=1

The Management Competency Indicator Tool is available free of charge in a self-report format from the Health and Safety Executive website. Managers are able complete the measure and the interactive spreadsheet enables managers to receive feedback on their responses:

- www.hse.gov.uk/stress/mcit.htm

References

Boyatzis, R.E. (1982). *The Competent Manager: A Model for Effective Performance*. John Wiley & Sons, Chichester.

Donaldson-Feilder, E., Lewis, R. and Yarker, J., (2009). *Preventing Stress: Promoting Positive Manager Behaviour*. CIPD Insight Report. CIPD Publications: London, available on the CIPD website: www.cipd.co.uk/subjects/health/stress/_preventing_stress

Flanagan, J.C. (1954). The critical incident technique. *Psychological Bulletin*, 51, 327–358.

Rankin, N. (2004). *The New Prescription for Performance: The Eleventh Competency Benchmarking Survey. Competency & Emotional Intelligence Benchmarking Supplement 2004/2005*. London: IRS.

Theorell, T., Emdad, R., Arnetz, B. and Weingarten, A.-M. (2001). Employee effects of an educational program for managers at an insurance company. *Psychosomatic Medicine*, 63, 724–733.

Tsutsumi, A., Takao, S., Mineyama, S., Nishiuchi, K., Komatsu, H. and Kawakami, N. (2005). Effects of a supervisory education for positive mental health in the workplace: A quasi-experimental study. *Journal of Occupational Health*, 47, 226–235.

Yarker, J., Donaldson-Feilder, E. and Lewis, R. (2008). *Management Competencies for Preventing and Reducing Stress at Work: Identifying and Developing the Management Behaviours Necessary to Implement the HSE Management Standards*. HSE Books, London.

Yarker, J., Donaldson-Feilder, E., Lewis, R. and Flaxman, P. E. (2007). *Management Competencies for Preventing and Reducing Stress at Work: Identifying and Developing the Management Behaviours Necessary to Implement the HSE Management Standards*. HSE Books, London.

5

Respectful and responsible: Managing emotions and having integrity (management competency 1)

The first competency we are going to explore is called 'Respectful and responsible: managing emotions and having integrity'. This competency is about treating staff with respect, including acting with integrity, managing emotions and being considerate. For example, managers must act calmly in pressured situations and take a consistent approach, as opposed to panicking or exhibiting mood swings. Ensuring deadlines are realistic, giving more positive than negative feedback and showing consideration for employees' work-life balance are other key elements.

The behaviours that are included in this competency fall into three different clusters:

1. Integrity
2. Managing Emotions
3. Considerate Approach.

Preventing Stress in Organizations: How to Develop Positive Managers,
Emma Donaldson-Feilder, Joanna Yarker and Rachel Lewis.
© 2011 John Wiley & Sons, Ltd. Published 2011 by John Wiley & Sons, Ltd.

In this chapter, each of these clusters of behaviours will be explored in turn, providing examples of the types of contexts in which both positive and negative behaviours may occur and providing exercises and case studies that can be used in training, coaching and consultancy to further explore the areas.

Integrity

The ultimate measure of a man is not where he stands in moments of comfort and convenience, but where he stands at a time of challenge and controversy. (Martin Luther King)

What does managing with integrity mean?

With the recent public furore over scandals such as that of the UK MP expenses, Fred Goodwin's (formerly RBS) pension and the uncovering of Bernard Madoff's Ponzi scheme, we are perhaps more acutely attuned than ever to both the concept, and importance, of ethics, integrity and values-based leadership.

The Latin root of integrity is similar to that of integer, meaning whole number. This concept of wholeness, or consistency of leadership is clearly relevant, and the concept of leading or managing with integrity is about a manager whose behaviour and decisions are in line with their, and our, principles; these principles being generally accepted to be both ethical and honest.

As reflected in the wider public perception, the academic literature has also recently begun to focus on the importance of integrity and ethics-based leadership. A small body of evidence shows the benefits of leading with integrity, with research linking perceptions of managers' effectiveness to perceptions of honesty, integrity and trustworthiness in the manager. It has been found that when staff believe their manager has integrity, they will be more likely to believe the information they receive from that manager, be more willing to commit to goals set by the manager, and be more comfortable engaging in behaviours that may put themselves at risk, for instance sharing sensitive information with their manager, or alerting them to impending issues in the team, therefore enabling the manager to manage more effectively and proactively. Conversely, if staff feel their manager cannot be trusted, or does not have integrity, it has been found that they will direct energy towards 'covering their backs', detracting from their work performance and only following the goals and objectives that have been set for them, thus creating an 'each for their own' mentality in the team.

Two quite different examples from employees in our research recalling manager behaviour that was lacking in integrity are presented here. In both, the long term ramifications of this behaviour are apparent.

This first example comes from a local government employee and relates to a manager that passed work off as her own.

"I came back to work after being on long term sick. While I was off, my manager had produced a report which had been taken from work I had been doing before I went off. This work I had done was very far reaching, and actually won a national award. The manager wrote this report as her own and even put a note on it that I had had no involvement as I had been off sick. But it was taken directly from my work. I asked her to change it, pointing out which bits I had done but she wouldn't. My manager then got to present this work nationally as her own. It really knocked me for six, I was feeling incredibly fragile after returning to work and this was awful. A few months later I had an opportunity to explain to the executive management team what work I had done around this. They acknowledged the work I had done but still my manager didn't. There was no apology even. I have a different manager now but would still hesitate before trusting them."

The second example relates to a manager being seen to lack integrity in their decision making, and also in their approach to sensitive information. The employee in this example works in a large financial organization.

"I had a good friend in my office called Katy. She worked in a different department to me but we were very close. I had worked in my area for a while, and through appraisals and meetings had made clear to my manager that I was keen to be given development opportunities to gain promotion. Katy told me that she was moving into my team. I found out from her that she was going to be second in command to my manager and therefore that she was being promoted. My manager knew I wanted a promotion and that I wanted to develop. He didn't communicate this about Katy to me and so I went to him when Katy told me and said how disappointed I was in not being considered for this move.

I didn't begrudge Katy the opportunity, but I did feel pushed out. Also, because she was my friend in the office and the one I normally confided in, I didn't have anyone to talk to about this. I couldn't talk to Katy as it would seem like sour grapes. Anyway, a week later, my manager was talking to Katy and he told her what I had said to him and had a moan about me. He betrayed my confidence. The things I said to him about my personal feelings about what had happened and how that impacted upon me he shared. I felt so betrayed. If he could say things to her, who else was he telling what I said?

In one-to-ones, he also made comments about my peer group and how he rated them and about their performance. He would say things to me that I guess were told to him in confidence. I became very distrustful of him. It had a very negative impact on the team. Rightly or wrongly, I was so disillusioned with him that I started letting everyone know the little things he was doing in terms of gossiping about others. It created a terrible atmosphere and no-one wanted to work hard for him."

Academic perspective on leading with integrity

Although the academic literature has an increasing focus on values-based leadership, no one framework looks specifically at leading with integrity. Of the traditional leadership models explored in Chapter 3, the consideration element of the task- and consideration-based leadership model has elements of leading with integrity, including manager's behaviours such as treating all staff members as equals. The transformational leadership model is more complex. Some would argue that although a key outcome of transformational leadership is its ability to engender trust in followers, it is not clear how this trust is gained. Some would argue that in fact, particularly when considering charismatic leadership, impact may not always be through ethical means, pointing to the opportunity for 'spin' and persuasion with this type of leadership. Despite this debate, transformational leadership, particularly the idealized influence component, has been positively linked with both perceptions of ethics and integrity in managers.

There are two more recent leadership models that focus on integrity-based leadership as their core construct. These are ethical leadership and authentic leadership. Ethical leadership has been defined by Brown and colleagues (Brown and Trevino, 2006) as 'the demonstration of normatively appropriate conduct through personal actions and interpersonal relationships, and the promotion of such conduct to followers through two-way communication, reinforcement and decision-making'. Research in this area has found that ethical leaders display that they are honest, trustworthy, fair and principled, and that they communicate on ethics and values by visibly and intentionally role modelling behaviour, in other words, practising what they preach.

Authentic leadership is a relatively new theory, first conceptualized in 2005. Key attributes of authentic leaders are that they are true to themselves, being motivated by personal convictions rather than success or status; that they own their own thoughts, feelings and actions but are able to consider and assess multiple perspectives in a balanced manner; and that they foster authenticity in their followers, by increased self-awareness, regulation and positive modelling.

The academic literature in this area therefore suggests that leading with integrity is not just about managers behaving in an honest, trustworthy and fair way towards employees, by not speaking behind people backs or passing on sensitive information, but it is also about role modelling these behaviours, encouraging their staff to behave in these positive ways and admitting mistakes when they occur.

The findings from our research

This duality is also reflected in our research findings where positive examples of behaviour included:

- ✓ Being a good role model
- ✓ Keeping employees' issues private and confidential
- ✓ Admitting their mistakes
- ✓ Treating all team members with equal importance
- ✓ Treating all team members with respect
- ✓ Being honest

Negative examples of behaviour (therefore not acting with integrity) included:

- × Speaking about employees behind their backs
- × Making promises, then not delivering on them
- × Saying one thing, and doing something different
- × Making personal issues public

Behaving with integrity is therefore not just about what a manager says, but, more importantly, their actions and how they role model the positive behaviours.

Here, a local government manager talks about their approach with his team and his commitment to integrity.

> "A long time ago, at the beginning of my career, I told a senior manager a problem that someone had told me. I ended up completely losing that person's trust because the senior that I told didn't keep it confidential. Not being open and honest with your team is the worst thing that you can do. It takes time to build trust in people. I make sure that from the beginning I build an atmosphere where everything is upfront, nothing is hidden and beyond conversation. If I have to convey something that is going to be negative, I make sure I know the full picture first and consider what this information is going to do to my team. I then tell them, I put across my point of view and the way I see it and I gauge the reaction. It is better out in the open where I can deal with the criticism and support them and work through it. I am absolutely commited to honesty".

This account highlights the fact that managers often need to convey and communicate negative information, for instance likelihood of redundancies or team changes. There are a number of learnings from this account that can be used as tips for managers in conveying negative information with integrity and honesty:

- Preparation – ensuring that the manager has all the information that is available, and also recognizes what information is not yet available or known;
- Considering the impact this information will have on the team and the long term ramifications;
- Conveying their opinion on it, therefore taking responsibility for the information rather than blaming 'senior management' or others;
- Expecting, allowing and accepting criticism; and
- Building in time to support the team following this information.

The difficulties of managing with integrity

Achieving the correct balance when managing in order to come across as a manager with integrity may be more difficult than it first appears. For example, managers who feel pressured themselves but want to appear to be friendly and supportive may make a commitment that, although they intend to keep, might be difficult – for instance 'I will change that deadline,' or 'I promise we will get some additional resource on board.'

The key thing is that managers realize the need to 'play the long game' and consider the long-term impact of their promises on the team before making any commitment. It may be that the commitment that they make is a more measured one for instance, 'I will put the case to senior management to try to get some additional resources on board,' or even avoiding promises or commitments if there is a risk they cannot be kept. If a manager is overloaded and is at risk of forgetting what they have promised, it might be worth them suggesting to their team that they remind them, possibly by email so there is a record, what they have said they will do.

A team will build up more trust for a manager who keeps their promises and whose word can be relied upon than someone who tries to appease team members by making empty promises or short-term decisions. Managing with integrity takes consideration and strength of conviction. There may be times when a manager cannot or does not keep their word. In this situation, the important thing is not that the manager hides this from the team, but rather is open and honest, and apologises for this. An example of this is provided by a central government manager:

> "One of my team came to me last week and asked if I had done that thing I said I would. I said 'Do you want the truth or do you want a lie?' They said they wanted the truth and I confessed that I had forgotten all about it. I said I had no excuse and I was sorry. People always prefer you to be honest. That is how you build trust and respect."

In our many discussions with managers, and upon exploring their upward feedback received from their direct reports, we found that managers were often concerned that they did not behave with integrity. . . despite their team members frequently disagreeing with this. One of the key issues we found was that managers felt that, to be an honest and ethical manager, they had to share everything with their team, particularly information that came to them from above. They also felt that if they were privy to sensitive information which they had been told not to pass on to their team members, that this was in some way unethical.

What are your thoughts on this?

The following case study arises from a real situation that occurred with a college.

Case study

This case study is taken from a college in the UK. At the beginning of the academic year, it was discovered that the head teacher was having an affair with one of the students. The student was of legal age and there was no question the affair had been conducted with an underage pupil. A senior teacher speaks of the situation, 'All the students in her (the head teacher's girlfriend's) class were upset about it and were worried that she was getting extra tuition, or that when it came to marking essays she would be preferred and they would be marked down.'

The senior teacher was sure that the head teacher would never do this as he was incredibly diligent and would not compromise marking. However she recognized that the students did not know this. She continues, 'As I was the next senior person to him, I was tasked with trying to resolve this problem over essay marking. Although he was meant to be doing this particular marking, I took it away from him and two or three of us did it. We then got an external examiner to check our marks, because we hadn't actually taught this subject. She was very under-standing, very sympathetic and supportive.'

The marks were returned to the students without an explanation of who did the marking or what had happened to resolve the issue. The senior teacher said 'I then told the head teacher we needed to tell the students what we had done to reassure them. He said no. He said he expressly forbade me from telling them anything. I had the students' trust but because I couldn't tell them what was done and how we'd done the marking to reassure them it had been done properly, they must have thought we were trying to hide things. That was not what I wanted to happen.' The senior teacher felt very distressed about the situation and noted that the distress and anxiety continued to be felt by the students.

She talks about the repercussions at the end of term. 'It had a tremendous effect on the students. Quite a number, who had been good students up until the start of term, failed their exams and didn't pass the year. Our pass figures were awful and you could tell what had done it. The students lost confidence in whether we had done the right thing and sign ups for the following year really dropped.' She talks of the fact that the relationship continued and that it was seen by both staff and students as being handled 'indiscreetly'.

When asked to consider why the head teacher acted in this way, the senior teacher said 'It must have been a huge stress for him to have his personal life coming out and it must have been embarrassing. He didn't want to make a big issue of it, and so didn't want to expressly address the students' concerns. In doing so, he completely under-estimated the strength of feeling, and lost the trust of the students for all of us.'

Do you think you would have acted differently as the senior teacher? Is there anything she could have done to ease the situation?

We recognize that line managers have an incredibly difficult role balancing the demands of their seniors as well as their team members. We also recognize that there is some information managers are unable, and would be unwise, to divulge to their team members.

Tips for how a manager can avoid feeling that they are behaving without integrity when they can't share key information with their team:

- The most important first step for the manager is recognizing their role as a manager and the responsibility they hold both to the organization (their seniors) and their team. Managers need to develop a strong sense of their own principles and values in order to make sure, whatever they do decide to do, it is consistent and they remain true to themselves. This will stop them feeling 'pulled' in opposite directions.
- Once they are clear about their role and their values, to make their team aware of what these are. This will be the first step in role modelling a team culture of integrity and authenticity.
- Be honest that there are some things that they are unable to share with the team. Communicate with the team.
- Avoid favouritism. Although it is human nature that certain members of the team will enjoy a better relationship with the manager than others, it is important that any message is conveyed equally and without judgement or favouritism.
- Refuse to provide information that is either false, or is against the values and principles that the manager hold.
- If information that is being withheld is incongruent with that manager's values and goals, in other words, the manager feels that it is ethically, or morally wrong to withhold that particular information from the team, the decision to withhold that information needs to be challenged upwards (or with whoever gave the manager the

instructions). This is where, as a practitioner you may have a role in helping the manager build a case, and, if this guidance has come from senior management, to help them to communicate upwards more effectively and assertively.

How do you feel this could be applied to the case study?

If a manager is able to convey information to the team according to these principles, they start to create a culture of trust in team members where the team recognize that the manager will behave in the way that they judge is best for the team as a whole, and due to this, won't need to challenge or question the information that they do receive. As a healthcare employee stated: 'You haven't got to be best friends with your manager, but you do have to know they have your best interests at heart.'

Managing Emotions

'If you can keep your head when all about you
Are losing theirs...' (Rudyard Kipling)

The importance of consistency

Within the meaning of the word integrity, came the concept of wholeness and consistency. The concept of consistency of managerial style is central to integrity. If a manager behaves differently and makes differing decisions dependent on their mood or the pressure that they are under, that manager is unlikely to be seen by their employees as one who is high in integrity.

Quotation from a manager working within education:

"You should appear calm as a swan even if your legs are swimming underneath. You are continually paddling but you stay calm. People will see you as being calm and laid back. Inside you might not be but that is what you need to show to your team. It empowers people. They think if I am calm, then they can do it, they think 'she said it will be fine, she will help me with this and we will work together.' Your manner and attitude rubs off on other people."

Recent academic research has pointed to how 'contagious' the manager's mood can be. Research has shown that 'high status' individuals are more likely to transmit their moods to 'low status' individuals than vice versa. Therefore managers (being hierarchically of higher status) are more likely to pass on their mood to their team rather than the team members affect their manager with their moods. Work of Sy, Cote and Saavedra (2005) found that when employees perceived their manager to be in a positive mood, they had more positive moods themselves, both at the individual level and at the group level. It was also found that the mood of the manager affected not just the well-being of the team, but also the performance – teams with managers who were in negative moods expended more effort in completing their tasks, and showed less coordination than those who had managers in positive moods.

The research, therefore, suggests that managers who do not control their negative emotions and moods are likely to impact negatively on both the well-being and the performance of the team. Below are two real examples of managers displaying this type of behaviour from the words of their employees. It is clear just how 'contagious' their moods, and particularly the impact of inconsistency, can be within a team.

This example comes from an employee working within a large financial organization:

> "It was almost like he had two personalities. He would tell you to do one thing one day, and then you would do it, and the next day he would ask you why you had done it. If you said to him that he had told you to do it, he would be adamant he hadn't and that you had done it wrong. It was horrible. It made me feel so bad I felt like leaving. I wasn't the only person that was experiencing this behaviour. The whole atmosphere in the office was always tense, you didn't know from one day to another whether he was going to come in happy and smiling or come in shouting. At the time we didn't say anything. We didn't speak to anyone about anything in case it got back to him and it would be blown out of all proportion. Although he left a year ago, even now you can see people are wary to be open and honest about things because they are worried something will come back to them."

This example comes from an employee working within a hospital ward:

> "Our manager can't handle the pressure being put on her. When she is stressed she gets frantic and changes personality. She is normally quite happy and friendly, but becomes very snappy and changes the boundaries. She gets intolerant of people asking questions and interrupting her with things that would normally be OK. When the pressure is on she passes it straight to us. Not just the work, but the stress and the anxiety which is felt by the whole team. You can see from her body language when she walks into the room and her stress and anxiety is felt by the whole team. You start to look after yourself more, you are not open, you start to take your terms and conditions by the rule, you won't do anything over and above your hours, you don't want to arrive early at work, or work slightly later. You withdraw into yourself, and only do what is defined by the role – and nothing more."

When negative outbursts happen

Sometimes negative manager emotion and mood can culminate in much more obvious and worrying outbursts directed towards employees. There is an emerging field of research in occupational psychology that explores the impact of negative leader behaviour, which could include negative mood and emotions, but which is more visible and concrete. There are a wide number of concepts that fall under the overarching concept of negative leader behaviour, including behaviours characterized as bullying, undermining, tyrannical, hostile, destructive and abusive. The strongest body of research refers to abusive supervision which is defined as 'the sustained display of hostile verbal and non-verbal behaviours, excluding physical contact' (Tepper, 2000) and may include behaviours such as using derogatory names, engaging in explosive outbursts, intimidating by use of threats and job loss, withholding needed information, silent treatment, and humiliating, ridiculing or belittling employees in front of others. Research conducted in the United Sates in 2005 by Harvey and colleagues suggested that 13.6 per cent of the working population are affected by abusive supervision (Harvey, Stoner, Hochwarter, and Kacmar, 2005).

An employee from a healthcare organization speaks of her manager who displays this type of negative behaviour:

"Her idea of motivating staff was to come in screaming hysterically. She would blame you for anything you did wrong or she lost paperwork. She would scream at you and you were, in her eyes the one responsible. All you could hear, almost every other day, was that she would be screaming at staff and that there were big arguments going on."

"This is a silly example, but shows you what she was like. One day she had a meeting with a more senior manager. I had arranged the meeting to be in a meeting room down the corridor. When she got to the meeting room the senior manager was in the room already, but on the phone. She had to wait 10 minutes to get into the room. When she did, she said she hadn't got time to have the meeting then, even though the meeting was due to last for 1 hour. She then turned round to me, in front of everyone and shouted 'In future, make sure all meetings you arrange are in MY OFFICE'. And she stormed out. It was devastating and humiliating.

Other times, she would have had a meeting with the chief executive and would come running in to our team and say 'You've got to do this, you got to do that.' Even if it was impossible and we would try and explain why it couldn't be done, she would scream 'I've told the chief executive that it will be done AND YOU MUST DO IT!' And we would then be left with an impossible situation. None of us wanted to do anything with her because she wouldn't listen to you. She just didn't understand the job. It meant the whole department literally got destroyed. It didn't run properly, it was inefficient'."

This example clearly shows the devastating effect of managers who display aggressive, belittling and blaming behaviour towards their team members. Research on negative leaders has related this type of behaviour to many negative outcomes such as job dissatisfaction, intention to leave, employee deviance behaviours, and a range of psychological outcomes such as anxiety, depression, burnout and somatic health complaints.

Research highlights the wide ranging and devastating outcomes of managers behaving in negative ways on employee well-being and performance. These behaviours may vary in severity from seemedly mild behaviours such as managers demonstrating the stress they are under, and perhaps being short with employees when approached, to severe behaviours such as explosive outbursts and intimidation. What the research suggests however is that any negative behaviour, mild or severe, will have an impact upon how employees evaluate that manager, and subsequently upon employee well-being and performance – both at the individual and the team level. Therefore it is vitally important that managers are able to manage their moods and behaviour and maintain an appropriate level of conduct in front of their team members.

The negative behaviours we found in our research to be important were:

× passing on stress to employees;
× acting aggressively;
× losing temper with employees; and
× being unpredictable in mood.

Positive behaviour is not just about the absence of negative

It is important to remember however that the behaviour that managers need to demonstrate is not just the absence of negative behaviour, for instance not shouting, but also more positive behaviour. These are the positive behaviours in this area we have found to be important:

✓ having a positive approach;
✓ acting calmly when under pressure;
✓ walking away when feeling unable to control emotion;
✓ apologizing for poor behaviour; and
✓ taking a consistent approach to managing.

Here is an example, from a large financial organization, of an employee talking about just how beneficial taking a positive and consistent approach can be in a team, particularly if that team is under pressure.

She walks round the team when we are really stressed and when we are going 'AAGGGHHHH!!!'. And she says, 'It is fine, don't worry about it, I will help.' Even if things are going wrong or we are under loads of pressure she will tell us that it is her responsibility and it is not for us to worry about and that all we need to do is our best. And it is so positive and wonderful just knowing that. When she is around she just has this aura, we just associate her with positivity. I am sure she has her own worries and that things aren't going as quickly as she would like, and I know her manager puts loads of pressure on her, but she always says she will cope and tells us not to worry. She keeps the team positive, she keeps us motivated, and she makes us want to do the best job we can for her.

What we found from our research, which is often forgotten in models of manager's mood or negative behaviour, is the understanding that, no matter how much training and development the manager has had, or how effective a manager is, there will be times when emotions will be impossible to control. In this situation, the manager may need to walk away and take time out to calm down and gain control to avoid the negative emotional content affecting the team.

If it is too late and the outburst has happened, the key thing is for the manager to retain their integrity. The manager needs to be honest and communicate with the team what happened, and apologize for their behaviour. Apologizing for poor behaviour, as long as it doesn't happen too often, will not damage the perceived integrity of that manager.

This example, from an employee in a financial organization, shows how beneficial taking this approach can be.

"My manager came into the office one morning and asked if he could have a word. I didn't know what it was about but when I went in he said 'I must apologize for yesterday, I was in such a mood and I really must apologizes.' I was so shocked! When someone is like that it really helps because you develop a better working relationship and when things are under pressure, you are more prepared to respond and you feel more valued."

What makes it more difficult to manage emotions?

Most managers, particularly if they are focused on their own development, will know that it is unacceptable to lose their temper with their team members or act aggressively towards them. Most will also aim to behave consistently, calmly and positively in pressured situations. Therefore it is often not the role of the practitioner to deal with those managers who consistently behave in abusive or hostile ways, but more commonly to work with managers who, for the most part, are respectful and responsible, but, on occasion, find it difficult or are unable to manage their emotions. It is your role to try and work through with the manager what might be the barriers to behaving in positive ways, and what might be the issues that cause them to behave in negative ways.

The following vignette is an excerpt taken from an interview with a local government manager where he describes a situation in which he was unable to control his emotions. The practitioner prompts the manager to reflect upon why this might have happened.

MANAGER: I try to maintain my professionalism at all times, but sometimes I can't hold onto it. One particular example is where I was very pressured in what I was doing. I was trying to get a document finished. I was saying to myself I had to get it done and worrying that it wouldn't be done in time. One of my team members kept coming up to me throughout the day and saying she needed to see me and she needed to ask me something. I just kept saying I was really busy and I would find her when I was finished. She didn't take the hint and it got to the seventh and eighth time and I said, or maybe snapped, 'Will you just go away. Leave me alone and don't bother me again'.

PRACTITIONER: What happened after you reacted like this?

MANAGER: I felt so guilty. She went back to her office and must have felt awful. I should have handled it better. I did then go out and see her and I did apologise and said I was very pressured. She said it was fine, but that it didn't make her feel good at all.

PRACTITIONER: What do you think you could have done differently?

MANAGER: 'I could have explained very early on that I had an important deadline to meet and that I would come and find her later. I could also have said, if it was a major issue, that she could speak to my boss or one of my peers who could have helped while I was tied up.

PRACTITIONER: What do you think was the barrier to you behaving in this more positive way?

MANAGER: The only barrier to me behaving differently was me. I got carried away. I felt like I was doing this piece of work and that no-one else could do it and no-one was helping me. I started thinking how unfair it all was that everyone always needed me, and I just got really selfish. I lost all perspective and rationality on the situation.

If you are running a training workshop you could facilitate a discussion around this where you might show the managers in the group the list of both positive and negative indicators, and then ask them to give examples of barriers they experience – the things that get in the way of them showing the positive behaviours, and the things that might cause them to show the negative behaviours. If in a coaching or one-to-one situation, you might want to explore with the manager a particular situation (perhaps the last time) where they felt unable to control their emotions, or felt that they had acted in a negative way towards their employees. Once the manager has recalled a situation, you can then work through an understanding of the context in which this occurred and facilitate a discussion around their barriers and issues.

In our research, we found the barriers or issues to fall within four themes: personal level, individual work/job level, team/relationship level and organizational/wider level barriers. These are explored in detail in Chapter 9.

Once the managers have identified their barriers to displaying positive behaviours (or issues causing them to display negative behaviours), it is helpful to get them to reflect upon the solutions to these. Whether one-to-one or in a group situation, you may well be faced with a response of 'There is nothing I can do about it', where managers perceive issues and barriers to be out of their control. It is important to encourage managers to think about solutions to issues in three ways: changing the situation, changing their reaction to the situation or managing the impact of their response to that situation. Even in situations, such as governmental legislation impacting upon their work pressure, where the situation itself cannot be changed, there is always a way to change and minimize the impact of the negative situation. Again, these are explored in detail in Chapter 9.

Considerate Approach

The final set of behaviours within 'Respectful and responsible: managing emotions and having integrity' is considerate approach. It could be said that displaying considerate behaviour is the umbrella that sits above all people management behaviour, particularly integrity and managing emotions – as it refers to a consideration of the needs, values, attitudes and reactions of others.

Considerate management in the academic literature

In Chapter 3, the leadership model of task- and consideration-based behaviour was explored. In this model, consideration refers to the degree to which a leader shows concern and respect for followers, looks out for their welfare, and expresses appreciation and support. Behaviours therefore include supporting employees, showing respect for employees' ideas, increasing cohesiveness, developing and mentoring, looking out for employees' welfare, managing conflict and team building. This type of leadership behaviour has been found to be associated with many positive employee outcomes, from performance and productivity, to reducing burnout and tension, and improving employee well-being.

The most commonly used conceptualization of transformational leadership by Bass and Avolio (1997) has one factor called individualized consideration, which although focusing attention on individual employees, is about attention in order to appreciate strengths, rather than concern for well-being. A UK-based model of transformational leadership was developed by Alimo-Metcalfe and Alban-Metcalfe in 2001. Interestingly, this model, which focused on line managers, found that one subscale '(having a) genuine concern for others' (displays sensitivity to the feelings of others, offers personal support, and communicates positive expectations) was the strongest predictor of ratings of effective stress management.

The academic literature therefore demonstrates that considerate manager behaviour has been consistently linked to well-being outcomes in employees, and focuses on behaviours related to having a genuine concern for others and their welfare, and upon appreciating others and providing positive feedback.

The findings from our research

The behaviours from our research parallel these findings.

The behaviours found to be important from our research again include both positive behaviours (considered here) and negative behaviours (considered below). The specific positive consideration manager behaviours we found to be important were:

- ✓ praising good work;
- ✓ acknowledging employee's efforts;
- ✓ operating a no blame culture;
- ✓ passing positive feedback about the team to senior management;
- ✓ being flexible when employees need time off; and
- ✓ demonstrating consideration of employee's need for work–life balance.

These positive examples from managers demonstrate how small changes in working arrangements can make a huge difference to the experience of employees at work.

This first quotation comes from a manager in a large financial organization:

"I joined as manager of a new team and straight away noticed that one, very junior, member of the team was very withdrawn from the rest of the group, very quiet and never raised any points in meetings. I took this person aside and took time to go through any issues that they had, and really tried to build their confidence up. He said that it was the first time anyone had ever said to him he was an important part of the team. I told him he was as vital and important as everyone else in the team. Very quickly I saw a change in him. I saw the spark coming back and he began to be more involved in the team. All it took was letting him know that I thought he was worthwhile and that I was willing to take the time to try and motivate him and develop him as a team member."

The second comes from a manager of a sales team who operated within an environment which, in his own words, was very target and output driven:

"What I do is note down every time anyone in the team achieves something, it might even be small things like finally managed to get through to a customer they had been trying to contact for a while. I then tell the senior manager about these once a month so that the achievement of every team member is recognized. The nature of our job in sales is we tend to focus on the negative. We tend to point the finger rather than give credit. We also get really focused on our target without considering all the other elements of our jobs that are important. I have found by doing this [recognizing achievement], I am better able to motivate the team, and my senior managers also see the good that my team is doing. I also encourage my team members to mirror what I do, and note down for themselves all their achievements. I really think this makes them do a better job as in focusing on the positives they are motivated to continue to do a good job. In sales it is all about confidence, and confidence comes from feeling good about yourself."

In terms of feedback and praise, from our research it is clear that employees are not expecting this to be every day and it certainly isn't about managers giving rewards and incentives. The important aspect seems to be that managers recognize how hard employees are working and the effort that they put in, as demonstrated by the following quotation from an employee working within a call centre.

"My manager always gives praise if things go well. She acknowledges and appreciates what I do. Even if things go wrong, she will still be supportive and try and focus on improving and staying focused. On a weekly basis as well she sends out an email saying who has done the most calls, and also specific things that we have done like dealing with a difficult caller or learning a new product. This congratulates those who have done a great job and promotes a bit of happy competition to get everyone in the team wanting to do their best for her. I had a manager before that never said thank you or well done. In this job, you do the same thing most days, and without that recognition sometimes it just feels like you are a hamster on a wheel, just running and running with no recognition."

The need for work–life balance

This area also encompasses managers who recognize an individual's need for work–life balance and the importance of personal life. These employee examples show how much this behaviour is appreciated.

"I was having a bit of trouble with my daughter. I needed to carry on working 37 hours a week, but wanted to work more flexibly, particularly making sure I could pick my daughter up from school at 3pm. My manager was great about it and let me come in very early in the morning so I could leave early. She also let me work late on the evenings when my husband could fill in. It has worked so well for me and really taken the pressure off me feeling I was letting my family down."

"Recently my sister was ill in hospital. I had been ill beforehand, and finding out how ill my sister was really made me feel unwell again. It all came to a bit of a head. My manager gave me time off without any fuss. She kept in contact with me and told me that I could take as much time as I needed, and that I should come back when I was better and not before. It really took the pressure off and stopped me feeling so guilty and worried about missing work. In fact I didn't take long off."

An interesting element of the research that emerged was how important it was for managers to also recognize their own limitations and need for work–life balance. There is a need for managers to recognize, just like team members, that being at work while feeling stressed or unwell will mean they are not as productive as they could be. Also, understanding from the 'managing emotions' section how contagious manager behaviour can be, it is worth remembering how important it is for managers to be able to present themselves in a consistent and in-control way. The following example from a financial manager demonstrates this issue.

"If I knew the team were under pressure and I was absolutely shattered myself and really tired, and feeling quite stressed myself, it would have been good to take say a Monday off, or have a long weekend, or just have a day to relax at home. But I went through several years of where I thought that if my team were putting up with all this and dealing with the work, I must be there too. I now realize that if I look after myself a bit better I will actually manage better. What I was saying was that I didn't think they could cope without me, and that is disrespectful. I wasn't doing a good job or helping anyone by forcing myself to come in. If I am indispensable then I am not doing my job right."

Examples of the inconsiderate approach

Many of the models that focus on considerate behaviour see negative behaviour as being the absence of positive behaviour, for instance not giving positive feedback, rather than giving negative feedback. We found from our research that some of the negative behaviours are actually different to the absence of positive behaviours. For instance, we found the following negative examples of behaviour to be important:

× making short term demands rather than allowing planning;
× creating unrealistic deadlines;
× giving more negative than positive feedback;
× relying on others to deal with problems;
× imposing 'my way is the only way'; and
× showing a lack of consideration for work-life balance

The following two examples demonstrate the impact of these negative behaviours, both upon employee's working lives and upon the perceived integrity of that manager.

> "I have no idea if I do a good job. All I get from my manager is that I am not doing my job properly or what I have done wrong. The only time they speak to me is when it is to bite my head off. I don't want a pat on the back every day. I know I am being paid to do a job, but it would be nice to be told once in a while 'thank you' or 'well done'. If this happened I wouldn't feel the job was so bad. I wouldn't feel like no one notices me. It might be a happier place to work."

> "I had a few days booked to go on holiday. I requested the days off but in the request book neglected to cover one of the shifts for them to take as holiday. I noticed my mistake 6 weeks in advance of my holiday and said how sorry I was but I needed that day off. I didn't see my manager for a few days but when I did, she said I couldn't have the day off because I hadn't booked it and I would need to come back from my holiday. It was a morning shift in the middle of my holiday so I would need to come back for 7 in the morning and then go back to my holiday at the end of the shift. It wasn't that she couldn't be flexible, it was that I hadn't gone through due process. I would have expected her to be more accommodating. Also, things she wouldn't let us do she would be more than happy to do for herself. She had no qualms about taking time off. It was a case of one rule for her and another for us."

Summary

This chapter has explored the competency 'Respectful and responsible: Managing emotions and having integrity'.

As described in Chapter 4, the research in Phase 2 refined the behaviours included in the whole stress management competency framework into a measure to enable both managers to self assess their own effectiveness and for use in 180 degree and 360 degree feedback programmes. Table 5.1 shows those behaviours within the measure relevant to this particular competency. You may want to use this table as a prompt for discussions in your work about displaying these types of behaviours.

Table 5.1.   Behavioural indicators for 'Respectful and responsible: Managing emotions and having integrity'

Competency	Cluster	Do (✓)/ Don't (×)	Examples of manager behaviour
Respectful and responsible: Managing emotions and having integrity	Integrity	✓	• Is a good role model • Treats team members with respect • Is honest
		×	• Says one thing, then does something different • Speaks about team members behind their backs
	Managing emotions	✓	• Acts calmly in pressured situations • Takes a consistent approach to managing
		×	• Is unpredictable in mood • Passes on stress to employees • Panics about deadlines • Takes suggestions for improvement as a personal criticism
	Considerate approach	×	• Makes short term demands rather than allowing planning • Creates unrealistic deadlines • Gives more negative than positive feedback • Relies on others to deal with problems • Imposes 'my way is the only way' • Shows a lack of consideration for work–life balance

Source: Adapted from Donaldson-Feilder, Lewis and Yarker (2009) © Crown Copyright 2009

References

Alimo-Metcalfe, B. and Alban-Metcalfe, R.J. (2001). The development of a transformational leadership questionnaire. *Journal of Occupational and Organizational Psychology*, 74, 1–27.

Bass, B.M. and Avolio, B.J. (1997). *Full Range Leadership Development: Manual for the Multifactor Leadership Questionnaire*. Mind Garden, Palo Alto, CA.

Brown, M.E. and Trevino, L.K. (2006). Ethical leadership: A review and future directions. *The Leadership Quarterly*, 17, 595–616.

Donaldson-Feilder, E., Lewis, R. and Yarker, J., (2009). *Preventing Stress: Promoting Positive Manager Behaviour*. CIPD Insight Report. CIPD Publications: London, available on the CIPD website: www.cipd.co.uk/subjects/health/stress/_preventing_ stress.

Harvey, P., Stoner, J., Hochwarter, W. and Kacmar, K.M. (2005). Easing the strain: The buffering role of supervisors in the perceptions of politics-strain relationship. *Journal of Occupational and Organizational Psychology*, 78, 337–354.

Sy, T., Cote, S. and Saavedra, R. (2005). The contagious leader: Impact of the leader's mood on the mood of the group members, group affective tone and group processes. *Journal of Applied Psychology*, 90, 295–305.

Tepper, B.J. (2000). Consequences of abusive supervision. *Academy of Management Journal*, 43, 178–190.

6

Managing and communicating existing and future work (management competency 2)

The second competency we are going to explore is called 'Managing and communicating existing and future work'. This competency is about managers proactively managing their work and the work of their team members, dealing with problems at work and decision making, keeping team members involved and encouraging participation across their team.

The behaviours included in this competency fall into three different clusters:

1. Proactive work management
2. Problem solving
3. Participative/empowering.

As with the previous chapter, each of the clusters of behaviours are explored in turn, with examples of the types of contexts in which the behaviours may occur, and exercises and case studies to enable their use and exploration in your work as a practitioner.

Preventing Stress in Organizations: How to Develop Positive Managers,
Emma Donaldson-Feilder, Joanna Yarker and Rachel Lewis.
© 2011 John Wiley & Sons, Ltd. Published 2011 by John Wiley & Sons, Ltd.

Proactive Work Management

"Organizing is what you do before you do something, so that when you do it, it is not all mixed up." (A.A. Milne)

This cluster is all about managers managing proactively. In the academic literature, proactive behaviours are referred to as *anticipatory, change orientated and self-initiated*; essentially meaning that managers will act in advance of a future situation to allow themselves to plan and organize their work and the work of others, rather than working reactively, or 'fire fighting'.

A vast body of research in the academic literature points to proactive behaviour being an important determinant of organizational success particularly in dynamic and uncertain environments. This is also reinforced by the leadership literature, which demonstrates proactive work management to be a core component of many of the key leadership models. For instance, taking those explored in Chapter 3, the transformational leadership model created by Alimo-Metcalfe (Alimo-Metcalfe and Alban-Metcalfe, 2001) includes a factor entitled 'Clarifying individual and team direction, priorities and purpose' and the initiating structure component of the Leader Behaviour Description Questionnaire (Stogdill, 1963) includes management behaviours of letting group members know what is expected of them, encouraging the use of uniform procedures, assigning team members to particular tasks, and scheduling work to be done. These directly refer to the importance of proactivity in management.

The findings from our research

The positive examples of behaviour that we found to be important are:

✓ clearly communicating employee objectives;
✓ developing action plans;
✓ monitoring team workload on an ongoing basis;
✓ encouraging the team to review how they organize their work;
✓ stopping additional work being taken on when necessary;
✓ working proactively;
✓ seeing projects/tasks through to delivery;
✓ reviewing processes to see if work can be improved; and
✓ prioritizing future workloads.

What is clear is that planning and organizing; or working proactively, is seen, by both academic and practitioner literature, as an essential component of good leadership and management. Importantly though, it is traditionally considered as being crucial for task management and performance, a way to enable the manager to keep control of work and make things happen in terms of hitting targets and deadlines; rather than as an essential component in preventing and reducing employee work-related stress. In our research, we actually found that the behaviours within this cluster were more commonly mentioned than those in any other competency – and therefore those management behaviours that were most frequently associated with preventing and reducing employee work-related stress and pressure.

Why might a lack of proactivity and forward planning cause employee work-related stress?

The following two examples from employees demonstrate the impact of a lack of forward planning on employees' experiences of the workplace. The first presents perhaps the most common scenario or cause of work-related stress, where work is delegated to employees with short deadlines: due to these deadlines, employees need to work long hours, under more pressure than usual, and feel that the quality of their work is being compromised.

> "A lot of stress is caused by a lack of forward planning. I am asked to do things there and then, and often it is already too late before you are asked to do something. Doing things at such short notice means it is difficult for me to do a good job and present my work the way I want to."

The second example, from a local government employee, demonstrates that a lack of forward planning can result in employees being unclear about what their objectives or their roles at work are, causing conflict and argument within the team.

> "There are always fierce arguments in the morning when vehicles aren't ready or someone has got in someone else's vehicle. It should be better organized so that people know in advance what is happening the next day. If managers took a couple of minutes to talk to teams and plan things out, everyone would know what they were doing, everyone would be happy, and there wouldn't be a sudden change in the morning – and it wouldn't all kick off and start arguments."

The following example demonstrates the problem caused by a manager's lack of forward planning:

> "In our department our funding is dictated by how much output we have and we collate this information every year in June. I need Jenny (my manager's) input for that. Nine times out of ten she is not in the office when I need her to

be, and everything is done at the last minute. It will be done the day before it is due to go in, or at 3 o'clock when the closing time for getting this information in is 5 o'clock. And it is a mad panic when we actually have three months to plan for this. It creates pressure unnecessarily. I don't think we need to have lists and lists of things to do, and dates to do things by, but if we could loosely plan so that her and I sat down for a day to thrash it out – that is all I need her to do. I need her to work backwards from the deadline and look at it realistically."

What does planning involve?

From the previous example it is clear that forward planning is not just about anticipating potential issues, barriers or emergencies, but also planning according to the regular requirements and timetabling of jobs.

From our research it is clear that forward planning is a balancing act and in order to manage this process, it is important for managers not just to set the plan for the year for the team, but to constantly review, consult, update and communicate on the plans and expectations. This way, the manager is able to monitor the team's progress on an ongoing basis as well as work proactively. This example from a call centre employee highlights the benefits of taking a long-term, action-based approach:

"In my last job we always got very busy at the end of the financial year. The call volume increased by 300 per cent which means we were taking call after call. Despite this, it was well managed in terms of there was lots of forward planning. Two months before the end of the tax year we had regular meetings each week to update us on what would be happening at the end of the year, and we also had extra training. It was communicated to everyone what was expected in terms of advice we should and shouldn't be giving. Although it was a really busy four week period, our morale was really high because we had all worked towards this."

Managers therefore may consider adding planning to team meetings where the opportunity is afforded both to create the plan, and, within a team setting, discuss any issues or problems with that plan. It may be that this is done in an informal way, for instance looking at the busy periods and discussing best ways to cope with and plan for this, or by using planning mechanics such as a SWOT analysis where the team would look at the strengths, weaknesses, opportunities and threats to both the work itself over a set period of time, and also the developing plan of action. Central however to the process of planning is for managers to make sure that the team members are all aware of what the demands and expectations of the role are. This way, team members can be equipped to deal with the demands both in terms of skills and time. It is also the manager's responsibility to set priorities and objectives for the team. One example from a healthcare manager highlights the importance of this:

> "We have a team meeting where we lay out all our objectives for the next month. If I am clear what I would like my team to do, but in this meeting, my team feel they can only fulfil 90 per cent of this, we can have a discussion and plan for this. I also make sure that the minutes of the meeting are distributed a couple of days later so that everyone knows what they are doing and what everyone else is doing."

So far in this chapter, we have highlighted the importance of forward planning for managers and the problems associated with a lack of planning. However, planning does need to be a balancing act: just as a lack of planning can be detrimental to employees, so can too much planning. John Lennon said 'Life is what happens to you when you are busy making other plans.' The realities of today's rapidly changing and developing workplace mean that it is not possible to be prepared for every eventuality or anticipate every problem. Not everything can and should be controlled. There are always situations in the workplace such as sickness or accidents that cannot be planned for. The following example from a local government manager demonstrates the issue of too much planning and suggests a way to plan 'with contingency'.

> "We plan for 100 per cent delivery – looking at our time and working out a percentage. This doesn't allow for sickness, down time, development or anything connected with improving the way that we work. If we worked to 85 per cent delivery, where 85 per cent was devoted to actually delivering what we were doing, and 15 per cent allowed for compensation for people being off sick or anything else, we would find we weren't under so much pressure, and would get a bit of flexibility into our plan. Having that 15 per cent allows a bit of leeway when we can calm down and also means if there is something desperately urgent it can be dropped into our lap and we can do it rather than having to drop anything else."

This example suggests the need to add a bit of leeway or flexibility into plans in order both to allow for changes in situations, and provide time and allowance for emergency deadlines and work pressures.

The link between autonomy and well-being is one of the most consistent findings in organizational work-related stress research, showing that where employees feel that they do not have control or responsibility over how or what work they do, well-being is negatively affected. If work is too planned, the impact upon employees may be that their autonomy and perceptions of responsibility over their work will suffer. The following example demonstrates the problems with over-planning from a call centre manager.

"I tried too many rotas – a rota for coming in, for going for breaks, for going upstairs and for having time out. I thought it would be better for them to know when they were going upstairs and when they were going for breaks. It didn't work out like that. They felt very under pressure to think 'Oh, I'm going for a break at 10.15 and so I need to hurry up with this customer.' Or thinking that if they didn't go at 10.15, the next person would be late for their break. They told me how difficult it was because of the nature of the work they did to put everything by the clock and also felt that they didn't always want tea or a cigarette at the time I specified they should have one. In the end I did away with it all together and just kept a rota for them coming in. It is working much more smoothly."

What then are the key learning points for managers around planning?

The following can be used as helpful tips and hints in your work with managers around planning:

- Planning is important not just for team performance, but for team well-being.
- Planning should be focused both on everyday work, and upon developing contingencies for emergencies.
- Planning is not a one-off task. It needs to be constantly reviewed, updated and monitored.
- It is key that employees know, and are in agreement, with the manager's planning and prioritiszation.
- Employee should be involved in the process of planning.
- Achieve a balance: make sure the work is not so tightly planned that it doesn't allow for changes in the team or the situation; or for employees to have control and responsibility over their working lives.

Exercise with managers

- It may be an idea to talk through with managers you are working with, particularly if you are working within a coaching context, how they go about planning.
- You might want to use prompts such as 'How do you prepare for busy periods at work?', 'Do you tend to leave work to the last minute?', and 'How much are you able to predict the workloads for you and your team?'.
- Try to get them to reflect upon the impact of their planning or lack of planning. One way to do this is to get managers to think about times when work was passed onto them with short deadlines, or they

were told about work at the last minute. If a manager is able to appreciate what the impact of this was for him/herself, it will then be much easier to have a valuable conversation about change and improvements.

You might want to use the list above as a prompt to explore if there are any improvements or changes that could be made to their planning process.

Why planning doesn't always happen

We found that most managers recognize the importance of forward planning – but were just not able to always achieve it. Our research demonstrated a number of common barriers that managers explained caused them to work in reactive rather than proactive ways. The most common reason cited was pressure of work, where managers were so caught up in the day-to-day demands of their role, that they were always reacting to the moment, rather than anticipating future demands. The following example from a manager demonstrates this:

> "A big problem I have is saying I will do something and then not doing it due to the pressures of the day. I had a planning meeting with my team four weeks ago when we discussed outcomes and agreed how to work as a team. I promised to deliver on a few aspects of that, essentially planning how we were going to work in the coming months; however with the day-to-day pressures I have not been able to do it. My team are getting really frustrated. I know I need to prioritize this over other aspects and other jobs."

This example demonstrated both that the day-to-day demands were a barrier to being able to engage in forward planning, and being able to fulfil their role adequately. The following example demonstrates how the latter can actually then impact on employees.

> "My poor planning ends up being other people's problems. Sometimes I am so busy that I don't have time to take a particular step in a process that I need to do to start a project. I then push work down to people at a lower level and give them less time to do the project because the deadline always remains the same. This must be very stressful."

Another common reason for managers not being able to forward plan is the pressure coming from above, in other words when projects or workloads are passed onto managers from senior managers, or from changes in government or legislative process. The following example from a local government employee demonstrates the impact of this:

> "My manager would go out and agree things with other managers and come back and say 'I have agreed that you will do X and Y', but never referred to what our workload already was. That used to put the team in turmoil. Everyone was jumping to that particular manager's wants and needs."

Finally managers talked about the lack of planning being due to their personality, for instance having a tendency to procrastinate and not take action in a timely manner. It is certainly the case that individuals that would be low in the personality trait of conscientiousness would be more prone to leave things to the last minute, and to feel more comfortable behaving spontaneously than in a more planned way. The following example demonstrates a manager who admits to a tendency to leave things to the last minute.

> "I am going to a meeting tomorrow and I just reviewed the last minutes of the meeting and the actions that we agreed should be taken and I found actions I had forgotten. So I went to someone in my team to take that action forward before I have the meeting tomorrow. It makes me always on the verge of a crisis because I don't do things in a timely manner. I need to try to do things on a regular basis that are important, but not urgent at that particular time. Taking the meeting example, immediately after the meeting I should have planned when to take action and negotiated with people their input into what needed to be done."

Some managers, either due to their personality, pressure of work, a lack of knowledge of the role, or lack of confidence in their ability can be indecisive. The impact of indecision will be explored further in the second cluster in this chapter called 'Problem Solving', however this example demonstrates an employee suffering due to a manager's indecision:

> "What also happens is that my manager changes his mind frequently. The problem is that he gives an instruction, but they hasn't sat down and got it clear in his head first – so then he changes his mind. Last week I spent a whole day preparing a schedule for him – all his papers, his itinerary, train tickets, how to get there, everything – and then he decided the night before he wasn't going to go after all."

You may want to explore with managers what the barriers to them acting in more proactive ways might be at work and possible solutions to these barriers. It is important that managers are encouraged to consider their own solutions to the issues. Tools and mechanics that you can use in this kind of work are explored fully in Chapter - which focuses on overcoming barriers to Positive Manager Behaviour more broadly.

What else does proactive management include?

In this chapter so far we have focused on proactive management behaviours around planning and organizing. There are however many other ways that managers can be proactive in their day-to-day management that will be beneficial to the health and well-being of their employees. In order for managers to be able to proactively manage effectively, they need to be aware of what employees are working on day to day, essentially monitoring the workload and resources of their team and team members.

This is highlighted by the following quotation from a financial employee:

"My managers are very aware of the deliverable within each area and are also aware of how many people and the expertise of the people delivering those deliverables. They will identify stress points, and continuously monitor what the stress factors are within the team."

The following quotation from a manager shows one way that they monitor the workload of their team:

"I take responsibility for the work that comes into the department so as it comes in I account for it by ticking it off and saying we have received it. Then I put it into date order so that when anybody is ready for another piece of work, I give them the oldest piece of work. This way I make sure that I manage the time and deadline bit of the work for them and their role is making sure they can do their work to the best of their ability."

We identified in our research that a common problem was that managers would delegate work to their team members without an awareness of how much work each team member already had on. This not only created issues of overload for some team members and unequal workloads, but also left team members feeling unsupported by their manager. The following scenario demonstrates how serious the repercussions of a lack of monitoring can be.

"We have a ceiling limit for caseloads that we can carry out defined by the organization. My manager kept on adding cases to my caseload without actually stopping, looking and saying 'What is the state of play?'. Before I knew it I had exceeded the limit and was overloaded – but still the work was continuing and my manager was loading it up. I tried to say something to my manager but he didn't seem to take any action. I knew I was at the point of breaking. The fact I was overloaded was brought up in a team meeting in my absence and it was only then that my manager took action. The problem was that we had people on long-term sick in our team and didn't have an outlet, or enough resources to offload cases – and therefore they were just being piled up on the people left in the team. What my manager should have done is go to his senior manager with an argument and said 'Look, we are currently budgeted and staffed for a certain number of people, and we are under that amount of people, but you are still expecting us to do the same amount of work. We need some relief, whether we have to move it off to another office, or bring resource from other areas to cover the workload for a couple of weeks."

This example demonstrates both the impact of a lack of monitoring and also introduces some of the options available to managers to proactively ease pressure and workload on their team members. This scenario suggests bringing in additional resources to manage the overload. Managing workload in terms of allocating resources can involve bringing in temporary staff; however, often budgets are not available for this. More commonly, resources can be used from another part of the organization, for instance using another team that are less busy; work can be re-allocated within the team so that work is more evenly distributed, or managers themselves can step in and take some of the workload. Another option available to managers is to increase the amount of time that their team members are paid to work, therefore enabling more work to be done and cleared. The following scenario demonstrates how this can be an effective strategy:

"We had a deadline whereby we had to meet a certain number of cases by the end of that week. By Wednesday afternoon it was obvious we weren't going to meet that number. My manager said that he was prepared for us to come and get paid double time on Saturday if need be to hit the target. Normally if someone mentions Saturday work I wouldn't be happy but he was great at motivating us. It relieved a lot of stress because if we had continued working to try and hit the deadline by Friday, we would have been under so much pressure."

What are your thoughts on this?

We now consider a case study taken from a real account by a manager working within an NHS trust in the UK.

Case study

The manager had been monitoring the workload of his team members, and recognized that they were all already at full capacity. The manager knew that there was no budget to pay for additional resources and due to the specialized nature of what they did, felt there was no option to get resources from other areas within the trust. The manager speaks 'The pressure for me is that I am so conscious of how much work my team have got on that I feel reluctant to delegate too much. I think it might crush them. I leave the pressure with myself, and don't delegate any more work. This means I am always struggling to keep on top of the huge mountain of stuff on my desk.'

The fact that the manager was struggling was noticed by his senior manager, who decided to set up regular Monday meetings for the manager to try and tackle the workload issue. The manager continues, 'I found these meetings very stressful because she (the senior manager) needed to know all my outstanding deadlines. I used to think that for me to compile all the deadlines into a list to tell her would take me two hours alone – and this really stressed me out. She also suggested I delegated my work to others, but some people in my team were already doing the work of two people and so I knew it wasn't the right approach to take.'

The senior manager was new in her role and although she had a little knowledge of the specialized work carried out within this team, she had no experience, and as a result was felt by the manager to make suggestions that were impractical, unreasonable and unrealistic. The manager continues 'In the end I started to lie about how much work I was doing. I could see that my manager was becoming stressed by the fact she hadn't sorted out the problem. She kept advising me to delegate away work, but I knew that even she knew this wasn't the right solution.'

Although the manager carried on like this for a few more weeks, he started to get symptoms of illness and was seriously worried that he was going to burnout.

How do you feel the manager could have dealt with this situation? Was there anything you think the senior manager could have done to ease the pressure?

One thing that this case study demonstrates is that it is not always appropriate or possible to proactively manage workload by re-allocating resources. An option available to managers is to prevent the workload piling up in the first place, essentially by using their role as gatekeepers to stop additional work being passed onto the team or by controlling the flow of work into team members so that the workload is regulated. This example from a local government employee demonstrates the efficacy of this solution:

"When I first joined the organization there was a tendency for lots of managers to come to me directly with work. It was putting me under pressure to have different people coming to me all the time with different tasks. My manager put in a system whereby everything had to go through him. At first this felt strange, but it is a great system because it takes the pressure off me. He regulates the amount of work that I get, and so knows how much I have got on, and how much I can cope with."

We recognize however that it is not always possible for managers to perform this gatekeeping role and that due to pressures from senior managers, or immovable deadlines from legislation or procedural changes, sometimes work has to be passed to team members. This does not mean that managers are then unable to manage the workload of their team. Managers are able to help and encourage employees to review the way that they work, particularly around how work is organized and prioritized. The following passage from a healthcare manager highlights this approach:

"Team members come to me with issues of workload, generally feeling that the pressures upon them are too great to deal with. My approach is to sit down with them following having identified what is on their agenda, agreeing what the priorities are, what can be put to one side, what can be delayed and what must be prioritized. In the last couple of months this has happened with one of my team members, who has various health problems. It was a case of going through with him what he felt he had to do in the period of time and where possible dropping some things back, agreeing new deadlines and agreeing deadlines where work was already overdue. We mapped it all out together and agreed what would be followed up on a regular basis. We were then able to meet the deadlines and timelines put in place. The team member stayed in work whereas arguably he might have gone off sick if we hadn't done that."

In this case the manager helped the employee to break his workload down, allocate priorities, set deadlines and develop an action plan, which allowed the employee to see the problem workload as more manageable. It may be that the manager can also help employees to review the way that they work and approach their work, perhaps identifying different or new ways of working that could improve the way they carry out their work. It may even be that the manager provides this support or encouragement by prompting employees on what they have coming up, as demonstrated by the following example from a central government employee:

"My manager reviews my milestones for me. I do my own reviews but he keeps on top of them and says 'Well, you've got a milestone coming up in three weeks, how is it going? Is there anything you would like me to do?' We have regular meetings to look at my workload which has been really useful. He checks if I have too much on, and asks me if I need to delegate more. This really helps me to deal with my workload."

This cluster has focused on proactive management by looking at actions that managers can take to monitor the workload and resources of their team. Underpinning all of this however is communication. This could be communication to employees around where the busy or stressful periods may be and how these will be tackled. It may be to communicate why work is being passed on to them or deadlines are being pushed. It may just be to publicly acknowledge and recognize the pressures that team members are under. The final example in this section demonstrates the power of that acknowledgement:

> "My manager is fantastic. She is aware of the pressure we are under and how hard we all work. Friday is the only day when we don't deliver any group work sessions. Last week she came into our office at 3pm on a Friday and said 'What are you all still doing here?' We said that we had lots of work to do but she said 'No, I want you to go home because you have had a really busy week and things have been very difficult.' It was wonderful to be told this."

Can you see how any of these behaviours may have been helpful in the case study introduced earlier?

Problem Solving

'I must do something' will always solve more problems than 'something must be done'. (Proverb)

There are reams of literature and management books focusing on the most appropriate strategies and guidelines for effective problem solving and decision making. For instance, the 7-point plan from Carter McNamara (2003) in the Field Guide to Leadership and Supervision for non-profit staff involves:

1. Defining the problem;
2. Looking at potential causes for the problem;
3. Identifying alternatives for approaches to resolve the problem;
4. Selecting an approach to resolve the problem;
5. Planning the implementation of the best alternative;
6. Monitoring implementation of the plan; and
7. Verifying if the problem has been resolved.

Other theorists such as Edward de Bono (1973) and Robert Heller (1999) have focused upon taking a creative approach to problem solving. Indeed much of what line managers are required to do in their role is solve problems and make decisions, therefore it is not surprising that the search for the 'holy grail' of effective problem solving has attracted many followers.

This cluster, however, does not attempt to focus on the process that managers should follow when engaging in problem solving; but rather the behaviours that are important for managers to demonstrate when presented with problems by their team members. It is, therefore, about the manager's approach to employee or team problems, rather than the process to solve those, or their own, problems.

The findings from our research

Positive examples of manager behaviour included:

✓ Dealing rationally with problems
✓ Following up problems on the team's behalf
✓ Dealing with problems as soon as they arise
✓ Breaking problems down into parts

Negative examples of manager behaviour included:

× Indecisive at decision making
× Listening but not resolving problems
× Not taking problems seriously; and
× Assuming problems will sort themselves out

It is also important that managers monitor their team's workload and resources on a regular basis in order to spot when potential problems and issues are likely to arise, and work preventatively or proactively rather than reacting to the problem when it arises. As the old adage states 'an ounce of prevention is worth a pound of cure.' The following excerpt from a manager demonstrates the pitfalls of not monitoring:

> "There have been times when I haven't realized there is a problem until it is too late and that is partly because of being busy myself, and partly assuming that if I don't get any questions, that everyone is coping. I have tended to assume that everyone is OK working at the same level and speed as me, and therefore I have ignored warning signs and had to deal with real problems in the team too late."

Of course, although in an ideal world, all potential problems would be flagged up and dealt with before they became problematic; we recognize that this can never be completely the case as so many issues arising within the workplace are unforeseeable, and managers are working under so many different conflicting demands. Therefore, the remainder of this section will focus on those behaviours that are important (or important to avoid) when dealing with problems that have arisen. It must be said that many of the behaviours explored in the previous section as part of 'Proactive Work Management' are also important for positive problem solving, particularly those around reviewing, defining and developing action plans around problems.

A problem shared is a problem halved?

Our research found that in terms of problem solving, positive action is important, and in the case of preventing and reducing stress in employees, it isn't enough to just listen to employee problems, as demonstrated by the following experience of a local government employee:

> "My manager is very cheerful and willing to chat about things. The problem is that by actually going and having a chat with him about a problem, he sees it as getting it sorted. It isn't – the problem is still there. It is all well and good chatting, but the problem doesn't get sorted out. I want him to take some action and do something rather than chat. He tries to be my buddy, but this just leaves the problem dragging on and on, and I find myself becoming more and more stressed."

The employee here talks about the need for the manager to take action. In some cases this might mean that the employee needs the manager to 'come to their rescue' and actually sort out the problem on their behalf. Although throughout this book we have talked about the importance of employees having autonomy over their work and therefore responsibility to conduct their work, and consequently solve their problems in their own way, some problems cannot be effectively dealt with by employees. Take for instance the example where a software system has broken down, or where a supplier is not fulfilling their promises and so some escalation and 'back up' is needed, or where a team member is experiencing problems with another member of the team, or where there is a piece of work that the team member does not have the capability to deal with . . . the list goes on. These are all examples where it is important not only that the manager steps in and deals with, and follows up on, the problem, but also does this quickly, rationally and openly.

In the next cluster we will explore the need for managers to work participatively and involve and consult the team on a day-to-day basis. It is clear from our research however that, particularly around problem solving, employees need their managers to be able to be decisive, as explained by the following education employee:

"I like decisive managers. I'm not someone who wants to sit around and discuss everything without making a decision. My manager used to say 'This is the problem, this is what I think we should do, does anyone have any objections?'. And we might say a few things and she would say 'OK, we'll try this. If it doesn't work, we will talk about it again and try something else.' Things do need to be discussed to a point, but you also need someone to take action. Good managers are those that know when to be decisive and just solve the problem. I would rather have a manager who is strong at decision making because at least they are trying to do something rather than just avoiding making a decision by asking everyone else what to do."

Taking action might not involve solving the problem for the employee, but rather encourage the employee to work through the problem and therefore solve it for themselves. The most effective way to do this that emerged from our research, was to break down the problem into smaller parts so that either the team member deals with one part of the issue at a time, or that team members are each responsible for a different part of the larger problem. The latter is demonstrated in the following scenario described by a local government manager:

"We had a burst main in one of our buildings which means that a lot of accommodation was taken out, and there were real health and safety issues with live electrical equipment stood in water. There were also service issues with the people who occupied the building being under pressure to solve the problem but didn't know how and didn't know where to start. I dealt with it by being as calm as possible, giving my people clear definitive things to do, so that they could work in blocks and know what they were responsible for rather than being faced with this huge problem. Then I tried to work with the people who occupied the building to get alternative accommodation. It worked really well. People were able to focus rather than looking at the whole problem and this really brought stress levels down. Dealing with a piece of something is much easier than trying to deal with the whole thing."

This strategy may also be useful for you to use in your practice with managers. You may for instance ask a manager to recall a crisis or problem in their team, and then work through both how they went about problem solving, and whether a mechanism such as breaking the problem down into smaller parts might have been useful. It may be that you use this in helping a manager to deal with their own problems in their working life.

What managers need to avoid doing when faced with employees' problems

We have ascertained that it is important for managers to be decisive, action oriented and quick when solving problems on behalf of employees – and, therefore, avoiding indecision, inaction or hesitation. This includes avoiding inaction in terms of just listening to the problem, essentially being a shoulder to cry on, but not trying to do anything to solve the problem. Our research also revealed other examples of unhelpful inaction. Interestingly, many of the behaviours that were found to be ineffective were actually where managers were either doing what they thought was right, or trying to be supportive and encouraging, as demonstrated by the following example from an employee:

> "I had this deadline to hit and I knew it was going to be an issue. I said to my manager that I needed to speak to him. When I told him of my problem, he just said 'I have absolute faith in you. Just do your best.' I absolutely lost it and said 'What do you mean? Do my best? What kind of advice is that?' At the time I needed practical advice. I was so worried about it and he did nothing to allay my fears but instead just upset me."

The manager here was being supportive in demonstrating their belief in the employee, however by their inaction in terms of problem solving actually left the employee feeling that their problem had been belittled. Managers may also seek to smooth issues over rather than solve the problem. This may be due to lack of confidence, or an avoidance of confrontation, but equally it could be because managers felt that this was the right thing to do. The following employee example demonstrates how keeping the peace can cause more problems within the team and wider organization:

> "My manager is one of those people who try to smooth things over and keep the peace and not rock the boat, but in so doing he allows himself and others to be exploited by people who don't adhere to the organizational policies and procedures and just do what they like. Instead of sorting this out, he tries to find a way not to upset them. It is not fair that people can get away with flouting the rules and causing problems. They should be sorted out for the benefit of everyone."

This example could be deemed as one where the manager is distancing himself from the problem and actually absolving responsibility. Managers ignoring, not taking responsibility for or walking away from problems in the team were perhaps the most commonly found causes of discontent and work-related stress in employees around problem solving. The following scenario from a financial employee demonstrates the impact of managers ignoring problems.

"My manager doesn't want to know. It is almost as if, if you are feeling under stress, or if there is a problem, it is looked on as negative. There is an attitude they don't want to see you as being negative but always want you to be positive. Sometimes this is hard when there is no one to go to. A few months ago I was constantly being given jobs that I didn't have the training or knowledge to do, and I felt very under pressure. I told my manager a few times but I didn't get any help. She didn't acknowledge there was a problem. She just kept saying 'you are expected to deal with this.' I got very stressed. I lost all confidence because no-one was willing to help, and I thought there was something wrong with me in that I couldn't deal with it."

What could the manager have done in this situation? Would the behaviours explored in this section have been useful in this scenario?

Once again, as highlighted at the end of the last section, underpinning all these behaviours is the need for communication. Sorting out problems within the team is not easy and may take time and lots of attempts to get the solution right. There are times when there might not actually be a solution to a problem. In all these circumstances, what is important is that the manager communicates with the team openly and honestly, letting them know that they are both acknowledging the problem, and attempting to come up with a workable solution.

Participative/Empowering

"You have to enable and empower people to make decisions independent of you. As I have learned, each person on a team is an extension of your leadership; if they feel empowered by you they will magnify your power to lead." (Tom Ridge, US Politician)

The following cluster explores management behaviours where the views, thoughts and ideas of employees are considered, and where managers provide responsibility, autonomy and empowerment to employees.

The findings from our research

The positive behaviours found to be important in our research include:

✓ Giving employees the right level of responsibility
✓ Trusting employees to do their own work
✓ Correctly judging when to consult and when to make a decision
✓ Keeping employees informed of what is happening in the organization
✓ Acting as a mentor
✓ Delegating work equally

✓ Helping employees to develop in their role
✓ Encouraging team participation
✓ Providing employees with the opportunity to air their views
✓ Providing regular team meetings

The negative behaviours found to be important in our research include:

× Giving too little direction to employees
× Managing 'under a microscope'
× Imposing 'my way is the only way'
× Making decisions without consultation
× Refusing requests for training
× Not providing upward mobility in the job
× Not allowing employees to use their new training

The behaviours in this cluster very clearly split into two groups – the first being those behaviours where employee participation is encouraged, the participative element of this cluster; and the second where employees are empowered both by the amount of control and responsibility they have in their job, and the opportunities to develop their skills further. Underpinning this whole cluster however is control, or autonomy. As mentioned throughout this book, the link between control and employee well-being is one of the most empirically sound in work-related stress management literature. Therefore, not providing employees with autonomy or responsibility in their role is very clearly linked to negative outcomes of employee ill-health and dissatisfaction.

Empowerment and participation in the leadership literature

One of the criticisms of the leadership behaviour literature has been that in conceptualizing leadership from a leader behaviour, or 'top down' viewpoint, the research has failed to account for the needs, wants and expectations of the follower. Although the Leader Behaviour Description Questionnaire (LBDQ, explored in Chapter 2) does include some participative behaviours such as putting suggestions made by the team into operation, and consulting the group; it wasn't until the transformational leadership models that emerged in the 1990s that the importance of the employee ('follower') in leadership literature was really considered. It could be argued therefore that only relatively recently have leadership models actually considered the employee, and their needs for a voice, for growth and for development, in their conceptualization.

A central tenet of transformational leadership is that the distinguishing feature of transformational leaders is their ability to transform employees so that they perform beyond expectations: this is therefore conceptualized in terms of the motivational and empowering effect of the leader upon the employee. The Bass model of transformational leadership (from which the MLQ, still the most popular transformational leadership measure, was created) does not refer to participative leadership at all, but does refer to empowerment in the individualized consideration component of the model. In this component, empowerment is fostered by the leader creating opportunities for employee development, coaching and mentoring. The later, UK-based conceptualization of transformational leadership by Alimo-Metcalfe (from which the TLQ measure was created) is much more strongly focused on empowerment and participative leadership, including many items within factors such as 'Showing genuine concern for others' well-being and development', 'Empowering, delegating and developing potential', 'Openness to ideas and advice' and 'Creating a supportive learning and self-development environment'

Participative management

At the heart of participative management is the belief that employees, or team members, have an important contribution to make in terms of providing ideas and suggestions for the smooth running of the day-to-day work and strategic functioning of the team. It therefore includes employees being involved in problem solving, as explored in the previous cluster, change management, and strategy development. The following example, described by a central government manager, demonstrates the power of involving employees:

> "Rather than me just saying 'OK, we are going to do this, this and the other', there was a bit of debate about what worked well, what didn't work so well and so on. The team felt self engaged that not only were they part of the problem, but they were part of the solution. It wasn't a 'them and us', but it was us as a team and seeing it as our responsibility. The spirit was that we were in this situation together and so we would work together to sort it out. It wasn't me as a manager telling them what to do, it was more me as part of a team and them as part of a team."

The following example describes a similar scenario, but where the employees were not consulted. This is from the perspective of an employee:

> "My manager would dictate the work that the team would do. Although that is fair enough, he would liaise with other people, set a timetable, agree and promise targets without consulting with us, or having any real understanding of the effort it was going to take. We were never privy to any discussions. The first thing we knew was 'Can you do this by this date?' There was no negotiation, discussion or even a real appreciation of what was involved.

And that makes me feel angry, frustrated and worried. I know that managers have to have conversations that we are not privy to, but it would have been nice to have been consulted and be part of the discussion following the initial one. And if the actual promises could come with a bit of collaboration with the team so that we could get our point across and explain the situation that would really help."

What the second example demonstrates is that without participation and collaboration, not only can employees become angry and frustrated about decisions, but also can become worried about their future and their position. This erodes the trust held in the manager and will subsequently affect performance.

How to foster a culture of participation

A key learning from our research was that participative management can only happen in a team where there is trust for the manager, and where employees feel safe to put across their views and ideas. This trust in the manager needs to be earned, and therefore managers need to be able to work towards building a team in which every employee feels valued and feels safe to contribute. In the last chapter we explored the behaviours associated with 'Respectful and responsible: Managing emotions and having integrity', and demonstrated the positive impact of managers keeping promises, being honest, considering their employee views and managing in a consistent way. It is these behaviours that will underpin a culture of trust where employees feel able to put their views and ideas across, as demonstrated by the following manager example:

> "If I am honest with my team, I expect them to be honest back. They know they can say anything to me. If they don't like what I am saying they can challenge it, and through discussion and communication we can come to a common ground. They do trust me though and they know there are times when I can't tell them anything. They know when I say it is not open for discussion that it is for a good reason."

This demonstrates that, with trust, employees will be comfortable with managers making the decision about when to consult employees and when to make a decision or to give an action without consultation. Without that strong base however, employees will be distrustful and negative emotions and behaviours will result.

In addition to developing a culture by the manager role-modelling behaviours of integrity, honesty and respect, there are a number of practical ways that a manager can create a culture of participation. The most common way to do this is by holding team meetings.

The 'rules' for team meetings

Not only do we recommend that all line managers hold regular team meetings, but, more importantly, that these team meetings are constructed following a number of guidelines. These 'rules' have been developed based on our extensive research with both employees and managers about what is and isn't useful.

1. Put time in the diary for team meetings, and stick to these times religiously

There is no rule about how regularly team meetings should be held. This will differ according to the type of work conducted and where the team are based. More importantly, though, the time for team meetings should be held as precious. A regular time should be put in where all, or most of, the team can attend. All team members should be encouraged not to put other meetings or annual leave in at these times.

The power of this regularity is demonstrated by the following employee example:

> "We had team meetings every week. Our manager got to know exactly what we all did and what our roles involved. He stuck to team meetings religiously. We got to discuss everything we were doing in that week, and together could sort out any issues or problems. It made us a really tight team. There was a good atmosphere. We all pulled together if there was a problem because we had built this culture where we were in it together."

We spoke to many managers who found that work priorities such as projects and excessive workload often impinged on their ability to hold team meetings and so these meetings could be delayed for several weeks. What we also saw was that these managers talked about problems of work-related stress, lack of communication and conflict in their team. In order to keep a routine of regular team meetings, it may be that they are not held every week, and that they are only half an hour long rather than two or three hours. It is important to help managers find a workable solution for them and their team that can be stuck to and therefore seen as a key part of their management agenda.

2. Build adequate space and time for discussion and sharing into the meeting

From our research, the key benefit of team meetings was seen to be giving employees the chance to offload their problems and issues, and to contribute ideas and thoughts on improvements to their work. What we also heard, however, was that team meetings were often highly 'agenda'd' whereby managers filled the time with communication about wider organizational issues, changes in policy and practice and other directives. The frustration with this approach is demonstrated by the following local government employee:

> "We used to have weekly team meetings where we could discuss cases and how we could improve things, and help each other out. Now we have meetings every 3 to 4 weeks. We never get the chance to talk about anything or even speak in our team meetings. They are press conferences; managers telling us about new initiatives, new policies, new bits of paper, new practices and so on. They are utterly and completing depressing and colleagues do their best to avoid them."

Although team meetings are an excellent time for communicating wider issues, there needs to be a balance between this kind of communication, and the knowledge sharing and participation element of the meeting. When considering the frequency and length of time of team meeting, is it worth getting managers to think about whether, with all the information they need to communicate to their team, they are still allowing for a balance between talking to, and talking with team members.

3. Demonstrate that employees' views are not just listened to, but acted upon

Getting employees' views and ideas needs to be more than paying lip-service. Although initially there will be positive benefits from getting employees' views and ideas; if these are not actioned, employees will quickly become disillusioned and stop putting forward their ideas. It is also likely that attendance to team meetings will diminish and performance will wane.

Although we recognize that implementing all ideas will not be possible, there will always be some ideas that are possible to action and managers should be encouraged to be flexible, moving away from a 'my way is the only way' position and trying out new ideas. It could be that actioning these ideas are communicated to employees as 'trials' so that managers commit to trying out a new way of working for a set period of time, after which the approach can be reviewed; or it could be that managers look for the 'quick win' ideas that can be actioned quickly and easily but which will show a real impact on employees' working lives. One financial employee demonstrates the importance of views being actioned:

> "At our team meeting we were asked our thoughts and opinions on a big departmental change. We were openly canvassed about how to go about this. When the plan came out, our views had been taken into account. It is really important we are listened to. Often managers can't actually action what you would like, or what you want, but if you feel you are listened to, and your views are taken into account, it will really help."

4. Communicate all ideas will be listened to without prejudice
A very quick way to reduce participation in team meetings is to pass judgement on employees' views, or belittle views of employees. Although some ideas may not be realistic or practical, they are unlikely to be irrelevant or useless. Often, as has been found by brainstorming methods, so called 'blue-sky' ideas or lateral thinking around problems, may actually lead the team to consider new and different ways of thinking and problem solving, and often then triggers a 'literal' solution to that problem. Managers should be encouraged to set the ground-rules for the team that no idea will be belittled or dismissed, and that no judgement will be made on communications. The following manager demonstrates how surprised he often is by ideas that result: 'Sometimes I think things aren't a good idea, but I will say let's trial it and see how it works. Sometimes these things turn out to be really really good ideas and work really well.'

5. Involve the whole team regardless of hierarchy or experience
It is important that all employees in the team are encouraged to partic-ipate and that managers communicate how valuable each and every contribution to the meeting is.

The following manager example demonstrates this point:

> "We were in a team of high achievers and also had an admin assistant. One day I said to the admin assistant 'Look, you are an important part of the team. You may not be a manager, but you are absolutely integral.' They said it was the first time that anyone had said anything like that. They were withdrawn about participating in team meetings and would sit quiet for fear of opening their mouth and not feeling that they were of any worth in the team. Very quickly after this chat, it was almost instanta-neous, you could see the spark coming back and the involvement in the team. It took just one person to say they were worthwhile to make a difference. Everyone in my team is important."

If the solution to getting participation from the team is not as simple as a chat, there are various ways that managers can encourage wider participation.

The following are some ideas:

- Have a presentation from a different area in the team in each meeting so that not only do the whole team get a perspective of what everyone is doing, but also those who are less likely to speak will have a chance to showcase what they do.
- Break the brainstorming element of the meeting into smaller groups of three to four people. People are usually happier to contribute in smaller than larger groups.

- Rotate the chairing and minuting of the team meetings each time so that everyone has a chance to be involved, and also so that the hierarchical structure of the team meeting is not so fixed.
- Consider having off-site team meetings in a less formal or structured environment for instance over lunch.
- Make use of team-building mechanisms to encourage team members to get to know each other better and therefore feel more comfortable participating.
- Focus on empowering management behaviour. The next section will explore the ways in which we found managers can empower employees within their team.

Empowering management

As discussed in the previous section, by encouraging participation from the team, the manager is actually empowering their team members by giving them respect and demonstrating that they value their opinions and ideas. The day-to-day way that managers can empower their employees is by providing them with the autonomy to conduct their work in their own way and in their own time. The following example from a central government employee demonstrates the importance of this:

> "The main thing my manager does is let me get on with it. I think sometimes we are our own bosses. Although their needs to be that overseeing, he just lets me get on with what I need to do – gives me the responsibility so that I can carry out my jobs when they need to be done. And that relieves a lot of the stress. In previous jobs when you feel like your manager is just watching over you constantly and telling you what to do and putting on a lot of pressure. Here it is completely different and you are able to just get on with the work you want to. That makes life a lot easier."

This provides an example of a manager allowing the employee to carry out her job in herheir own time, but autonomy also extends further. It may include the manager encouraging employees to sort their own problems out rather than dealing with them on their behalf (as introduced in the cluster on problem solving). The following financial manager excerpt demonstrates the power of this approach.

> "One of my team let a situation carry her away at work and wasn't dealing with it. I took her into an office and said 'OK, how did you handle that situation?' She said not very well. I said 'OK, what did you want to gain from the situation?' She said she wanted her team to leave her alone to do her work. I said 'OK – and how can you do this?' She gave me the

answer: that she should actually go away from her desk and work in a quiet place where people couldn't put pressure on. By answering her own question she felt much more in control. It was like she had taken control back. I hadn't done it for her, I had just encouraged her to think differently about her approach."

This example clearly demonstrates that the manager is empowering employees to feel that they are able to solve their own problems and therefore improving their confidence in their work. As discussed in the section on problem solving there will be times when employees won't have the answers, or won't be able to solve their own problems. In these cases, the manager will need to problem solve on their behalf. It is, however, the manager's role to work out when the employee could be encouraged and prompted to solve their own issues, and use this whenever possible to empower the employee.

Finally, along with allowing employees to conduct work in their own way and giving them the support to solve their own issues, empowerment may also include allowing employees to conduct their work where they want. In certain jobs, organizations and sectors it may not be possible for employees to work in any place other than the designated place of work, so there will be situations where this is not the case: however, managers should be encouraged to provide employees with the tools to be able to carry out their work elsewhere, if possible. This may be on the train on the journey to and from work and could involve providing employees with smart phones to be able to access emails. It could be to allow employees to work from home on certain days or to complete work at home rather than return to the workplace if an offsite meeting finishes early in the afternoon. The following employee example describes this approach:

"My manager says if we are going to be away, or want to work from home, just put it in the office diary that we are working from home. I live a long way away and sometimes, rather than travel all the way in, I work from home – and actually am able to get much more done. As long as he knows where I am, he is fine with it, and trusts me to do my job in the way I see fit."

When managers do not display empowering behaviour

The first example explored in this section described previous managers who were micro-managing; constantly watching over work and asking questions. In our research we found that micro-managing was one of the most commonly reported issues when employees were talking about empowerment and autonomy. This interfering may involve frequent checking up on employees' work and excessive monitoring, having to sign off all materials (even if not necessary), feeling that the only way is the manager's way and therefore complaining or finding fault in all other approaches, and questioning employees.

Rather than interfering, some managers disempower employees just through a lack of delegating, where managers keep the work for themselves rather than give work for their team to do. One of our interviewees commented that it represented a scenario where managers 'had a dog but barked themselves'. We found that this made employees feel stressed, and as a result of feeling that their manager didn't have faith in them or trust them, made employees question their own competence in their role. The following scenario demonstrates this.

"My manager was unable to give you work without actually then going ahead and changing it or doing it himself. You would be sitting there and he would ask you if you had done the work and you wouldn't be sure whether you were supposed to have done it, or whether he had done it himself. It was very confusing. I never knew what I was meant to be doing. I would do the most straightforward thing and he would ask me to make changes. Even if they were simple changes, he would spend half an hour explaining all the changes he wanted you to make. In this half an hour he could have done it himself. He didn't say what the objective of what he was asking for was.

He then wouldn't give you time to do it – he would be interfering all the time to find out if it had been done and then he would go ahead and do it himself without telling you. It was very stressful. I didn't know where I stood. I felt I couldn't do anything right. My work wasn't going anywhere and I wasn't developing."

In our research some managers acknowledged that they either interfered, or did not delegate as much as they should or could do to their team. Reasons cited for this were: not having faith in their team members' ability, not knowing how team members worked and therefore not having faith in them, and, most commonly, not realizing that they were actually not providing autonomy to their team members. The following example from a manager describes the latter:

"Sometimes I think I am the only person that can ever do anything and that if you want to get something done it is best to do it yourself. I don't always realize the effect this has on other people. Perhaps this makes people think that they are not good enough to do anything. I remember a comment being made about that and taking a good look at how I did begin to delegate work and include people. I remember someone making a comment to me by saying 'Oh well, you trust me to do that do you?' It hadn't dawned on me until then that I must be perceived as someone who thought only I could do something. I thought I was trying to protect people from having too much to do, but actually the lesson was that people blossom and flourish when, in the right context, you give them something to do."

There is such a thing as too much autonomy

Just like with forward planning, as discussed at the beginning of this chapter, there can be too much of a good thing. Managers can provide their employees with too much autonomy, or in other words too little direction, and as a result can detrimentally affect employees' experiences. There is a very careful balance between providing employees with responsibility and autonomy to conduct and complete their own work and leaving employees feeling unsupported, unstructured and therefore as if they are floundering. It is also a fact that some employees want to have more support and direction than others. The concept of individual differences is explored more fully in the next chapter, however it will be the case that some team members want to be managed closely day by day, but others will want to be left to complete their own tasks.

Our research with managers suggested a number of ways managers can achieve this balance. You may want to suggest these pointers to managers you work with in training or coaching interventions:

- Encourage managers to work out what their team want and how they like to be managed, recognizing that achieving the right balance will be different for everyone in the team.
- When delegating tasks, ensure managers check with their team that they are happy and that they know how to go about completing that task.
- When delegating tasks, set and agree timescales and deadlines to provide employees with structure around the task.
- Build in time to meet and discuss task progress (if appropriate, generally for a large project) at regular intervals.
- Convey to employees that the manager is there for support and advice whenever needed.
- When employees need advice on problems from managers, encourage managers to question if that employee can answer that problem themselves. If they can, encourage managers to steer employees in a direction, or facilitate the employees to solve their own issues rather than providing answers.

Finally, we found that not all managers are aware of their behaviour and the impact it has upon their team members. It may be useful, therefore, either to encourage them to engage in an upward feedback process, or to facilitate a discussion with team members about their management behaviour.

Empowering growth and development

The final part of empowering behaviour that we found to be important from our research was where managers supported team members' development and skill growth. We found that empowering development needs to include a three part process (see Figure 6.1):

Step 1: Identifying development needs and wants
The manager needs to take time with each employee to find out what would be most helpful for them. This will differ for each employee. Some will want to be challenged and will want to progress and develop into the next stage of their careers; whereas others will be happy and will aim to master their current role before moving onwards. It is important that managers do not impose training or development schedules on employees but develop a schedule that is mutually beneficial and achievable for both parties. It could be that this stage is actioned via informal discussions, or in conjunction with one-to-one meetings with the manager; or it could be part of a more formal appraisal, development or audit process.

It is key that this step is revisited on a regular basis. With the pace of change in our working lives, training and development needs also change regularly and, therefore, however managers choose to do this, regular development update meetings should be planned in with employees. The following excerpt from a manager highlights the importance of this approach:

> "I have a new member of staff who had, in a previous team, had a few periods of stress-related absence. She was new to the way we worked and so I tried to make it as easy as possible for her, tried to develop her own training plan based on the way she liked to learn things. I ensured this was done on a one-to-one basis and we didn't move on until she was comfortable. There were times when she did express that she was feeling rushed and that she wasn't ready to move on. Each time I spoke to her and we worked out a new plan or a revision to the plan so that she was constantly being developed, but only to the point that she felt comfortable with."

Step 2: Providing development opportunities
Perhaps the most obvious way to provide development opportunities is by providing training for employees. Employees in our research commented how training helped them to feel more professional and more confident in their role. It may be that following Step 1, the manager will have designed a formal training plan for the employee. In this way, the employee will decide with the manager in advance what training they will attend over a year or financial period. Equally, though, our research demonstrated that some managers took a more informal approach to

finding training courses once the development needs had been identified, as shown by the following example:

> "My manager is always on the look out for training courses. He comes up with loads of training courses and says 'Oh look – this might be useful for you.' He'll just see something and run up to me and say 'What do you think?' It is great, it shows he is willing to look out for me and for my development."

Another example was that managers identified the training and development needs across their whole team, and then put on a schedule of training that all team members could choose to attend or not. It may have been for instance that one team member needed time management training, but others didn't. The manager however took the decision to offer the same training to everyone which they could opt into or out of. This gave employees the autonomy to choose their training and also avoided 'singling out' development needs in the team.

It may be that training courses are not appropriate for development of team members. Many employees talked of ongoing coaching and mentoring from managers and the importance of managers' time to be able to share ideas and suggestions for different ways of doing things. These sessions may also include employees scoping out their plans and career options for the future to encourage employees to develop responsibility and autonomy for their development. The following example from an employee demonstrates the benefit of this approach:

> 'He treats me like a peer and gives me a lot of respect. He gives me a lot of feedback and pushes me to be in front of the right people to help with my career going forwards. He gives me a lot of support in the area of career development.'

It may be that rather than providing development opportunities through training, employees are given greater responsibility at work, encouraged to get involved in different projects at work to expand their skill base, or encouraged to work within new teams to expand their experience and visibility within the workplace.

Finally, the opportunity to meet development needs may not be provided within and by organizations. In our research, employees discussed the benefits of managers encouraging self-learning, for instance employees completing college courses or examinations, and even employees being able to take time off work for career counselling and development.

You will notice on Figure 6.1 that there is an arrow from Step 2 leading back to Step 1. This again points to the need for managers to review and monitor development on an ongoing basis. Providing employees with training and development in one area may highlight a gap or a need in another area, or may highlight to employees that an alternative path would be more suitable.

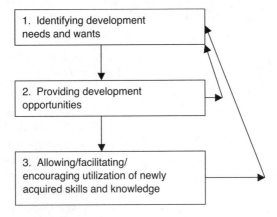

Figure 6.1 Process in empowering development

Step 3: Allowing/facilitating/encouraging utilization of newly acquired skills and knowledge

The final step is the key to empowerment, but perhaps the one that is most overlooked when developing employees. If employees are not able to use their newly acquired skills and knowledge in the workplace, the impact on motivation will be lost and employees will feel more dissatisfied than before the development opportunity was provided. It is imperative therefore that the manager sees development as integral to their work, rather than as a perk in addition to their work. It is the role of the manager to facilitate, encourage and allow the employee to use their new skills and knowledge in their work. This may mean providing the employee with different types of projects, more responsibilities or, in some cases, with a promotion.

Summary

This chapter has explored the competency 'Managing and communicating existing and future work'.

As described in Chapter 4, the research in Phase 2 refined the behaviours included in the whole stress management competency framework into a measure to enable managers to self assess their own effectiveness and/or for use in upward and 360 degree feedback programmes. Table 6.1 shows behaviours within the measure relevant to this particular competency. You may want to use this table as a prompt for discussions in your work with managers to help them display these types of behaviours.

Table 6.1. Behavioural indicators for 'Managing and communicating existing and future work'

Competency	Cluster	Do (✓)/ Don't (✗)	Examples of manager behaviour
Managing and communicating existing and future work	Proactive work management	✓	■ Clearly communicates employee job objectives ■ Develops action plans ■ Monitors team workload on an ongoing basis ■ Encourages team to review how they organize their work ■ Stops additional work being taken on when necessary ■ Works proactively ■ Sees projects/tasks through to delivery ■ Reviews processes to see if work can be improved ■ Prioritizes future workloads
	Problem solving	✓	■ Deals rationally with problems ■ Follows up problems on team's behalf ■ Deals with problems as soon as they arise
		✗	■ Is indecisive at decision making
	Participative/ empowering	✓	■ Gives employees the right level of responsibility ■ Correctly judges when to consult and when to make a decision ■ Keeps employees informed of what is happening in the organization ■ Acts as a mentor ■ Delegates work equally

Table 6.1.   (*Continued*)

Competency	Cluster	Do (✓)/ Don't (✗)	Examples of manager behaviour
			■ Helps team members develop in their role ■ Encourages team participation ■ Provides regular team meetings
		✗	■ Gives too little direction to employees

Source: Adapted from Donaldson-Feilder, Lewis and Yarker (2009)
© Crown Copyright 2009

References

Alimo-Metcalfe, B. and Alban-Metcalfe, R.J. (2001). The development of a transformational leadership questionnaire. *Journal of Occupational and Organizational Psychology*, 74, 1–27.

De Bono, E. (1973). *Lateral Thinking: Creativity Step by Step*. Harper Colophan, New York.

Donaldson-Feilder, E., Lewis, R. and Yarker, J., (2009). *Preventing Stress: Promoting Positive Manager Behaviour*. CIPD Insight Report. CIPD Publications: London, available on the CIPD website: www.cipd.co.uk/subjects/health/stress/_preventing_ stress

Heller, R. (1999). *Essential Managers: Making Decisions*. Dorling Kindersley, London.

McNamara, C. (2003). *Field Guide to Leadership and Supervision for Non-Profit Staff*. Authenticity Consulting, LLC, Minneapolis.

Stogdill, R.M. (1963). *Manual for the Leader Behavior Description Questionnaire*. The Ohio State University, Columbus.

7

Managing the individual within the team (management competency 3)

The third competency we are going to explore is called 'Managing the individual within the team'. This competency points specifically to the human side of people management. Traditional leadership models generally assume that leaders treat all employees the same, based on the idea that there are a core set of behaviours that leaders need to demonstrate to all their employees. The implication from this approach is that the same behaviours will work, or be effective, for every employee. What we know however from a wide research base (for example, that focusing on individual differences, moderators of leadership effectiveness, and the stress process) is that not all employees react the same way to the same stimulus, and not all employees want the same thing at work.

For instance:

- One employee in a team may want a manager to give them very clear guidance and instructions in their work; whereas another might want to take a much more independent approach.
- One employee might find the concept of hot desking (not having one particular desk but moving according to availability) unsettling and

Preventing Stress in Organizations: How to Develop Positive Managers,
Emma Donaldson-Feilder, Joanna Yarker and Rachel Lewis.
© 2011 John Wiley & Sons, Ltd. Published 2011 by John Wiley & Sons, Ltd.

stressful; whereas another may enjoy the change and the opportunity to meet and socialize with a wider base of colleagues.

- One employee in a team might come to work purely to earn money to spend socially; whereas another may see their job as their vocation and gain personal satisfaction from their work.

The behaviours covered in this chapter can help a manager understand the members of their team and how they work. By doing this, they will be in a better position to understand the potential work-related stress triggers of team members and the pressures they may be under; they will, therefore, be better able to work with their team to prevent stress-related problems. As well as this, by understanding the motivations of team members, managers will be better able to design their work in such a way as to get the most productive and satisfied working team.

The behaviours included in this competency fall into three different clusters:

1. personally accessible;
2. sociable; and
3. empathetic engagement.

As with the two previous chapters, each of the clusters of behaviours are explored in turn, with examples of the types of contexts in which the behaviours may occur, and exercises and case studies to enable their use and exploration in your work as a practitioner. What is different however about this competency is that each cluster of behaviours may be considered as a slightly different angle from which managers can seek to understand their team members and their motivations. It may be that some of these clusters are more appropriate for some working environments and others for others – in other words, it is possible that you will need to emphasize different parts of the competency depending on the managers' workplaces.

Personally Accessible

"If you sit in your office and don't come out of it, how do you know what your staff are doing or what your customers are saying? Unless you get out there and talk to people, you won't be able to do your job. You need to get the balance right and not interfere – just show them that you are there and that you are available for them." (Senior Central Government Manager)

This cluster is all about managers being available, approachable and accessible to their team members when they need them. The most well known interpretation of this approach is the 'Open Door Policy'. This was actually an approach initiated by Thomas Watson Snr in the 1920s as a way to deal with employee grievances. The ethos was that if employees were not able to get satisfaction from their line manager, they would be free to approach their senior manager and so on up the organizational hierarchy. Therefore it actually refers to employees being able to approach managers at any level of the organizational hierarchy. Moreover it was originally conceptualized that the correspondence was to be confidential. Although many organizations do have a formal open door policy that refers to the 'open hierarchy' approach, more commonly when an 'open door policy' is referred to by managers and team members, it refers to the ability to communicate with the line manager when needed or when a problem arises; essentially therefore the manager being available and approachable to team members.

Personally accessible in academic literature

The body of academic literature that would most closely refer to personally accessible or available management would be that of manager support, broadly defined by Anderson and Williams in 1996 as 'the availability of broad helping behaviours from the direct supervisor'. This literature has been criticized for a lack of specificity, in other words, the lack of understanding of the actual behaviours underpinning manager support. However, it could be argued that, for managers to be able to display helping or supportive behaviours, they would need to be accessible, approachable and available. One of the strengths of the research that we have conducted and are exploring in detail in this book, is that it does enable the unpicking, or unravelling, of the specific behaviours managers need in order both to be supportive, and to prevent and reduce stress in their team members.

Following a review of the leadership models explored earlier in this book, it appears that both transformational and the behavioural leadership models refer to the importance of accessible line management. In the Leader Behavior Description Questionnaire (see Stodgill (1963)) (or LBDQ, the main operationalization of the Behavioural leadership model), both a positive item of 'Friendly and approachable' and a negative item of 'Keeps to him/herself' are included. The Transformational Leadership Questionnaire (or TLQ, developed in the UK by Alimo-Metcalfe (Alimo-Metcalfe and Alban-Metcalfe, 2001)) has a factor called 'Accessible, approachable and in-touch' which refers to managers being approachable and not status conscious, preferring face-to-face communications and keeping in touch. Interestingly the Multifactor Leadership Questionnaire (the operationalization of Bass' Transformational Leadership Model (Bass and Avolio, 1997)) refers to personally accessible only in the negative: within the laissez faire component of leadership, it refers to management behaviour that is passive, and to avoidance, including avoiding involvement and being absent when needed. The academic leadership models therefore refer to personally accessible behaviours both in their presence and their absence, or negative, as being important. This mirrors what we found in our research to be key within this cluster: it is important for managers not only to show positive accessibility behaviours, but also to avoid negative ones.

The findings from our research

The following list demonstrates the behaviours highlighted in our research which are key for managers to be personally accessible:

✓ Speaking to team members personally rather than using email
✓ Providing regular opportunities to speak one-to-one
✓ Returning calls and emails promptly
✓ Being available to talk to when needed
✓ Communicating that employees can talk to them at any time
✓ Having an open-door policy
✓ Making time to talk to employees at their desks

The behaviours we found to be important for managers to avoid (in other words, the negative behaviours) were:

× Being constantly away from their desk
× Being constantly in meetings
× Saying 'don't bother me now'
× Not moving from their office

How to be personally accessible

As can be seen from the behaviours above, being personally accessible is not just about being available for team members by having an open door; it is about managers being proactive in making time to talk to employees and demonstrating their approachability and availability. The following two manager quotations highlight this approach:

> "I make time to talk to people whether it is just one or two minutes and I just say 'Hello, how are you', or talk for longer. It is about making time to talk and being seen as approachable so that if a problem does arise they are comfortable coming to me. And it shows I am not just talking to them when I want something or when there has been an issue."

> "I get to work at quarter past seven in the morning to make sure I see the night staff and check they have had a reasonable night. I know all their

names and what is going on with a few of them. When you get to that level of conversation, they get confidence in you and they know you take an interest. Being there, talking to people, not just about work but all sorts of things, being visible, knowing that your door is always open and you won't turn anyone away when they knock at the door. Making sure that everyone knows you are there to help if there is a problem."

These manager examples both demonstrate two key points.

1. It is important that the manager proactively encourages conversation with their employees to develop a relationship where issues can be discussed. An open door policy will not be effective if employees don't feel comfortable approaching their manager. Therefore 'floor walking', taking time to talk to employees at their desks, saying 'Good morning' when employees come into the office, and going to the canteen at lunchtime are all great ways to foster this perception of approachability.
2. Conversations with employees should not always be about work issues or problems. It is much easier to build a relationship of trust with employees if managers know a little about them and are able to talk more informally. Further, by getting to know employees on a deeper level, managers can begin to understand their motivations and needs at work. Through this, when employees do have issues or problems, managers will be in a much better position to suggest and develop appropriate strategies and solutions.

Case study

The following case study with a manager demonstrates how serious the impact of non-availability can be for employees. It takes place in a local government organization. The manager involved had been put on secondment to another team to work on another project. The manager did not have a choice in this secondment and the new project was crucial for the future of the organization. The manager speaks 'Working on this other project meant I had to be away from my team for eight months. This other project was crucial, but in working on it I left my team under a lot of pressure to deliver work with no manager to support them. I ignored some of the communication I was getting from my team because at the time I was under so much pressure myself.'

The manager goes on to describe how, although she did try to touch base with the team, the demands of the new project made it very difficult; 'My new project was based in another site quite a long way away from my old team. When I did manage to get in to see the team it was always before they came in in the morning or after they had gone at night. They didn't know I had been in or had been around most of the time.'

Eight months later she returned to her team and encountered a very different working environment; 'Before, you could have a laugh, and there was no laughing. People used to talk about their weekend, but there was none of that. I don't think it was an intentional personal thing, it was just that they had got out of the habit because I hadn't been there. I had lost credibility and their trust.' The manager then describes a few very hard months where she tried to rebuild the relationships and trust of the team. She says in summary 'I learnt never to leave people on their own and let them think they can't communicate with you – the damage was just too great.'

What do you think the manager could have done differently to improve the situation whilst working on the project and on her return?

Managing accessibility in modern times

Ideally managers would be available on site or within the office for employees to be able to contact when necessary. However, more and more managers are tasked with managing remote teams, home workers, or teams based in different geographical areas. This means that face-to-face communication on a frequent basis may not always be possible. Our research provides many examples where managers were managing within these contexts, but were rated by their employees as being highly accessible and available.

So how did they do this? The following list, prepared from examples gathered across our research, provides suggestions for managers to improve accessibility and availability:

1. *Make face-to-face visits to team members as regularly as possible*: How often this is possible will depend on the team. Ideally face-to-face visits should include both one-to-ones with employees, and team meetings. Moreover, in these visits it is beneficial if managers are able to build in both work and project correspondence with more informal contact to establish and solidify manager–team member relationship.

2. *When face-to-face visits are not possible, encourage managers to talk to employees on the phone rather than use email*: In our research we found that email was regarded as an impersonal way to communicate. Employees felt more supported and in touch with their managers when they could talk regularly on the phone. Moreover, this regular phone call should not be to deal with specific problems or issues, but just to demonstrate that managers are there for employees and are interested in their experiences at work. The following quote from a financial manager demonstrates this approach:'

My team are based all around the UK so we don't have regular face-to-face contact. We try to speak on the phone a lot. I speak to them as often as I can to make sure they know I haven't forgotten about them.' Even better, managers may consider use of video-conferencing so that face-to-face conversations can be achieved remotely.

3. *Create opportunities for team meetings and get-togethers*: It is important that managers managing remotely recognize the importance of the working environment and culture for a healthy and successful team (Please note: Sociability will be included in more detail within the next behavioural cluster and the benefits of team working were explored more in Chapter 5). In environments where managers may not be physically available at all times, a strong team culture will buffer the negative effects and provide a supportive and nurturing environment. This is even more important for managers to proactively focus upon in teams where both the team and the manager are remote. Managers could organize regular team meetings that include team building and social elements to foster the team relationships. One manager describes their approach:

> 'My team are dotted all around the country. When we have team meetings, I make sure they all come up the night before so that we can all have dinner together. It is difficult but I try to make them feel like they are all part of a team and together.'

4. *Communicate and agree response times*: One of the key sources of work-related stress in employees was when managers were contacted, but did not respond quickly either to emails or to phone calls. It is essential, therefore, that managers agree response times with their employees. This may differ depending on the managers commitments on certain days of the week, or with communication received at particular hours of the day. Whatever the appropriate arrangements, it is important that managers agree the response arrangements with all team members – and review the appropriateness of these arrangements on a regular basis.

5. *Make sure all team members know where the manager is at all times*: One of the issues with managers not being physically present is that employees may not know when would be appropriate to contact them, and so avoid doing so. It is important, therefore, that managers communicate to employees at all times where they will be and how they can be contacted. This might be utilizing phone, email, and pager. The following demonstrates a manager using this approach:

> 'The danger with me working across different sites is that problems occur and I don't get to hear about them and they escalate. So I make sure my staff know where I am and how to get hold of me even if I am not there. I have got a pager and a mobile and I always respond to

emails. It can be demanding because I feel like I am at their beck and call all the time, but it is a better approach than saying I don't have time for them.'

This approach will also ensure that team members recognize when it may take longer to respond to their enquiries or questions. You could suggest the manager consider the use of an electronic diary that can be shared and viewed by all team members; or the publication of a weekly rota that highlights the manager's key meetings, visits and appointments.

Setting boundaries around accessibility

Point 5 in the last section described a manager who worked remotely but who worked hard to be constantly accessible and available to their team members. The quote hinted at the pressures of this approach on the manager themselves. In our research we met many managers who decried the amount of pressure they felt that being available to their team members had created, giving examples where managers were not able to complete their own work due to constant interruptions, or where managers deliberately stayed away from the office to enable them to get their work completed.

How then can managers achieve a balance whereby they are perceived available and accessible to their team, but also protect themselves from adverse pressure to enable them to also complete their work and manage their own demands?

From our research and experience working with managers and teams, we have developed a few ideas that may be useful for you to discuss with managers who are suffering from this issue.

1. *Create protected time everyday where team members cannot contact managers (unless in emergencies)*: This may for instance include the early morning hours such as 8 to 9.30am where managers will be able to focus their energy on the day and deal with any urgent tasks and demands. It may also include the end of the day, for instance 5pm onwards so that both managers and employees see a direct end to the day and to enable managers to achieve a work–home life balance. However it is not recommended that too many hours of the day are blocked out as protected time.
2. *Make use of 'surgery hours'*: Although managers may want to make themselves available for employee issues and problems all day, it may be the case that managers only want to deal with urgent problems and issues on an adhoc basis rather than general feedback or less urgent issues such as development needs or training. If this is the case, one idea is to make use of a surgery hour that could be every day, or once a

week (or whenever is suitable for the manager) whereby employees are able to book time with the manager to discuss these non-urgent issues. This surgery hour is recommended to be consistent and to be protected time for employees; therefore managers would not arrange other meetings within this time.

3. *Devise a way to demonstrate non-availability:* Within a team environment where the manager is in the office, this may be as simple as a shut office door, or may be the manager could make use of a 'not available' sign or a nameplate that can be moved between 'Available' and 'Engaged'. There will be times when a manager will be in a meeting or on a call where interruptions will not be possible. If this is the case, a manager should communicate timings to their employees about when they will be available and out of the meeting/off the call. This could be done via a sign that includes timings on the door, or even a clock. Another idea would be for a manager to go and work in another room, but leave the sign/statement on their office door. In remote teams, this could be done via out of office email or voicemail stating non-availability and time when available.

   If it is the case where managers are in the office but working on a deadline or key project and don't want to (rather than can't) be interrupted, the same mechanism could be used, but managers could also state that interruptions via email could be made in emergencies. This way the managers can be kept in touch and be made aware of any urgent issues. In order for both of these to work, managers need to use them sparingly. This way, employees will learn to use and respect the non-availability.

4. *Set time parameters:* Where managers prefer to be always available for employees, the use of time parameters are recommended. It is important these are stated and agreed at the beginning of meetings, and that these are imposed and stuck to by the managers. An example might be 'Yes, let's talk about this now. I only have 15 minutes for this meeting though. I think this should be sufficient to cover everything, but if you think we need more we can agree another time at the end of the meeting.' Towards the end of this time, managers can use signals such as stating 'Before we finish. . .' or 'As our time is nearly up for this particular talk. . .' In this way managers are able to maintain a level of control over their day.

   Similarly, if a manager cannot deal with an employee's request or issue at that moment, rather than suggesting 'come back later' or 'I'm busy now', a time should be agreed when the manager will be available and can deal with the employee. Again, it is crucial that this agreed time is stuck to so that the manager is able to both build and maintain the trust of their employees.

5. *Communicate!:* If managers communicate their work demands and arrangements to employees consistently so employees are kept

informed of the managers' workloads and meetings, employees will be much more likely to demonstrate empathy and not interrupt managers for non-urgent issues when they know that they are busy. Similarly, if managers can also encourage as much team communication as possible so that their team has a 'working together' attitude, the impact of managerial non-availability can be lessened by team members actually helping each other to sort out problems and issues.

Essentially, these ideas are about enabling managers to set boundaries and parameters and to recognize their needs, limitations and work demands. Being effective managers and preventing and reducing work-related stress in team members does not involve managers being at the beck and call of their team as this could compromise both productivity and health.

Sociable

"Interdependence is and ought to be as much the ideal of man as self-sufficiency. Man is a social being." (Mahatma Gandhi)

This cluster is perhaps the most contentious in our research findings, and is one that raises both the most vehement support and vehement rejection. As said at the beginning of this chapter, it may be that in some working environments, or for some managers, not all of the behaviours will be appropriate. However, what we have found is that managers adopting and demonstrating friendly and sociable behaviours to their team is a very powerful way to gain the trust of their employees and in so doing understand more about what their employees need and want. In understanding more about employees' motivations, managers are in the strongest position to be able to get the best out of their team members both in terms of productivity, happiness and job satisfaction.

Sociability in the management literature

In reviewing the leadership models reviewed in Chapter 3 of this book, it is clear that sociable leadership is not seen as a key component of the transformational leadership models or the behavioural leadership models (apart from one use of the word 'friendly' in the latter). In fact the only model that was found that did touch upon sociable behaviours was the model created by Gilbreath and Benson (2004). This was a leadership model which focused on the outcome of employees' well-being and, therefore, is perhaps the closest to the model found in our research. Their scale includes the management behaviour item 'Fun things to keep morale up'. It is interesting that these behaviours are key for the health and well-being of employees, but are perhaps not seen as relevant to productivity outcomes (which are the central focus for the transformational and behavioural leadership models).

Although the leadership models don't directly refer to sociable and friendly behaviour, the central tenet of one leadership theory, that of leader-member exchange (or LMX), is upon the quality of the relationship between managers and the employees. The basic premise of LMX is that managers do not adopt a single leadership style to their employees, but rather behave differently towards different members of the team, developing closer relationships with some than others. These closer, or higher quality relationships tend to be characterized by mutual trust, respect, commitment and bonding. The theory suggests that employees in good quality relationships with their managers display more positive behaviours and performance. In addition, a growing body of research points to the positive effects of high quality LMX on employees' well-being and health. The theory of LMX, therefore, suggests that it is beneficial for employees and their managers to have a good, close, high quality working relationship.

The findings from our research

The behaviours that we found to be key in this cluster include:

- ✓ Bring in treats
- ✓ Socialize with the team
- ✓ Be willing to have a laugh at work
- ✓ Regularly have informal chats with employees

The behaviours that we found were important for managers to avoid (in other words, the negative behaviours) include:

- ✕ Doesn't attend social events
- ✕ Doesn't join employees for lunch
- ✕ Uses a harsh tone of voice when asking for things
- ✕ Pulls team up for talking/laughing during working hours

Being a sociable manager

The key focus of this cluster is managers behaving in a sociable and friendly way towards employees. These three examples from managers demonstrate the types of behaviours and actions that this cluster consists of:

> "I like to speak to everyone, say good morning in the morning and just walk round and say hi. We usually have a coffee break in the morning and a tea

break in the afternoon where we all get together and have a chat and talk about things that are going on at work as well as social things. We have the usual Christmas outing, team outings and we plan social lunches – just lunches in the week where we all go to the pub and have a team bonding session."

"As a general way of managing when our work gets stressful, I am very upbeat, very positive and very bubbly. It is amazing how far a box of doughnuts or a night out will go. Things like that show we operate as a team and my job is to reinforce that, keep the team going and keep them as happy as possible. We have team meetings once a month and are very positive and motivational. We have team lunches every month as well where we go to the local pub together and have lunch. We do lots of things together as a team to make sure we are all happy, open and friendly."

"I try to keep a positive spirit in the team and lead from the front. We work in a very busy branch and when we close the branch doors at 5 it is a great time for us to relieve the pressure. There is always lots of laughing and clowning around and I encourage this. Although we have a lot of pressure in our work, there is a really good team spirit. We all keep our sense of humour and this helps us to manage our workload. I also make sure we have regular outings after work – get togethers and team events where we can all let off steam. This really helps with the team spirit."

These examples demonstrate that being a sociable manager doesn't just involve social events or outings, but more importantly is about a general attitude and behaviour towards the team which:

- is friendly, including asking about both their work and their life outside of work;
- is thoughtful, including bringing in treats and gifts on birthdays, special occasions, at the end of a project or in times of pressure; and
- uses and encourages humour and informality at times.

The benefits of the sociable approach

At the beginning of this section about the 'Sociable' cluster, we explored how these types of behaviours could help managers to understand more about each team members' motivations, needs and wants. The examples above however demonstrate the power of this approach in easing pressure and helping team members to work through difficult and pressurized times at work. Therefore this approach can act as a motivator in itself. The following scenario described by a healthcare manager highlights this in more detail:

"The six of us in our team are quite noisy. By the nature of our work it is mainly constant telephone work. One of the other teams, when we first moved to this building said 'There is always a lot of laughing from your team.' I said 'Oh, does it disturb you?' They said 'Yes, it can be really off putting.' I said that although I appreciated that, what they had to understand was that my team deal with very negative stuff on the phone and they have to have a vent for that. If that vent is that they chat about what they did at the weekend or where they are going; or even if it is to laugh at something someone said on the phone, that is fine. I told him that rather than telling them to be quiet, I would need to look into moving elsewhere. I am not going to tell my team to work in silence. It is a very demanding and a very upsetting job. To be able to laugh and have a chat relieves the stress and tension and enables you to look at the situation more rationally. It is either that, or shout, scream, stamp your feet or burst into tears."

This scenario again demonstrates the power of humour and informal chat to relieve tension and pressure in the team, and act as a kind of coping mechanism. What it also introduces it the concept of respite. This suggests that to have a break from focusing on work and the task can help employees to be able to see the situation, or the problem, more rationally and objectively. This employee quotation demonstrates the use of informal chat to do this:

"I find if I do something else for a little while or I go and talk to someone and have a chat, I come back with fresh eyes and sometimes see the solution that maybe I wouldn't have seen before. My manager encourages this rather than thinking 'my staff need to be quiet and sitting at their desk working'."

Therefore the sociable approach within the team can not only help the manager to learn more about what makes their employees tick, but can also be a way to relieve work-related stress and as a coping mechanism at work, as well as encouraging problem solving. This approach also has a strong effect on the team. In the previous chapter we explored the cluster of 'Participative/empowering' and the strong motivation element of team working. A sociable manager can also, while strengthening the relationship between each team member and themselves; also strengthen relationships within the team. The following example from an employee highlights the benefit of this:

"Our manager is really good at getting the team to get to know each other, not just on a work level, but as people. By doing this, it encourages us all to worry about each other and pay more attention to what they are doing and how they are – and what impact our actions might have on colleagues. So just by encouraging that closeness and togetherness in a team, it is a good way of helping the team not to suffer stress."

What if the manager is not 'the sociable type'?

In our research we came across many managers who felt that they were just not the sociable type. Reasons given were either having an introverted personality, feeling that there needed to be a barrier between employees and managers, having a long commute and therefore not having time to attend social functions, that it was too 'feely touchy' or just feeling that it wasn't part of their job role.

Although we recognize that not everyone has the same management approach, we did see how significant the effects of a manager not displaying the positive behaviours could be. The first example describes an employee's experience of their manager:

> "In my team we are very insular. Where I sit, which is opposite the HR team I can see they all get on and laugh and joke. They don't interact with us. Our culture is fostered and led by our line manager. He is quiet and insular and unsociable, and it breeds in the team. In the HR team they go out to lunch, or after work for a drink, or just sit down and discuss how they are getting on and how they are feeling. There is nothing like that in our team. In fact I could have my head on the table if I am unwell, and no-one will actually even ask if I am OK."

The following example describes a teacher's experience with their head teacher:

> "He used to come into the classroom and say 'Lovely wallboard, you have spent so much time on it.' He would go out the room and we would say 'sod off'. It was like he had read a book that said 'Talk to your staff in a very positive way', but it just wasn't from the heart. You just thought he had said it because the textbook told him to. Sometimes he would walk past and blank you, and other times he would smile at you. He would also call you into his office and say 'Sit down, I need to talk to you', as if you were one of the pupils, and the next day say 'It's Friday, lets go to the pub'. Of course we didn't want to. He made us so uncomfortable. There were so many tears. It made us all feel down and sad. The leader sets the tone for the whole organization."

Both examples show how the behaviour of the manager can be contagious in that if managers do not display positive behaviour, or are inconsistent in their management style, their teams are also prevented from displaying positive behaviour.

We are not suggesting that managers should be 'friends' with their employees, or that all managers should go to the pub with their employees after work on a regular basis. This is not appropriate in some organizations, or in some teams in recognition of diversity, but more importantly, many managers would not feel comfortable with the sociable element of these behaviours. Rather, managers may prefer to join their employee's for lunch in the office canteen, or talk informally to them during the day or in breaks.

If the manager is not 'the sociable type' here, are some suggestions of how they might display some of these behaviours while still being comfortable with their appropriateness:

1. *Accept the different needs and wants of employees*: Although the manager may themselves not be comfortable with use of humour in the workplace, or informal conversations, they can still recognize how important and beneficial these types of activities can be for employees and therefore accept, tolerate and encourage these behaviours. Although the ideal would be for managers to role model this behaviour, being able to role model encouragement and an acceptance of 'different strokes for different folks' is the next best option.

2. *Realize that being sociable doesn't have to mean 'nights out'*: Not all managers will feel comfortable, or that it is appropriate to join staff on nights out. The aim of the display of sociable behaviours is both to understand more about employees' motivations, and give employees 'breathing space' from their work. Therefore, rather than nights out, a sociable behaviour could be to join employees in the canteen for lunch, or organize a walk at lunchtime, or initiate an activity that is not work related, but which the manager is comfortable with. It could purely be that managers always ask employees about their weekend, or say 'hello' in the morning – or even make tea for the team every day. The key is to help non-sociable managers to find sociable, warm and friendly activities or behaviours that they would be comfortable displaying at work and introducing into their management style.

3. *Above all, demonstrate both consistency and authenticity*: We would never recommend managers display behaviours they are not comfortable with, because this will inevitably result in either the manager appearing disingenuous, or showing inconsistency in their behaviour. The example earlier citing the head teacher's behaviour demonstrates the negative impact of inconsistency. We also feel though, that every manager, no matter how 'unsociable' they feel they are, can introduce more sociable, friendly and warm behaviours into their repertoire that they would feel comfortable with, and therefore be able to continue consistently with their team.

Empathetic Engagement

"People will forget what you said, people will forget what you did, but people will never forget how you made them feel." (Bonnie Jean Wasmund)

The *Oxford Dictionary* definition of 'empathy' is that it is 'the power of understanding and imaginatively entering into another person's feelings', therefore seeking to understand how another person feels, or what makes them tick. Much research has been conducted in areas of developmental, neurological, social and abnormal psychology around the construct of empathy, and found that its roots within humans are cognitive, affective and dispositional.

Empathy in the leadership and management literature

In recent leadership and management literature, authors have tended to focus upon the construct of emotional intelligence, rather than empathy. Emotional intelligence was defined by Mayer and Salovey in 1997 as 'the ability to perceive and express emotion, assimilate emotion in thought, understand and reason with emotion, and regulate emotion in self and others'; it is, therefore, the ability to reflect upon the emotional content of both our own thoughts and the thoughts of others. Mayer and Salovey (1997) argue that emotional intelligence is a cognitive ability that involves the processing of emotions, and is therefore something that individuals or managers either 'have' or 'don't have'. In the practitioner sphere, more popular models of Emotional Intelligence have viewed it as either an array of coping abilities – including theorists such as Bar-On (Bar-On and Parker, 2000) – or a set of management and leadership competencies (such as the concept popularized by Goleman in 1995). The latter types of models suggest that emotional intelligence in managers is a skill that managers can learn. Research, in both the practitioner and academic fields, points quite clearly to the benefits of emotional intelligence for both team and individual success and well-being.

While emotional intelligence refers to the emotions of self and others, empathy refers to the feelings of others; it is, therefore, conceptualized, in the main, as the ability to understand others' feelings, rather than to understand one's own feelings. In reviewing the management and leadership models, although empathy is not directly referred to, two of the models do include relevant behaviours. The Leader Behavior Description Questionnaire for instance includes items of 'does little things to make it pleasant to be a member of the group', 'treats all members as his or her equals' and 'looks out for the welfare of group members'. The Transformational Leadership Questionnaire (developed in the UK by Alimo-Metcalfe), in a key point of difference from the Bass model of Transformational Leadership, includes a factor called 'Showing genuine concern for others': here it is the central factor in the model, and includes showing a genuine interest in staff as individuals, valuing contributions, developing strengths, coaching, mentoring and having positive expectations. What then do we refer to when we talk of 'Empathetic Engagement'?

The findings from our research

The behaviours that we found to be key in this cluster include:

✓ Encourage employees' input in discussions
✓ Listen when employees ask for help
✓ Make an effort to find out what motivates employees at work
✓ Try to see team member's point of view
✓ Take an interest in the team members' lives outside of work
✓ Regularly ask 'How are you?'
✓ Treat all team members with equal importance

The behaviours that we found it is important for managers to avoid include:

× Assume rather than checks employees are OK
× Refuse to believe that someone is becoming stressed
× Insensitive to people's personal issues
× Maintain a distance from employees – 'us and them'

Seeking to understand and 'know' team members

The behaviours in this cluster concern managers proactively seeking to understand the feelings, motivations, needs and wants of their team members. It could be said that the previous two clusters ('Personally Accessible' and 'Sociable') are mechanisms by which to foster empathetic engagement, in that if managers are able to communicate and engage with their employees in more informal ways and if managers behave in approachable, friendly and accessible ways, they will be given more opportunities to understand the feelings and motivations of their team members and communicate with them at a deeper level.

The following example describes a manager who appreciates the importance of empathy.

> "The most important thing is to be mindful of who people are. More than work issues about them, being able to refer to them so that they feel I know details about them, for instance what annoys them. You don't have to know everything about everyone, but it really makes a difference if you can refer to something you know is relevant and important to them. Personal touches, congratulations, flowers, pictures, plants, buying them some orange squash when it is hot – whatever really. It may not cost much money or much time but it really makes a difference to people's attitudes in the workplace. If people feel they are noticed, then it provides a real cushion which enables people to cope with an awful lot of stress."

This example demonstrates that not only does the empathetic approach to management help managers understand more about those who are in the team and therefore how to get the best out of them, but also makes the team members feel valued and important and happy and this can then act as a buffer to pressures and stresses in people's working lives. What is clear is that, although this may be a personality style of the manager, behaving in an empathetic way involves the manager being proactive, and also highly cognizant of what may be underneath the surface of an employee. The following example demonstrates this need to explore a bit deeper:

> "There was a particular person on reception who was not dealing with customers effectively and wasn't talking to them in the right way. I mentioned it to him a couple of times and said that this is what I was seeing and that this was not the right way to deal with customers. He took what I said, but continued with his behaviour. I called him one day and said 'After the conversations we have had, what are the issues?' There was a complaint about the way that he had talked to the customer so I gave the complaint to him and showed him what the customer had said. I said 'What I am seeing is that this is not your normal behaviour, what is it that has sparked this off?' I was just thinking it would be work issues, but what came out was that it was personal stuff about his home, his finances and issues with his partner. From that day, any time he has an issue he has come to talk to me and we work through it."

This example demonstrates the manager making an effort to understand what the cause of the poor behaviour was, rather than purely reacting to the presenting behaviour – in other words, treating the cause rather than the symptoms. If we take this medical analogy further, taking this approach with focusing on the cause, or the person themselves, allows managers to take preventative action and spot issues, and warning signs, as demonstrated by the following employee's quotation:

> 'My manager is very astute in terms of reading people and picking up on what she would perceive to be the warning signs. If I am looking tired she will say so and explore it and see if I am OK and am coping.'

These examples demonstrate managers being proactive and actively checking upon employees' welfare. The following example describes a management approach in direct contrast to this:

> "My manager is not at all demonstrative and is very analytical. When he is busy he forgets us. He is of the opinion that unless people shout, they are OK, instead of paying a bit of attention to them. He will never realize if someone has a problem. He wouldn't dream of thinking about what to do to motivate his staff, or to keep them happy. The most he would do is say 'good morning', but that doesn't always happen either."

It was clear from our research that not only did it take time for managers to be able to understand and 'know' their team members, but that it was an approach which needed to be seen as part of everyday management, and therefore revisited on a regular basis, rather than as a one off or at team development events. For instance, it could be that although generally a particular employee would prefer to work under their own steam, they might have particular issues with certain aspects of the role or situations and, therefore, at times prefer a more hands-on approach. Further, the way an employee reacts generally, and how they react under pressure or work-related stress may actually be different to the expectation, again pointing to the need to avoid assumptions. The following example from a manager describing an employee demonstrates the latter situation:

> "One employee on the face of it was coping. I failed to pick up the signs over two or three months and then she went off sick with stress. I misread the fact that she was an extrovert and talked a lot. In a lot of cases I would see her talking and think she was OK and happy. But it was a sign of stress. She would talk uncontrollably when she was stressed. Due to her being so extrovert I just thought that was her and that was normal."

Recognizing the difference

When managers do take efforts to understand their employees' motivations and needs, they will start to appreciate that everyone is different, and, therefore, one employee will be motivated and made happy by different things to another. The empathetic manager is, therefore, the flexible manager in terms of being able to display a range of differing behaviours to team members depending on their personality and their motivations.

The following examples demonstrate line managers recognizing this:

> "Some people in my team are more personable than others. I know from my team I have got both extremes of people who are very personable and people who are equally good at the job but just want to get on with it, and don't want any kind of chit chat or small talk."

> "I have someone in my team who is chatty, one who is reserved, and one who is really outspoken. I have to balance that dynamic. In a team meeting I could say one point and the reserved person might not say something because the outspoken one is going for it. And then you have the chatty one who talks all the way through. I have learnt I can't treat everyone the same. I have to get to know my team as individuals as well as as a team."

> "You have to recognize staff and make them feel important, and you have to understand what it is that makes them feel important. Some people like public demonstrations – saying well done and everyone clapping. Others just like to be taken aside and privately told that they have done a really good job. It all comes down to understanding your team as individuals."

Exercise for Managers

When working with managers, it may be helpful to use an exercise with them to explore the extent to which they understand the different motivations of their team members. We have found the following exercise very powerful in our group workshops and coaching.

1. Get the manager, on a landscape A4 piece of paper, to write down their name in the top left corner of the page, and then to write the names of three or four of their team members across the top of the page.
2. Ask them to think about what motivates them to do their work to the best of their ability and to write this under their name. You may need to prompt them with suggestions such as pay, pension, feeling valued, getting positive feedback, the opportunity to travel, flexible working hours, geographical locality, sees the work as important/significant, pride in the organization. The manager may come up with different suggestions to this about why they come to work.
3. Once the manager has done this, ask them to repeat the same exercise for each of their team members, thinking about what they think motivates each of their team members.

You can then guide the manager in reflecting upon what they have written. You might want to probe around the following types of questions:

- How easy did you find it to do the exercise?
- Was it easier to think about the motivations of some team members than others?
- Those team members for whom you were not sure of their motivations, what impact do you feel this may have on the way that you work together?
- How do your team members' motivations affect their approach to work and the team?
- If your team members have different motivations to you, how does this impact upon your relationship?

By probing around these areas, you will be able to get the manager to see the link between motivations towards work, and the types of approaches and attitude towards work.

The 'similar to me' effect

Within occupational psychology a concept termed the 'similar to me' effect has been explored. Research has shown that we tend to rate or regard people we perceive as similar to us more highly than those we regard as dissimilar to us; similarity may be in terms of biographical details (such as the area we came from, the school we went to and other background details), age, gender, ethnicity, attractiveness, cognitive style, attachment style, and many other parameters. Therefore, if managers have team members that they perceive as similar to them, in this case in terms of their approach to work and their motivations towards work, they are more likely to have a good relationship with those team members, and perceive them as being effective at their role.

The exercise above will have got the manager to reflect upon this. Did you find for instance that those managers that perceived a particular team member as having similar motivations to them also stated that they had the strongest working relationship with that team member? Likewise, did you find that those team members whose motivations the manager found difficult to identify, or who had motivations very different to those of the manager, were described as having a less effective or close working relationship? The following example from a manager demonstrates the impact of different working styles and motivations within a team.

> "My own style is that I like to get things done and I like to in a timely manner. I put deadlines on myself and on my team. So, I used to expect everybody to behave in the same way, so if I want to get something finished I make sure I get it done that week or that day. Some people don't work like that, and in the past I have put unrealistic expectations on certain people. I didn't consider that not everyone works using the same method as I do, which is to put everything to one side and complete that task; they might have put the task in with something else, or completed things in a different order. It didn't help those individuals, and what I have learned is that I can't expect everybody to work in the same way, so everybody has to have a different timespan and different ways of working. My problem was I was expecting everyone to be the same as me and wanting the same things and the same things to drive them. It doesn't. I am not driven by money, but other people are – so they will only do more work if they get more money. I would say 'Just do it because you want to do a good job', but they don't feel like that. I have to understand and appreciate that."

Managers need to be encouraged to appreciate that having a different motivation towards work is valid, and also can be useful and effective in a team environment. It would be useful to work through with the manager how different work motivations and styles are beneficial and advantageous to the team, as well as exploring ways in which they can best utilize and work with those differences.

Summary

This chapter has explored the competency 'Managing the individual within the team'. As described in the previous chapter, the research in Phase Two refined the behaviours included in the whole stress

Table 7.1. Behavioural indicators for 'Managing the individual within the team'

Competency	Cluster	Do (✓)/ Don't (✗)	Examples of manager behaviour
Managing the individual within the team	Personally accessible	✓	■ Speaks personally rather than uses email ■ Provides regular opportunities to speak one to one ■ Returns calls/emails promptly ■ Is available to talk to when needed
	Sociable	✓	■ Brings in treats ■ Socializes with the team ■ Is willing to have a laugh at work
	Empathetic engagement	✓	■ Encourages employee input in discussions ■ Listens when employees ask for help ■ Makes an effort to find out what motivates employees at work ■ Tries to see team member's point of view ■ Takes an interest in team's life outside work ■ Regularly asks 'how are you?' ■ Treats all team members with equal importance
		✗	■ Assumes rather than checks employees are OK

Source: Adapted from Donaldson-Feilder, Lewis and Yarker (2009)
© Crown Copyright 2009

management competency framework into a measure to enable both managers to self-assess their own effectiveness and for use in upward and 360 degree feedback programmes. Table 7.1 shows those behaviours within the measure relevant to this particular competency. You may want to use this table as a prompt for discussions in your work about displaying these types of behaviours.

References

Alimo-Metcalfe, B. and Alban-Metcalfe, R.J. (2001). The development of a new transformational leadership questionnaire. *Journal of Occupational and Organizational Psychology*, 74, 1–27.

Anderson, S.E. and Williams, C.J. (1996). Interpersonal, job and individual factors related to helping processes at work. *Journal of Applied Psychology*, 81, 282–296.

Bar-On, R. and Parker, J.D.A. (2000). *The Handbook of Emotional Intelligence. Theory, Development, Assessment and Application at Home, School and in the Workplace.* Jossey Bass, San Francisco.

Bass, B.M. and Avolio, B.J. (1997). *Full Range Leadership Development: Manual for the Multifactor Leadership Questionnaire.* Mind Garden, Palo Alto, CA.

Donaldson-Feilder, E., Lewis, R. and Yarker, J., (2009). *Preventing Stress: Promoting Positive Manager Behaviour.* CIPD Insight Report. CIPD Publications: London, available on the CIPD website: www.cipd.co.uk/subjects/health/stress/_preventing_ stress.

Gilbreath, B. and Benson, P.G. (2004). The contribution of supervisor behavior to employee psychological well-being. *Work and Stress*, 18, 255–266.

Goleman, D. (1995). *Emotional Intelligence.* Bloomsbury, London.

Mayer, J.D. and Salovey, D. (1997). What is emotional intelligence? In P. Salovey and D. J. Shuyter (eds). *Emotional Development and Educational Implications.* Basic Books, London.

Stogdill, R.M. (1963). *Manual for the Leader Behavior Description Questionnaire.* The Ohio State University Press, Columbus.

8

Reasoning/managing difficult situations (management competency 4)

The final competency we are going to explore is called 'Reasoning/ managing difficult situations'. This competency is perhaps the only one of the four explored within this book that refers to behaviours that may not be 'everyday' behaviours, but those that managers would be required to display during difficult situations such as conflict in the team, or through incidents of bullying and harassment.

It is important to be clear that although when the mention of conflict or managing difficult situations is raised, we automatically tend to think about incidents of bullying and harassment; more often managers will be faced with minor arguments or bickering between colleagues, or 'bad atmospheres'. These minor arguments are common within teams, but must not be neglected. These situations demand manager behaviour, focus and attention to ensure that the situation does not escalate from a minor 'bicker' to a more serious incident.

There are many resources and packages available within the learning and development domain that are designed to equip managers with conflict management skills. The behaviours covered in this

Preventing Stress in Organizations: How to Develop Positive Managers,
Emma Donaldson-Feilder, Joanna Yarker and Rachel Lewis.
© 2011 John Wiley & Sons, Ltd. Published 2011 by John Wiley & Sons, Ltd.

chapter highlight the importance of a consistent behavioural process whereby managers seek to spot and resolve the conflict quickly and fairly, consult with others on appropriate solutions, and follow up on the team relationships after resolution of the conflict. They are designed to help managers approach conflicts and difficult situations within the team. They *do not* provide a full conflict management training for managers, and we strongly recommend that if an organization or manager you are working with does have issues of conflict, bullying or harassment, it would be key to provide further conflict management training which would approach issues such as managing aggression, assertiveness training and mediation skills that will not be covered within this chapter.

The behaviours included in this competency fall into three different clusters:

1. Managing conflict;
2. Use of organizational resources; and
3. Taking responsibility for resolving issues.

Once again, each of the clusters of behaviours is explored in turn, with examples of the types of contexts in which the behaviours may occur, and exercises and case studies to enable their use and exploration in your work as a practitioner.

Managing Conflict

"Washing one's hands of the conflict between the powerful and the powerless means to side with the powerful, not to be neutral." (Paulo Freire)

This cluster is all about managers being able to step in and manage conflict within the team environment fairly, objectively and quickly. Managing conflict is becoming an increasing challenge within organizations with the Chartered Institute of Personnel and Development (2007a) reporting in their guide *Managing Conflict at Work: A Guide for Line Managers*, that the number of employment tribunals in the UK in 2006–7 had increased to 132,577, an increase of 17,538 on the previous year. It is thought that this increase is both due to an increased awareness of employment rights and litigation among employees, and also the introduction of the 2003 new employment legislation which prohibited discrimination on the basis of age, sexual orientation and religion (adding to those already in place to prohibit discrimination on the basis of race, sex and disability). The CIPD survey report *Managing Conflict at Work* (CIPD, 2007a) highlighted results finding that the regulations had increased the number of disciplinary and grievance procedures, but not affected the amount of employment tribunal applications, suggesting that employers were more likely to rely on legal advice to resolve disputes since the regulations than address them internally. In addition, this survey also found that managers were increasingly reticent to address conflict within their team for fear that they would do or say something that could be held against them legally. This suggests that, more than ever, line managers should be equipped with the skills, knowledge and capacity to both identify and manage workplace conflicts.

Unfortunately, however, not only may line managers be part of the solution in terms of employee conflict, but they are also often the cause of employee disputes and conflicts. In the beginning of this book we explored research demonstrating the link between manager behaviour and employee stress; research by the CIPD (from the *Managing Conflict at Work* report, CIPD, 2004) found that line managers are most likely to be the source of bullying within organizations. Many of the behaviours explored over the last three chapters, for instance behaving with a lack of integrity, behaving aggressively or inconsistently, not acting with consideration towards employees, among others, could be seen to contribute to this issue.

Conflict in the academic literature

In the academic literature, interpersonal conflict is either operationalized overtly (for instance being rude to a colleague) or covertly (for instance speaking behind someone's back or spreading rumours about a colleague) and may range from minor disagreements with colleagues, to physical assaults. Although there is not extensive research, it is suggested to be one of the main sources of stress at work. In 1985, Keenan and Newton used the Stress Incident Report, which was an open ended method, to collect stressful incidents that occurred at work in the past month, and found that interpersonal conflict at work was one of the most cited sources of stress at work (Keenan and Newton, 1985). A further study by Bolger, DeLongis, Kessler and Schilling (1989), which looked at employee's experience of daily stressors, found that interpersonal conflict was one of the most upsetting stressor of all, accounting for more than 80 per cent of the variance in daily mood. Similarly, Smith and Sulsky (1995) conducted a study of 600 participants in three organizations and found that 25 per cent of respondents rated interpersonal issues as their most upsetting job stressor. It appears, therefore, that interpersonal conflict is an important and influential stressor in the workplace.

The academic literature has also explored the consequences of interpersonal conflict at work, finding clear links with an employee's intention to leave the organization, higher absenteeism and job dissatisfaction; psychosomatic complaints such as frustration, anxiety and psychological strain; in addition to having a negative impact upon both performance and productivity for employees.

A related body of research is that of the workplace bullying and workplace violence and aggression literature. Workplace psychological aggression has been found by research to be commonplace, certainly more so than violence – although it should be recognized that psychological aggression is often a precursor to physical violence. The effects of aggression have been found in research to be similar to those of violence; ranging from psychological impacts such as strain, intention to leave the organization and dissatisfaction; physical complaints; and behavioural outcomes of decreased performance and productivity.

The concept of workplace bullying has, not surprisingly, received a fair amount of attention in the workplace stress literature. As found in the CIPD research, academic research also shows that although bullying is sometimes perpetrated by peers of the employee, it is more common for the perpetrator to be the supervisor. A comprehensive review of the bullying literature was conducted on behalf of the UK Health and Safety Executive in 2006 by Beswick, Gore and Palferman. This suggested that there were significant associations between employees' experiences of bullying, even if they are not directly victims but rather witnesses to bullying, and psychological strain, physical strain and sickness absence.

This review provided a list of 'bullying behaviours' by both managers and employees. A review by Rayner and McIvor in 2006 added to this, suggesting that not only was it important to focus upon the negative behaviours, therefore the behaviours that managers should avoid, but also to focus upon behaviours that they should engage in and encourage. This review suggested managers should be encouraged to demonstrate awareness of employees' behaviours, listen to employees' issues, communicate effectively, mediate, and apply early conflict resolution. The need for both positive and negative behaviours to be focused upon when seeking to manage conflict was mirrored in our research findings.

The findings from our research

The following demonstrates the behaviours highlighted in our research to be key for managers to manage conflict effectively:

✓ Act as a mediator in conflict situations
✓ Deal with squabbles before they become arguments
✓ Deal objectively with conflicts
✓ Deal with conflicts head on

The behaviours we found to be important for managers to avoid (in other words, the negative behaviours) were:

× Trying to keep the peace rather than sort out problems
× Taking sides
× Not taking employee complaints seriously

Addressing conflict in the team quickly

Our research demonstrated that one of the most important ways for managers to be able to manage conflict was to do so quickly, by both noticing and intervening promptly. In any team there will always be occasions where tensions, disputes or conflicts occur between team members. It may be as a result of serious incidents such as discriminatory behaviour, theft or bullying; but it is more likely to occur as a result of team members preferring to work in slightly different ways, or where unfair conduct is perceived such as one team member taking credit for another's work, or not pulling equal weight within the team or not including a team member in pieces of correspondence or social events. A manager's role is to be able to monitor the team relationships and watch for any signs that more serious disputes or conflicts are developing. As Max Lucade said 'Conflict is inevitable but combat is optional.' Often squabbles may appear to be resolved and forgotten quickly, but when the same squabble reoccurs regularly, or is not resolved and so begins to fester away, the manager needs to intervene and talk to the team members to try and resolve both the conflict and the source of the conflict.

The following example from a Healthcare manager demonstrates this approach:

"I make sure that if I do pick up on anything, because I do get wee squabbles and things sometimes, that I actually pick one out and ask what's wrong because I can see there is an atmosphere. I try and get them through it in the best way without interfering too much. Often, it might be that somebody have been not helping with a clinic that day, or not training and they are doing their own thing. It is silly things sometimes, but silly things like somebody looking at the Internet when they should be doing something else can cause a disagreement."

For managers to be able to pick up on squabbles, tensions and disagreements before they become conflicts, managers need to know each team member as an individual and understand both their motivations and the way that they work. There are many reasons why managers knowing their team will really help with being able to intervene in disputes quickly. Here are just some of those reasons:

- Certain employees will place more importance on situations, and therefore be more likely to be upset by a situation than others. An example might be where a team member borrows an item of stationary from another team member's desk while that team member is away. While some team members may be happy for their items to be borrowed and returned, others would be upset to have had their possessions touched. The manager, if they are aware of each of their employee's drivers would be able to understand and explain if conflict did arise.
- Due to either home or work issues, there will be times when team members will be more sensitive to the behaviour of other team members and therefore may have a propensity to over-react, or react differently to usual. For instance if a team member makes a comment that could be seen as critical, or if a team member is excluded, whether intentionally or not, from an email or social engagement. The manager would be able to intervene to explain the situation to both parties.
- Some employees will have different ways of reacting to conflict than others. Some would confront the situation openly, making their displeasure known, whereas others may become withdrawn, quiet and brooding. Others may generally be laidback and relaxed, but if annoyed, may become excessively angry. The managers, if understanding the way that their team members react, would be able to spot the early warning signs in each of them and react accordingly.

Of course there are lots of different reasons why a manager knowing their team members will help them to intervene quickly. Most importantly it will allow the manager to spot small changes in the behaviour or appearance of that employee which may alert them to potential issues. All the behaviours discussed and explored in Chapter 7 around 'Managing the individual within the team' will be useful to help the manager to get to know their team members better.

You may find when you are speaking to a manager that they feel worried or reticent to intervene quickly in case they come across as either interfering, or as 'making a mountain out of a molehill'. We are not suggesting a formal intervention. How the manager approaches the team members will depend upon the relationship between the manager and the employee, and the personality of the team member; but generally it would involve a quiet word rather than anything more organized or formal. In our experience it is so much easier to resolve a conflict or issue when there are early signs or hunches and where the habits have not been formed and the source of tension not cemented, than where the manager tries to resolve a situation that has been festering and growing for longer. In the latter situation, not only will the employees themselves be more aggrieved with each other, but are also likely to have formed impressions about whether the manager's behaviour to date has been fair and equitable (for instance that they haven't stepped in, or have been seen to give tacit approval to the conflict). Due to these added issues, resolving long-term conflicts is generally much more problematic than resolving issues that are emerging and smaller.

Dealing with conflicts head on

The last section introduced the issue of managers sometimes preferring to avoid conflict and confrontation. Although we recognize it can not only be daunting, but counter to the personalities of the managers, to confront and intervene in conflicts; we have seen so many times in our practice and our research where if managers do not intervene, problems escalate and spread from those initially involved, to the whole team. Avoiding the issue makes it more likely that the end result will be a disciplinary process or grievance procedure. Even if it doesn't go to this extent it will make it much harder for the managers to resolve. The following example from a manager demonstrates how the conflict issue may spread if left unresolved:

> "There have been a few flare ups in the staffroom which I tend to, I know this is a fault, I tend to avoid confrontation. While I am aware that sometimes confrontation is no bad thing and it can be a positive thing, I tend to avoid it. There was a situation where a colleague was being very critical of other colleagues and was trying to get people to take sides on this. I knew this behaviour wasn't right but unfortunately by the time I became aware of it, and came to look at it, the sides had already been taken. It would have meant dealing with whole groups rather than just one individual – and so I avoided it again."

The next example is described by an employee. In this situation, due to the manager's non-intervention, the employee themselves have to step in and try and resolve the conflict.

> "My first instinct was to keep well out of the argument between the two other people in my team, but I had to get involved and I then acted as an intermediary between them while trying to get on with my own work. I wouldn't say I tried to avoid the conflict, but there was no reason for me to be involved with it . . . I just wanted to get on with my work. It was obvious though that this was going to affect my work as well, so I tried to act as the go-between to see if I could make them compromise and sort it out. My manager should have done something. The level of anxiety and conflict going on was really visible. He should have stepped in earlier. When I pointed it out, he just said 'Right, what can we do about it?' – and again left it to me."

Your role may be about providing the manager with the support and confidence to address and respond to conflict within their team. This may be within a coaching environment, or you may recommend some formal training for the manager in conflict management and negotiation skills. It is also important to remember that although it may seem daunting for a manager to deal with team conflict, it is part of their job role and responsibilities and therefore does need to be addressed and taken seriously. The following sections around addressing conflicts may also provide some insights for your work with managers.

How to address the conflicting team members

The manager's role within a conflict will be to help to resolve the problem and to get both 'sides' to reach an amicable solution. This needs to be done with objectivity, fairness and without the manager taking sides. Effectively the manager will be acting as a mediator, an impartial within the conflict. As a mediator the manager will aim to get to the heart of the issue, before helping the individuals concerned understand what needs to be done to resolve the issue and move forward. This process of resolving the conflict could be approached in a sequential way.

The following suggests a six-step process for the conflict resolution:

1. *Identify the problem*: Identify what the heart of the conflict is and what the issues arising from it are.
2. *Consider all perspectives*: This stage is about the manager being clear what everyone's perspective may be and who is, or could be, involved or affected by the conflict. By taking this step, a manager will be more likely to be able to generate a fair solution that includes all parties.
3. *Generate possible solutions*: Ideally potential solutions would be generated in a participative way, with a manager either having one-to-ones with each team member directly or indirectly involved in the conflict; or if possible, within a team meeting session. The latter may not be possible depending on the emotional content and severity of the conflict. At this stage the manager should also involve and consult with organizational resources in order to effectively utilize existing policies and practices. This will be explored further in the 'Use of organizational resources' cluster.
4. *Evaluate proposed solutions*: Again ideally the evaluation of solutions would be conducted in a participative way whereby team members examine and evaluate each of the solutions generated. It would be useful for the manager to lead the evaluation and encourage team members to evaluate based on objective criteria such as how realistic the solution is, the risks and the benefits offered by the solution. By setting objective criteria, the manager will reduce the amount of emotion-based decision making.
5. *Create an action plan*: Once a solution has been decided upon, an action plan will need to be developed to set out who will be involved in

each stage of the solution, the time-frames and the criteria for judging success. This action plan would need to be agreed and bought in to by all parties involved.

6. *Develop a contingency plan*: We would recommend a manager also develops contingency plans that will set out alternative solutions if things go wrong or if unforeseen situations arise. In the case of conflict resolution, often solutions are not as simple as they seem and resolving one issue can actually create another. Therefore, it is important that managers are prepared to be flexible in their plans and direction, and have thought reasonably and rationally about alternatives beforehand, in order to avoid reactive management decisions at a later stage.

Despite going through these steps, often managers find the hardest thing to do is to be objective and not themselves take sides. The following example from a local government manager highlights this, talking about a conflict between team members:

"As a manager you have to intervene to sort it out but it is very difficult to not at least mentally think who is to blame. You tend to get into a mindset. I know on a number of occasions when I have resolved something, what I should have actually done is given more time to one of the aggrieved parties. Even though they weren't getting what they wanted or even if they had been proved wrong. It is about me failing to deal with the feeling content of people and treating something as a rational and concrete problem. Rather than thinking 'OK, I have resolved that bit of it, but I need to go back to that person in a few days and give them half an hour to say how they are feeling', I just don't do it. There are a million reasons for this. Sometimes it is awkward, sometimes I don't like them and it is hard to give personal attention on someone I am not keen on. It doesn't help though – it just means that they feel more aggrieved and build up more stress."

This very honest account demonstrates the difficulty in remaining objective when a manager's views, likes and dislikes are involved. What you may notice about this account is the use of the word 'I'. The manager states 'When I resolved. . .', 'What I should have done . . .' and 'I have resolved that bit . . .' Our experience is that when managers seek to resolve conflicts participatively, in that they involve the aggrieved parties in developing their own solutions and compromises, rather than telling them what to do, or creating solutions for them, there is less chance that the situation will be affected by the managers' viewpoint and subsequently more chance of an amicable solution. We would, therefore, strongly recommend managers take the approach whereby they seek to gather together both sides to communicate and act as an objective broker or mediator who will find common ground, aiding the team members in coming to a solution, rather than giving them solutions and in doing so taking sides. The following example from an employee demonstrates this:

> "If a difference of opinion arises between me and another member of staff, my manager (who has responsibility for both of us), would sit down and listen to both sides, or all sides of the issue. Without making a judgement she would listen to what we had to say and acknowledge that we had different concerns, but not necessarily come down on one side or the other, or saying 'you are right' and 'you are wrong'. It sent a really clear message to us that we were important and that she was interested in what we had to say. It gave us the opportunity to put across our point of view and maybe consider things from a different perspective."

Essentially, managing conflict is about managers behaving with integrity. This involves managers maintaining their professionalism and acting as a role model for their teams by being consistent in their approach and avoiding favouritism. This is particularly important in a conflict situation where managers need to treat both sides of the conflict equally, regardless of whether one side is 'the victim' and the other 'the protagonist'. It also means setting a team culture where backbiting, gossiping and office politics are not encouraged or tolerated; meaning that respectful behaviour towards all team members is demonstrated. In a culture where disrespectful behaviour or backbiting is seen as acceptable, it will not only be harder for managers to 'nip issues in the bud' and tackle conflicts before they escalate, but it is also likely to mean that the managers will be seen as less trustworthy and therefore less likely to be able to resolve conflicts fairly and quickly within their teams. Managers also need to act with honesty and integrity by keeping employees' issues private and confidential. The following example from an employee demonstrates the manager acting with a lack of integrity in a conflict situation:

> "When I was working as a trainee I experienced a bit of bullying within the team. The manager dealing with us didn't handle it very effectively and actually tended to create more problems as a result, making it quite public where the complaints came from. When I went to the manager, their automatic reaction, rather than try and bond the team, was to pull in individual members of the team and try and explain what comments had been made about them and by whom. It made things so much worse for me."

The behaviours around 'Acting with integrity', explored in detail in Chapter 5, are therefore very pertinent here. It may be worth going back to that chapter and thinking about the behaviours in the context of managing conflict.

To prompt your memory, Table 8.1 lists the behaviours explored in the 'Integrity' cluster:

Table 8.1.   Behaviours explored within 'Integrity'

Positive examples of behaviour	Negative examples of behaviour
Being a good role model	Speaking about employees behind their backs
Keeping employee issues private and confidential	Making promises, then not delivering on them
Admitting their mistakes	Saying one thing, and doing something different
Treating all team members with equal importance	Making personal issues public
Treating all team members with respect	
Being honest	

Use of Organizational Resources

"He who can take advice is sometimes superior to him who can give it."
(Karl von Knebel)

This cluster is about managers who are prepared to ask for advice and seek information from others. There are so many phrases in our language about how difficult it is to accept advice from others, and it is certainly not a modern issue, as highlighted by the following quotation from Publilius Syrus in 100 BC of 'Many receive advice, few profit from it.' As discussed in the beginning of this chapter, when dealing with conflict or disputes at work, there is not only the issue that this conflict may impact upon other team members, negatively affecting productivity and well-being across the group; but also that there are legal ramifications such as the discrimination legislation, and policies such as grievance procedures to consider. This means that taking correct action in these situations is even more important.

It is the manager's role to seek to resolve the conflict – but that does not mean that the conflict resolution itself must be done by the manager. Certainly, in the last section we explored how managers acting as an objective mediator, encouraging and allowing the aggrieved parties to resolve their own conflict, could actually be more effective than where managers tried to develop their own solutions to the issue. There will be conflict situations that managers have not had experience dealing with and it is important that the managers not only realize what organizational resources are available to help them in resolving the particular issue, but also that they use and seek advice from these resources.

Use of organizational resources in the literature

When reviewing the management literature it becomes clear that the majority of leadership models focus upon managers being able to give advice and being able to persuade and influence others – rather than being able to take and accept advice from others. In fact, the only leadership model that included any reference to accepting, or taking, advice was that of the TLQ, the UK Transformational Leadership Scale developed by Alimo-Metcalfe. The TLQ has a factor called 'Integrity and openness to ideas and advice' which describes consulting and involving others in decision making. This is however, non-source specific and, therefore, is likely to refer to taking advice from team members and involving them in decisions (as explored in Chapter 6 in the Participative/ Empowering cluster), rather than seeking advice from peers, and organizational resources such as Human Resources, Occupational Health, and Health and Safety. The section below describes the particular sources of advice we found to be important within our research.

The findings from our research

The following demonstrates the behaviours highlighted in our research to be key for managers to make use of organizational resources:

✓ Seeks advice from other managers when necessary
✓ Uses HR as a resource to help deal with problems
✓ Seeks help from occupational health when necessary

Seeking advice from other managers

We have focused within this book on developing the skills for managers to be able to prevent and reduce stress in their team members. In the next four chapters the focus will change to understanding the barriers to managers both receiving and using those skills in the workplace, and the support that managers could and should access in order to demonstrate more positive behaviour.

Whether managers are working within a large or a small organization, there will almost always be other managers within the business that could be utilized as a peer support group. This financial manager demonstrates how he uses this peer group for managing conflict at work:

> "I use a network of colleagues. I talk to people in similar roles to see if they have come across similar issues. If they have, I find out what they did, what was good and what was bad and what they learnt from it, so that I can approach the conflict in my team with more knowledge and more confidence."

Managers involved in our research often said their first point of call was to ask other managers about how to deal with conflict. The reasons for this varied, but most commonly it was because it avoided making a conflict issue too official or formal, and that peers were likely to be more familiar with the working context and therefore give more relevant advice. The following example from a central government manager highlights this feeling:

> "We have a very good HR department here and they would be very proactive in giving advice if I phoned them with a workplace issue and that they would be willing to support me in trying to sort it out. I would probably first ask other managers as they would be more familiar with the way we work on a day to day basis and the pressures that we are under. My direct line manager is also really supportive. I use him as a sounding board about what I should be doing. I say 'This is what I am thinking of doing, what do you think?'"

This example also introduces the idea of not just using peers, but also line managers (the manager's manager) to get advice and information. In this example, the line manager was used as a sounding board, essentially double checking that the manager was taking the right action and going about the conflict in the correct way. It may also be useful for managers, if not to get the advice of line managers, to communicate the situation to senior managers. By doing this, managers will set up a 'paper trail' with the senior managers, creating a formal record of the conflict. Although the conflict would hopefully be resolved without need for formal procedures, by alerting senior managers at the beginning of the conflict, means that if the process does become a formal disciplinary or grievance procedure, line managers will have demonstrated their consistent and professional approach to the situation.

Where might you play a role in encouraging managers to use their colleagues for advice and guidance?

Here are a number of suggestions of interventions or strategies you could set up within organizations to help managers use their peer network:

- *Encourage regular 'manager' meetings*: These would be informal events whereby managers within an organization would meet to network and build relationships. These could be interdisciplinary but would ideally be for managers within the same hierarchical level, to allow for free discussion. Ideas to increase opportunities for building networks would be to have meetings themed around particular issues or problems, where managers present case studies of their experiences of working on and solving problems. If interdisciplinary or where teams are dispersed across the organization, it might also be useful to encourage one or two managers per session to present the work they have been doing in their teams or areas.

- *Set up Communities of Practice (CoP):* This term was coined by Lave and Wenger in the 1990s and refers to a group of people who share an interest or profession, and has been proven to be extremely useful for the goal of gaining knowledge related to work. Communities share information and experiences with the group and learn from each other. These communities can meet in real life, for instance in regular meetings, or increasingly commonly, online. Social networking sites such as LinkedIn, or protected sites such as Ning can be used highly effectively for groups to share information, to ask questions, and to receive advice from the community of practice within a supportive environment.

- *Develop mentoring or buddying programmes*: Many managers would find benefit from supportive mentors within their organizations who did not have specific line management responsibility over them. Identifying and matching suitable mentoring or buddying relationships could be a useful intervention to aid problem solving and supportive manager relationships.

- *Develop action learning sets*: These have proven to be highly effective in a number of organizational settings for problem solving. They provide managers with the opportunity to learn from others, reflect on their current practices, deal with problems not easily resolved by other means, build relationships and create innovative problem-solving strategies. For more information on action learning sets, see the text box 'Spotlight on action learning sets'.

Spotlight on Action Learning Sets

What are they?

'A deceptively simple, yet amazingly intricate problem solving strategy that has the capacity to create powerful individual and organisational changes.' (Marquardt, 2000)

What are they for?

Essentially action learning sets are based on the relationship between reflection and action. The focus is upon the issues that individuals bring, and planning future action with the structured attention and support of the group.

Where did they come from?

They originated in higher education and were developed by Reginald Revans in the 1920s. Revans used them in working with eight Nobel

Prize winners who would meet weekly to 'see if we can understand our own difficulties'.

The action learning equation

Learning = Traditional Knowledge + Questioning to gain insight

Revans felt that through constant questioning, individuals are able to see more clearly what the issue is, and in that, become more capable of accepting and responding to change.

How many people and how often?

Groups of 6 to 8 people meet regularly to discuss issues of mutual or personal importance. Generally sets would meet every 6 to 9 weeks.

What is the process in each set meeting?

1. *Ground rules are set*: agreements are made concerning confidentiality, encouragement and support, along with logistical agreements.
2. *One individual in the group shares a problem*: This problem needs to be open ended – not a puzzle or a technical problem but one where there is no 'right answer'. It should be a challenging question, involving action and generally having an impact on performance or well-being at work.
3. *The group ask questions*: The central tenet is the group members ask questions NOT give advice. The aim is to use the questions to move an individual to understanding their own problem. It should be encouraging, supporting and challenging.
4. *First individual summarizes what they have learnt and commits to action.*
5. *Second individual presents a problem*: The group move through steps 2 to 4.

The second meeting will involve the step 1 being reported and reflected upon with each individual in turn talking about what action they took, what they learned and what they will do next.

(For more information: International Foundation of Action Learning: www.ifal.org.uk)

Seeking advice from other organizational resources

Most medium to large organizations and some small organizations will have a Human Resources Department, Occupational Health and a Health and Safety area. These can be hugely valuable resources for line managers to use in helping to resolve conflict or difficult situations.

Although we have explored in the first cluster, 'Managing conflict', how, ideally conflict should be tackled and resolved at an early stage, there will be times when conflict is more serious (such as harassment, bullying, verbal abuse or physical intimidation) and where formal disciplinary actions should be taken. In these situations, it would be important for managers to demonstrate to their teams that these incidents will be taken seriously and be properly investigated and dealt with using the formal disciplinary and grievance procedures. Although managers may think that they are up to date with these procedures, it is always advisable to check with HR. Incorrect or out-of-date guidance could have serious ramifications in a formal process. Further, a line manager's credibility and perceived effectiveness is likely to suffer if they are seen to pass on incorrect advice and guidance to their teams and to the aggrieved parties. It is important to remember that the policies and guidance are in place to protect all employees within the organization, and therefore line managers showing that they follow and use the procedures and policies available will be highly reassuring to staff.

There are also times when conflict may have arisen due to, or may result in outcomes of, physical or mental health issues for team members. Although a manager is expected to be able to address and manage conflict as part of their role, they are not expected to diagnose, treat and, therefore, manage physical or mental health issues. An example might be that an employee had developed an anxiety disorder as a result of an ongoing conflict; or an employee, due to an existing disorder such as obsessive compulsive disorder, may have been making working life very difficult for the team and, therefore, been a cause of dispute and conflict.

For conflicts resulting from or resulting in mental or physical health issues, managers should always be advised to consult with their occupational health or health and safety advisors. Again, second-guessing in these situations would be highly inadvisable for managers and potentially dangerous for the health and well-being of both the affected employees and the wider teams. If managers are working within a small organization where there are no occupational health or health and safety resources, they could make use of an employee assistance programme (EAP), or consult the many websites and organizations that provide detailed, relevant and practical advice. Such websites and organizations in the

UK include SHiFT (www.shift.org.uk), Mind (www.mind.org.uk), the BBC (www.bbc.co.uk/headroom/) or the NHS (www.nhs.uk).

The behaviours that we have been exploring in this book aim to help managers to prevent and reduce stress. Managers can also make use of organizational resources such as Health and Safety to explore the risk factors within their teams and prevent not only stress, but also potential areas of conflict and dispute which may arise in them. Generally the more managers can keep an open dialogue with both their teams, and with the wider organizational resources, the better.

Therefore use of organizational resources such as HR, Occupational Health, Health and Safety or even union representatives does not have to just be about making the conflict process formal, but can be used, as suggested for peers, as a sounding board for managers, to provide alternative perspectives and to back up and double check correct courses of action. The following manager example demonstrates this approach in action:

'I like to get reassurance that I give the right information and deal with situations in the right way. I get some HR advice and I find that the union representatives are really supportive on some issues with staff.

Knowing who to go to

Worryingly often in organizations we come across the situation where although all the correct policies, practices and programmes are in place to help all employees (such as counselling, employee assistance programmes, occupational health checks and education around health and well-being) neither managers nor employees are aware of them. Therefore the programmes do not get used in the right way, or as much as they should, and managers and employees are left not knowing who to go to if a problem arises. Further, with widespread organizational change and departmental restructuring, employees can get confused as to where to access resources within new and changing structures. The following example from a manager demonstrates this:

"As a manager I feel on my own sometimes. You have HR and Personnel, and they are changing their role and remit and so are much more hands off – they are more about policy and written guidance, and less about hand holding and saying 'This is what you do.' I feel a bit like 'So where are the experts now? Who do I go to?' I don't think it is appropriate to look on the intranet and see what the guidance is. I work within OD and communications but it has a much different feel from the old Personnel Officers who took you as a manager and held your hand and talked you through it. This can be a real source of stress. You have to spend time working out who to go to and who can help."

You could play a useful part, either as an external or internal practitioner, finding out within the organization where you are working whether there is an issue of lack of knowledge around organizational resources, programmes, policies and practices. If you find this is the case, you could help the organization to develop awareness building initiatives, programmes and communications to make sure that all employees and managers understand who can help in resolving issues, or conflicts, within the workplace. It would also be useful to encourage managers to communicate the information and organizational resources available to their teams' members.

Taking Responsibility for Resolving Issues

"When a man points a finger at someone else, he should remember that four fingers are pointing at himself." (Louis Nizer)

This section is all about managers stepping up to the job and taking responsibility for resolving the conflict, both at the point of the conflict or resultant formal procedure by supporting all parties involved, and after the conflict appears to be resolved, or where the formal process has been completed. Many of the behaviours explored in the 'Problem solving' cluster in Chapter 6 would be relevant here. The text box 'Problem-solving behaviours' provides a reminder of these behaviours covered in Chapter 6. It may be useful for you to encourage managers to reflect upon these and the discussions within Chapter 5 when applied to the situation of managing conflict. The remainder of this cluster however will focus on taking responsibility applied to the specific example of managing difficult situations and conflicts.

Problem solving behaviours

Positive examples of manager behaviour included:

✓ Dealing rationally with problems
✓ Following up problems on the team's behalf
✓ Dealing with problems as soon as they arise
✓ Breaking problems down into parts.

Negative examples of manager behaviour included:

× Indecisive at decision making
× Listening but not resolving problems
× Not taking problems seriously
× Assuming problems will sort themselves out

The findings from our research

The following demonstrates the behaviours highlighted in our research which are key for managers when taking responsibility for resolving conflict issues:

✓ Follows up conflicts after resolution
✓ Supports employees through incidents of abuse
✓ Makes it clear they will take ultimate responsibility if things go wrong

The behaviours we found to be important for managers to avoid (in other words, the negative behaviours) were:

× Doesn't address bullying
× Saying that the conflict is 'not their problem'

Addressing conflict, bullying and harassment

In the first cluster in this chapter, 'Managing conflict' we stressed the need for managers to act quickly and step in to resolve conflict situations before they went on for too long or became more serious. We explored reasons why managers may have been reticent and how avoiding confrontation can actually cause situations to escalate, and create difficulties for resolution. What we didn't approach however was the need for managers to step in when the situation demands immediate attention, or is immediately serious, for instance in situations such as bullying or harassment.

We also discussed earlier in the chapter about how important participative management was in solution-focused conflict resolution. As found however in the 'Problem solving' cluster earlier, although generally getting participation from the aggrieved parties, and encouraging them to develop their own solutions to their issues is often very helpful; sometimes a manager needs to be decisive, strong and take action around the conflict.

There are a number of reasons why the manager may be called to do this. Below are some examples:

- The manager may witness an event occurring and need to take immediate action to remove an employee from that situation to avoid a conflict taking place. The following example from an employee demonstrates this:

I was sitting opposite my manager and I had a patient on the phone shouting at me so loudly that my manager could hear what he was saying. He told me to put the phone down on the patient, which I did. My manager then called him back and had a discussion with him. Afterwards, he told me the patient was completely out of line and that if I ever found myself in that situation again, that he would be more than happy to deal with it for me.

In this situation the manager has seen the employee is in a difficult situation and acts quickly to avoid either a conflict, or unnecessary upset to their employee.

- The manager may decide to take an employee out of the situation or away from the person that the conflict is with, if the situation has become heated and tempers are being lost. When people lose their temper, the ability to think and react rationally is compromised. This means that it is more likely that the conflict will escalate. In this situation therefore, rather than bring the sides together to talk through solutions, the manager would be encouraged to take responsibility by separating both parties and giving them time and space to calm down and regain perspective on the situation.
- If an employee continues to cause conflict in the team, or if there has been an incident of bullying or harassment, the manager may take responsibility for protecting the rest of the team from the source of the conflict and therefore remove that individual from the team, either to a new team or job role, or perhaps through disciplinary action. The following example demonstrates the detrimental impact that one person can have on their team. It describes a situation where a new manager came into a team that had very high levels of conflict, and low levels of morale.

Most of the issues centred around one person, and the effect that person had on the team. There were lots of arguments, lots of bitching, lots of issues that weren't being addressed and that hadn't been addressed for a long time. The new manager was more or less put into the lion's den to see how she would cope. It was pretty unfair on her but she came through it and turned our team from one of the most unproductive, to the best in the department. She started with a clean slate, didn't listen to the 'tittle tattle' that had gone on. She had a one-to-one with everyone, allowed everyone the opportunity to air their views, get the rant out. Then she watched us, watched how we interacted, and on a couple of occasions got people to move seats. It was trial and error, watching how people worked and interacted with each other. She became really involved with the people in the team, and she made a real difference.

In these situations, the manager demonstrates that they will take ultimate responsibility for conflicts in their team, and, if necessary, will step in and take decisive action. This serves to reassure employees and increase the credibility of and respect for the manager.

Case study

The following case study describes a local government employee who gets involved in a verbally abusive conflict with one of their team mates. The employee describes the conflict:

"I had a conflict with one of my team mates. He lost his temper at me and was shouting at the top of his voice and putting me down. Then he started picking up on personal things like 'Oh you come to this office and don't smile, you are always miserable.' Because at the time I had some personal problems, I wasn't the happy jolly person I normally was. He even picked up on me and said 'Who wants to look at your miserable face?' He was so rude. It took a lot for me to not lose my temper and try to be professional and not shout.

The employee then goes to speak to her line manager about the incident, still upset about what had happened. 'I was in tears and said how humiliated I felt to have had him shout at me in front of about twenty people'.

The line manager accepted that the situation was serious, and said that the incident would be investigated. The next day, both the employee and the other employee involved in the conflict were interviewed by a senior manager. Later, she was called in and told that as the other employee involved had given a different story, no further action could be taken. The employee continues, 'I said that I had witnesses, and that they could speak to others. My manager said she didn't want to though. When I asked why, she just said 'Time is passing and we are very busy.'

The impact of this lack of reaction on the employee is significant. She continues, 'I was still upset and felt something should be done. Nothing was though. I lost so much respect for my manager. She tried to wash her hands of responsibility. I needed her help and she didn't give it to me.'"

What action did the manager take that was correct in this case study, and what would you say she could have done differently? How could the behaviours explored in this chapter have helped?

After the 'resolution'

It would be lovely to think that once the conflict has been resolved, either through employees developing their own solution, through management action, or through disciplinary processes, the problem has gone away. Unfortunately it is rarely the case. Human nature is such that after a conflict, even if it has been resolved, we will still cogitate over it. It might be that we continue to bear a grudge against the other person involved in the conflict, or we might feel that we behaved in ways that we were ashamed of, or that let ourselves down. For whatever reason, even though in a practical sense the conflict may be over; the emotional content and impact of the conflict is often alive and well for many more weeks or even months.

It may also be that the conflict has resulted in a change in team structure, for instance if a team member has been removed from the team, or if roles have changed to avoid two members of the team working together. This will result in a change in team dynamic that will take both the manager's engagement, and time to embed and settle.

It is not just those directly involved in the conflict that would be affected by it long after it has been resolved. The bullying literature tells us that those employees who witness bullying at work actually experience similar psychological strain to those who experience the bullying. Therefore the conflict may still 'live on' in the wider team.

It is vitally important therefore that the manager sees conflict resolution as a process with an unclear end point that is far in advance of the 'practical' resolution. The manager would be advised to keep checking with the whole team in regular one-to-ones, or during discussions around performance or development appraisals to see if the conflict really has been resolved, if it is being managed, or if new conflicts and tensions have emerged as a result of the original conflict. The manager being vigilant and aware of team members' behaviours and responses is especially important during the weeks and months after a conflict in the team. The behaviours explored in Chapter 7 under 'Empathetic engagement' would be useful here to help managers to monitor and keep a 'temperature check' on the tensions and issues within their team.

Summary

This chapter has explored the competency 'Reasoning/Managing difficult situations'. As described in the previous chapters, the research in Phase 2 refined the behaviours included in the whole stress management competency framework into a measure to enable both managers to self-assess their own effectiveness and for use in upward and 360 degree feedback programmes. Table 8.2 shows the behaviours within the measure relevant to this particular competency. You may want to use this table as a prompt for discussions in your work about displaying these types of behaviours.

Table 8.2. Behavioural indicators for 'Reasoning/Managing difficult situations'

Cluster	Do (✓)/ Don't (✗)	Examples of manager behaviour
Managing conflict	✓	■ Acts as mediator in conflict situations ■ Deals with squabbles before they become arguments ■ Deals objectively with conflicts ■ Deals with conflicts head on
	✗	■ Acts to keep the peace rather than resolve issues
Use of organizational resources	✓	■ Seeks advice from other managers when necessary ■ Uses HR as a resource to help deal with problems ■ Seeks help from occupational health when necessary
Taking responsibility for resolving issues	✓	■ Follows up conflicts after resolution ■ Supports employees through incidents of abuse ■ Makes it clear they will take ultimate responsibility if things go wrong
	✗	■ Doesn't address bullying

Source: Adapted from Donaldson-Feilder, Lewis and Yarker 2009 © Crown Copyright 2009

References

Beswick, J., Gore, J. and Palferman, D. (2006). *Bullying at Work: A Review of the Literature.* Health and Safety Laboratory. (www.hse.gov.uk/research/hsl_pdf/2006/hsl0630.pdf, accessed 23 September 2010).

Bolger, N., DeLongis, A., Kessler, R.C. and Schilling, E.A. (1989). Effects of daily stress on negative mood. *Journal of Personality and Social Psychology*, 57, 808–818.

Chartered Institute of Personnel and Development (2004). *Managing conflict at work: A survey of the UK and Ireland. Survey Report October 2004.* CIPD Publications, London.

Chartered Institute of Personnel and Development (2007a). *Managing Conflict at Work: A Guide for Line Managers*. CIPD Publications, London.

Chartered Institute of Personnel and Development (2007b). *Managing Conflict at Work: Survey Report February 2007*. CIPD Publications, London.

Donaldson-Feilder, E., Lewis, R. and Yarker, J., (2009). *Preventing Stress: Promoting Positive Manager Behaviour*. CIPD Insight Report. CIPD Publications: London, available on the CIPD website: www.cipd.co.uk/subjects/health/stress/_preventing_ stress

Keenan, A. and Newton, T.J. (1985). Stressful events, stressors, and psychological strains in young professional engineers. *Journal of Occupational Behavior*, 6, 151–156.

Lave, J. and Wenger, E. (1991). *Situated Learning: Legitimate Peripheral Participation*. Cambridge University Press, New York.

Marquardt, M.J. (2000) Action learning and leadership. *The Learning Organization*, 7 (8), 233–240.

Rayner, C. and McIvor, K. (2006). *Report to the Dignity of Work Project Steering Committee*. Dignity at Work Report, Portsmouth University.

Smith, C.S. and Sulsky, L.M. (1995). *An investigation of job related coping strategies across multiple stressors and samples*. In L.R. Murphy (ed.), *Job Stress Interventions*. American Psychological Association, Washington, DC.

9

Overcoming barriers to positive manager behaviour

While most managers *intend* to behave in ways that are positive and conducive to staff well-being, it is not always easy actually to do so. One of the findings of our research was that there are a range of barriers to, or things that get in the way of, showing positive behaviour; these may even lead to managers showing negative behaviour. Our research suggests that these barriers operate at different levels:

1. personal level;
2. individual work or job level;
3. team and relationship level; and
4. organizational and wider level.

Managers need to be aware of the barriers that are significant for their own situation and how they can be overcome. If you are working with managers through training or coaching to help them show Positive Manager Behaviour, you will need to acknowledge and explore these barriers in order to ensure that they are overcome appropriately. It is likely that each manager will have a different set of barriers with which they have to contend. However, if you work with a group of managers in a

Preventing Stress in Organizations: How to Develop Positive Managers,
Emma Donaldson-Feilder, Joanna Yarker and Rachel Lewis.
© 2011 John Wiley & Sons, Ltd. Published 2011 by John Wiley & Sons, Ltd.

particular organization, there may be common barriers, particularly at the organizational and wider level; and, where common barriers exist, managers may be able to support one another in finding solutions.

When you help managers to identify their barriers to displaying positive behaviours (or issues causing them to display negative behaviours), you may find that managers feel that these barriers are insuperable ('There is nothing I can do about it'). To help managers get through this and start to see options, it may be useful to think of three different approaches to resolving the situation: can the manager...

- change the situation?
- change their reaction to the situation?
- manage the impact of their reaction to the situation?

Even in situations where the situation itself cannot be changed, such as when governmental legislation or the economic climate increases work pressure, there is always a way to change and minimise the impact of the negative situation.

In this chapter we look in more detail at each of the four types of barrier and explore examples and exercises to help managers overcome them.

Personal Level Barriers

In this first category, our research suggests that managers experience personal level barriers relating to: issues in their personal or home life; feeling stressed or under pressure themselves; and a lack of confidence in their own ability.

We all have times when our non-work life, stress levels or 'internal world' present us with challenges: our relationship is breaking down, we are organizing a wedding or big event, a friend or relative is ill, we are moving house, our own health is problematic ... the list is endless. Of course, managers are no exception to this and it can be hard to avoid these kinds of issues impinging on the way managers manage people. It may be purely that they have less time available for people management as they have to get away to attend hospital appointments or take time off to move house. Or it may be that they are distracted by non-work issues and less able to give their attention to managing people even though they are present in the workplace for the same amount of time. Or it may be that health or stress-related symptoms, such as reduced cognitive functioning or poorer memory, directly affect their capability to manage people.

Many managers will have times when they lack confidence in their own ability, whether this is caused by personal issues or other factors. This is particularly likely to be true when a manager is new in post or has been through a period of change. There can be a negative spiral effect, where lack of confidence leads to stress and being stressed has a negative impact on self-confidence.

The first step: Helping managers acknowledge personal issues

Every situation will be different, but there are some common themes for helping managers overcome personal barriers of this kind. The most important first step is to help them recognize when there is an issue – when something in their personal life or 'internal world' is impinging on their work and particularly on their people management. It is easy to be so caught up in what is happening that we don't notice the impact it is having, so helping managers gain greater self-awareness is fundamental. Finding ways to encourage them to be more mindful and in touch with their current state can be valuable in all sorts of ways.

One important facet of increasing self-awareness is to help managers gain greater understanding of what their own personal signs of stress or discomfort or low self-confidence are. A potential first step towards this could be getting them to think about how they are feeling right now and analysing how they know this. For example:

- Ask them to rate on a scale of 1 to 10, where 1 is 'I feel calm/confident' and 10 is 'I feel stressed/unsure of myself', what level of discomfort or lack of confidence they are currently feeling. (In a training workshop, you can get them to mark a cross on a line drawn on a piece of paper or, if there is sufficient trust in the group, actually get them to stand on an imaginary line across the room, where 1 is at one end of the room and 10 at the other.)
- Ask them how they knew that they were at that rating – what were the thoughts, emotions and physical sensations that allowed them to make that judgement?
- Ask them to think of times when they have been higher up and lower down the scale and what thoughts, emotions and physical sensations they had at those times.
- Pulling the information together, they can note down the signs or indicators that they have for low, medium and high levels of stress, discomfort or lack of confidence. This then is their 'personal indicator scale' and they can use it to monitor themselves on an ongoing basis.

The next step: Finding solutions

The aim is that individuals can use their personal indicator scale to catch their early warning signs and quickly identify times when personal issues risk impinging on their people management behaviour. The next step is for the manager to explore what they can do to prevent these situations from getting in the way of Positive Manager Behaviour or even causing negative behaviour. This is when the three-step solution-finding process mentioned earlier may help: what can they do to a) change the situation, b) change their reaction to the situation and/or c) manage the impact of their reaction to the situation?

As a practitioner, you can support managers to explore solutions through workshop exercises or coaching. It can be particularly helpful to get individuals to commit to specific action plans, so that they are clear what changes they will make. The ideal is also to provide some kind of follow-up through coaching, action learning or a review workshop to give them an incentive to carry out the actions planned and to discuss how they are progressing. The following case example illustrates how this might work.

Case study: Helping a manager overcome personal level barriers through coaching

Tim (name and details changed for confidentiality) was the manager of a delivery unit within a large local authority, responsible for a team of 30 people. He had been with the organization for 10 years and had recently been promoted into his current role. His previous jobs in the organization had been initially in different service-user-facing roles, and then in managing a small team within the unit, so promotion to manage the whole unit was a considerable step up in terms of responsibility. Tim had received some management training in his previous role, mostly focussed on implementing specific processes, such as appraisal and absence management. Around the same time as his promotion, Tim's wife gave birth to their first child. While Tim was enjoying fatherhood, he found that the lack of sleep caused by the baby waking up frequently through the night was leading to a build up of fatigue that made him feel sluggish and 'fuzzy-headed' at work.

Tim volunteered to participate in a programme on 'Positive Manager Behaviour' being rolled out by the local authority, as part of which he received upward feedback from his team on his management behaviour, a face-to-face feedback session and two follow-up coaching sessions. The upward feedback revealed some pleasant surprises for Tim in terms of how team members saw his management approach as they gave him more positive scores in a number of areas than he had given himself; it also showed that he was perceived as not managing his emotions as well as he might, which could lead to him passing stress on to his team and being unpredictable in mood. The discussion in the feedback session revealed that Tim was really struggling with the new role: he felt very unsure of his ability to manage 30 people, was worried that he was going to 'fail' as a manager and felt overwhelmingly tired, which was leading to anxieties about his functioning at work and home. The one-to-one time with an occupational psychologist in the feedback session and the coaching sessions provided a chance for Tim to talk through these concerns, develop an action plan and receive support as he put the plan into practice.

The discussions focused on practical solutions aiming to make changes where he could and better manage the things he couldn't change. Looked at from the perspective of the three options outlined earlier, the following emerged:

- *Change the situation*: Part of Tim's lack of confidence was due to his limited experience of and familiarity with the management role. Following the initial feedback session, Tim took time to discuss with the council's learning and development manager what management and leadership development was available to him: he asked to be included in a new pilot programme for managers that involved a series of workshops over the period of a year. As a result of talking about the degree to which being woken in the night was creating problems for him, Tim recognized that he and his wife needed to find ways for each of them to get some quality sleep during the week. In the coaching sessions, he explored a range of options he and his wife could consider for dealing with the baby at night, which enabled him to have a constructive discussion with his wife and come to an agreement about taking turns at being responsible for going to the baby and ways of minimizing the disruption to the person who was not responsible.

- *Change their reaction to the situation*: During the feedback session and subsequent coaching, one of the issues Tim explored was how his perfectionist nature led to him being critical of himself and 'giving himself a hard time'. While attending management development workshops would increase his understanding and familiarity with people management, thereby building his self-confidence, Tim was aware that he needed also to address his self-criticism and the anxiety associated with it – both for his own benefit and to stop him passing his anxieties on or being moody at work (and at home). Through the coaching sessions, the occupational psychologist coach introduced him to 'mindfulness' as a technique for: a) being more present in the moment (rather than worrying about the past or future); and b) acknowledging the anxious thoughts and feelings and thereby having more scope to make a choice about how to behave, not just being drawn automatically into anxious behaviour. Between sessions, Tim practised a range of mindfulness techniques, such as stopping regularly to bring his awareness into the present moment by focusing on his breath, and learning to observe his thoughts and feelings as if they were appearing on a screen. The increased mindfulness these techniques generated allowed him to be more effective at managing his emotions – both at work and home.

- *Manage the impact of their reaction to the situation*: Despite learning to manage his emotions better, Tim still found that some situations at work were inclined to lead to him feeling panicky; in addition, some days were harder than others due to lack of sleep. In the coaching, Tim explored a range of ways to prevent his reactions impacting on the people he managed. The solutions he generated included: being more open with his immediate direct reports (who each managed a small team within the unit) about areas in which he needed their support – particularly in generating reports on the team's activities for submission to the Senior Executive Team; learning to take a break and go out for a walk or breath of fresh air when he felt his anxiety levels rising; and spotting when a particularly sleepless night was making him moody, so that he could avoid doing too many people management activities on those days.The points discussed in this section are summarized in Table 9.1, which can be used to help prompt your memory.

Individual Work or Job Level Barriers

The second type of barrier are those operating at the level of the individual's work or job. It is almost always the case that managers have to juggle their people management responsibilities on top of a busy and demanding 'day job'. Indeed, one of the things managers told us during our research is that they would like more time in their schedule to focus on Positive Manager Behaviour and people management generally. Heavy workloads, conflicting and multiple priorities, short deadlines and lack of resources, whether they are the manager's responsibility or implicate the whole team, can all be barriers to managers showing Positive Manager Behaviour and/or lead to negative behaviour.

The first step: Awareness and monitoring for problems

Once again, a key first step is for the manager to be aware of these issues and the problems they present for their people management behaviour. Awareness and mindfulness exercises, to provide ongoing self-monitoring can help managers to identify when these kinds of job and work issues are impacting on their people management approach/ activities. Establishing routines for reviews and monitoring mechanisms can help them regularly to check whether they need to take action to prevent problems escalating.

Clarity about the situation then allows for analysis of how to overcome the barriers. Again looking at the three options can help; can the

Table 9.1. Solutions identified in our research – Personal level barriers

Barriers to displaying Positive Manager Behaviour	Suggestions for how this barrier might be overcome
Personal/home life issues	o Recognize and acknowledge your own behaviour o Talk to peers/manager/team/trusted colleague/mentor about it o Use Employee Assistance Programme/ organizational support such as coaching and mentoring o Take time out/off
Feeling stressed/under undue pressure yourself	o Speak to someone (peer, manager, coach) o Seek support for yourself o Take a break/holiday/deep breath o Recognize your emotions and know your stress triggers o Apologize to your team and, if possible, be honest about how you feel o Try to manage your own expectations of yourself o Be realistic about what you can and can't achieve at work o Focus on one thing at a time o Take time before reacting o Prioritize and plan o Keep fit and healthy
Lack of confidence in own ability	o Ask for training and development o Talk to/ask for help from peers/line manager o Manage the expectations of your team o Clarify what your role is to the team o Set clear boundaries with your team o Recognize your strengths and limitations o Aim to be honest in all communications – say when you don't know!

Source: Adapted from Donaldson-Feilder, Lewis and Yarker (2009)

manager: change the situation; change their reaction to the situation; and/or manage the impact of their reaction to the situation. The following sections focus particularly on how you might help managers change the situation, but also other solutions.

The next step: Helping managers be assertive to change the situation

The modern work environment and current economic situation mean that a high proportion of workplaces are 'lean', pared to the minimum in terms of staffing and resources. In a recession, when many organizations have gone through programmes of redundancies and job-freezes, many feel 'stuck' doing the workload of two (or more) people, juggling enormous demands with very limited resources. Work pressures can feel inevitable and, fearing for their own roles, people are reluctant to admit that their job is not manageable. However, organizations that want sustainable long-term productivity have to recognize that overloading their employees is counter-productive. While people may be able to perform under excessive pressure in the short-term, over time this will lead to burn-out, mistakes, distress and, in the long-run, the consequences are likely to be reduced performance, disengagement, ill-health and staff leaving the organization.

As a practitioner working with managers in these kinds of situations, you can help them identify what is and is not reasonable in terms of demands and support them in developing the assertiveness skills needed to challenge overload situations. It is not always easy to work out what is a reasonable workload or deadline, so it may be necessary to look, in as objective a way as possible, at the range of demands, priorities, deadlines and resources over a period of time: this information can then be used to determine whether, with good planning, prioritizing and time management, the situation can be managed or whether an upward challenge to 'push back' is appropriate. If this analysis leads to the conclusion that 'pushing back' is appropriate, then some assertiveness and negotiating concepts can be useful.

The 'assertiveness pendulum' can be a helpful concept to understand the difference between passive, assertive and aggressive behaviour (see Figure 9.1).

A classic pattern is to get into the habit of swinging from passive to aggressive:

- We start by being passive, over-accommodating, saying 'yes', doing everything we are asked to do.
- The pressure builds up and up as we get more and more overloaded and we start to feel put-upon.
- Then we reach a point where we can't bear it anymore, we feel angry and resentful and become irrational.
- This prompts a swing across into aggressive defence or attack, so we lash out in angry and irrational ways.

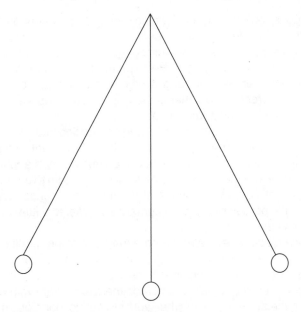

Passive	**Assertive**	**Aggressive**
Putting others' needs and rights above our own. Giving in to others' demands whether they are reasonable or not. Not standing up for ourselves. Withdrawing from conflict. Allowing others to 'walk all over' us ('doormat').	Giving respect to both our own and others' needs and rights. Doing things for others when it is reasonable and negotiating or saying 'no' in a calm and respectful way when appropriate. Not threatened by conflict. Expressing requests clearly and calmly.	Not respecting others' needs or rights and putting our own above others'. Behaving in irrational, angry, irritable and/or hostile ways in our interactions with and demands of others. Can be abusive (physically, verbally, emotionally).

Figure 9.1   The assertiveness pendulum

- Then, when the anger passes, we feel guilty and cowed, leading us to swing back into the passive mode and start the cycle all over again.

The healthier approach is to stay in assertive mode throughout. This involves keeping a watchful eye both on the demands being made of us and the reactions we are having to them. It also involves being able to negotiate on demands, priorities and deadlines in a calm, reasonable and respectful way. Some negotiating tips to help stay in the assertive zone might include:

- *Seek really to understand what the other person needs from the situation*: Look for what both you and the other person need, including perhaps getting to some of the underlying motivations. For example, if a manager's own manager is loading ever greater demands on them and giving multiple priorities, you can encourage the manager to explore in more detail what their manager needs to deliver and what their underlying concerns are. Perhaps the more senior manager is themselves under pressure and can be helped to tease out what will best relieve pressure on them, thereby establishing which of the 'priorities' is really most important.

- *Look at a range of options*: Rather than getting tied into all-or-nothing situations, aim to come up with a number of different options and explore the consequences of each. For example, when a manager is negotiating on competing deadlines, encourage them to come up with a selection of timescale options and explore the consequences of each with the person making the demands in order to settle on the one that works best for everyone.
- *Clarify consequences*: When someone is making additional demands, be clear with them about the impact that will have. For example, if a manager receives a new piece of work that conflicts with their current work-plan, encourage them to be clear with whoever is making the demand about what work will not get done or what other deadlines will have to get pushed back in order to deliver.
- *Be mindful of emotions*: Emotions are important indicators of the impact situations are having on you, so they provide useful information. On the other hand, being in a highly emotional state can get in the way of rational, calm negotiation, so it may be helpful to work through the emotions or take time out to let emotions subside before going into a negotiation or 'push back' situation.

Other solutions

Not all situations will require the manager to say 'no' or negotiate in order to make them manageable. In some cases, good planning, time management, prioritization, communication and/or delegation will be more appropriate ways of managing the situation. In other cases, the best solution is to help the manager change the way they are reacting to the situation or how their reaction is impacting. For example, it may be that the manager is actually well able to deal with the workload in practical terms, but gets highly anxious and feels overwhelmed when given a new piece of work: in this case, helping the manager recognize and reframe their emotional reaction may help. Other managers may need to explore how to look after themselves in order to be best able to manage work demands: here, encouraging the manager to take regular breaks, eat healthily, take exercise, etc. may be the key to enabling them to cope.

The points discussed in this section are summarized in Table 9.2, which can be used to help prompt your memory.

Table 9.2.   Solutions identified in our research – Individual work/job level barriers

Barriers to displaying Positive Manager Behaviour	Suggestions for how this barrier might be overcome
Workload	o Planning o Prioritizing o Challenge upwards and negotiating o Delegate/find extra resource where possible o Communicate honestly to the team what you are doing/trying to do o Diarize time for reflection/contingency time o Use 'surgery hours' rather than open door policy for team o Protect time to communicate with team o Take 15–30 minutes each day to get free time/fresh air and think/reboot
Short-term deadlines and demands	o Challenge upwards: request priorities and explain consequences for team o Anticipate and plan for regular deadlines o Communicate the strategy behind the deadline to the team o Thank the team for their efforts
Conflicting pressures and multiple priorities	o Clarify expectations o Challenge upwards o Say 'no' when necessary o Filter the work and prioritize o Focus on the 'quick wins' o Deal with work straight away o Create an action plan o Set out milestones – plan the year ahead o Keep communicating with the team
Lack of resource	o Make a strong case to senior management o Encourage team-work o Step in when necessary to get 'all hands on deck' o Communicate honestly with the team o Get advice from others o Gather evidence on the problem

Source: Adapted from Donaldson-Feilder, Lewis and Yarker (2009)

Team and Relationship Level Barriers

The third type of barrier is those relating to team and relationship issues. Here managers who participated in the research told us about situations where people were getting in the way of them behaving positively. In some cases this was difficulties with the people they were managing, in other cases it was relationships with those in more senior positions. In either case, some effective communication and sensitive handling is likely to be necessary. We now consider ways of dealing first with team issues then with issues created by senior managers.

The first step: Identify and understand the problem

The kinds of team issues that might be problematic are where team members lack motivation and/or capability or where they are showing problematic behaviours and/or attitudes. It may be that there is one person in the team who falls into this category and is causing problems for the whole team, or it may be a more widespread problem. Yet again, it is vital for the manager to be able to identify what is going on: this involves both clarifying their own perspective and also finding out others' perspectives. For example:

- If it seems that a particular person is not performing well, it is important to tease out what might be causing this issue: does the person lack skills, motivation, understanding...? To clarify the situation, it is important to have a discussion with the individual about their perspective on their performance and the reasons for any problems.
- If the situation is one where a team member appears to be creating problems by their behaviour, such as conflict or difficult dynamics in the team, it may be helpful to get other team members' perspectives to see if the manager's perceptions are borne out by others.

Making assumptions in these situations or not getting others' perspectives can lead to generating inappropriate solutions or implementing solutions in an inappropriate way.

The next step: Taking action

One of the messages from participants in our research was that it is important to address these issues and not assume they will go away of their own accord. It was also suggested that the earlier they are addressed the better, so as not to let them fester and build up. Clear, honest and open communication is vital. While sensitivity to people's emotions is important, trying to be overly 'kind' is unhelpful if it gets in the way of clear communication. It is not 'kind' to anyone to let someone under-perform or behave in disruptive or destructive ways. The person involved, the rest of the team and the manager themselves all suffer the consequences.

It could be said that using Positive Manager Behaviour is actually one way to overcome these barriers to Positive Manager Behaviour! In particular, the management competency, 'Reasoning/managing difficult situations' may be helpful – see Chapter 8. It is important to recognize that handling these situations is not easy and that managers may need support to help them do so: one of the clusters covered by this management competency is the manager's willingness to seek support from others in the organization.

Dealing with issues caused by the behaviour of those at a more senior level

Barriers to Positive Manager Behaviour may also be generated by the way senior managers in the organization behave. Participants in our research often tell us how difficult it is to show positive behaviour if they are on the receiving end of negative manager behaviour from their own manager or others in senior management positions. This is why the ideal is to have (or establish) a culture of Positive Manager Behaviour from the top of the organization, so that each part of the management hierarchy is role modelling Positive Manager Behaviour to those at the next level. As a practitioner, finding ways to take a systemic approach and work across the whole organization can help reduce the likelihood that managers will be exposed to barriers resulting from unhelpful behaviour by more senior managers. For example, if management or leadership development interventions can start with the top team and then be cascaded through the management hierarchy, they can potentially have a more widespread and effective impact.

In Chapter 10 we will look at some of the organizational factors that enhance the success of interventions to increase Positive Manager Behaviour, including exploring ways of gaining senior manager buy-in. Here, we consider how a manager might reduce the impact of negative senior manager behaviour or poor relationships with their own manager.

The first step: Clarity about the problem

As before, managers need to be aware that there is a problem in order to be in a position to find solutions. Almost everyone finds their boss difficult sometimes: the key is to be clear when this is more than just an occasional frustration, where there is a pattern of problematic behaviour by a senior person. It can be helpful to check with others to see whether they have identified the same pattern/issue – particularly as support is likely to be vital for finding and implementing solutions.

The next step: Seeking support to implement solutions

As with overcoming barriers caused by team members, part of the solution to difficulties with a senior manager may be about good, clear and open communication. However, the power-dynamics involved in dealing with difficult behaviour up the hierarchy are generally different to those down the hierarchy. This means that, where the issue relates to a more senior manager, it may be particularly important to seek support so as not to feel isolated and vulnerable.

Going back to the three options (changing the situation, changing the reaction to the situation or managing the impact of the reaction) it may be hard for a manager alone to have an effect on a more senior manager's behaviour – though in some cases some frank and specific feedback may make a difference. Getting support from someone higher up the hierarchy (at a level above the problematic manager) might be helpful, though it would need to be very sensitively handled; or it may be possible to achieve change through a peer group effort.

Alternatively, when the senior manager won't change their approach, it may be that getting support can help with handling the situation more effectively. Support may be available from a number of channels, including peers, the team, and specialist functions, such as Human Resources, Occupational Health and Health & Safety practitioners. Once a manager feels that they are not alone in handling the problem, their reaction to it may change and it may seem less threatening. There is research to suggest that peer support is especially effective if the individuals involved are exposed to the same stressors.

For example:

1. If a senior manager says things that are critical and undermining:
   - an isolated manager may find it damages their confidence and self-efficacy;
   - whereas a manager who has talked it through with peers and knows that others are having the same experience may be able to take the perspective of 'there he/she goes again saying undermining things' (changing reaction).
2. If a senior manager is being inconsistent and making things difficult:
   - an isolated manager may find that they get frustrated and this spills over into their people management approach, making it harder to behave positively;
   - whereas a manager who is able to get support from others (even if this is just a chance to get the frustration off their chest and talk it through with someone else) may find they can put their feelings to

one side when it comes to people management responsibilities (managing impact of the reaction).

The points discussed in this section are summarized in Table 9.3, which can be used to help prompt your memory.

Table 9.3. Solutions identified in our research – Team and relationship level barriers

Barriers to displaying Positive Manager Behaviour	Suggestions for how this barrier might be overcome
Lack of progress/capability within the team	o Deal with poor performance o Make use of organizational policies o Communicate honesty with the team member involved o Increase one-to-ones with all team members o Communicate objectives clearly
Problematic behaviours/ attitudes of team members	o Face and take action about the situation o Deal with poor performance o Develop a case/note down all incidents o Seek to find out the cause of the behaviour/ attitude o Reflect back to the team member on their behaviour and your feelings about it o Role modelling o Seek external advice and discussion o Take a step back to enable reflection and preparation o Clarify both their and your objectives o Recognize your feelings and your behaviour o Use of humour
Senior/line managers (pressure, inconsistent management, lack of direction, undermining)	o Ask for directions in writing and clarify what is required before taking action o Know which directives to challenge, and which to accept o Communicate the situation to the level above the problematic manager o Get involved in working groups and action planning sets to seek solutions o Talk to peers about solutions o Take a team approach to solving problems o Communicate the situation to the team o Recognize your emotions and take time to get perspective before reacting

Source: Adapted from Donaldson-Feilder, Lewis and Yarker (2009)

Organizational and Wider Level Barriers

The final type of barrier identified in our research was those operating at the level of the organization and the wider context. A number of different barriers were mentioned in this category, including organizational processes and the way IT is used in some organizations, handling confidential issues, and pressures caused by the wider market or political context.

Processes and IT Issues that get in the way of Positive Behaviour

While working in a large organization can have a range of advantages, it may also lead to difficulties such as cumbersome processes and bureaucracy. In a different domain but similar vein, modern technology provides us with great advantages in the workplace, but also brings its own difficulties such as over-use of emails and information overload. The pressures imposed and the time taken up by these factors can get in the way of Positive Manager Behaviour.

To overcome these barriers, as a coach, trainer or consultant, you can help managers:

- *Change the situation:* Are there ways of challenging and changing the status quo? What are the communication routes for providing feedback on processes that aren't working or about a culture in which emails are getting out of hand? Are there others in the organization who are finding the same problems and, if so, would it be possible to take a joint approach to achieving change?
- *Change the reaction to the situation:* If the processes or email culture can't be changed at an organizational level, what can an individual do to make the situation manageable? Are there ways of getting round the processes, taking valid shortcuts, working better within the system? Would some training make it possible to manage emails or other IT issues better? Can some emails be deleted without reading or filtered into separate folders for dealing with later (e.g., when they are for information only)?
- *Manage the impact of the reaction:* If they can't change the situation or how they manage the situation, can managers ensure that the fact they are having these problems doesn't impact on their management approach? Can they be mindful of their reaction to these issues, take a deep breath/break/pause and set the issue to one side rather than let it impinge on their team?

Confidential information

Particularly during organizational change, managers can find that they receive information that they are not allowed to share with their team. As a manager, being privy to confidential information of this kind can be a real challenge to the desire to be open and honest with employees: it may feel like it conflicts with their natural management style and with the management competency 'Respectful and responsible: managing emotions and having integrity', see Chapter 5.

How can you help a manager behave with integrity when they are being asked to keep 'secrets'?

- *Change the situation*: One approach is to see if the manager can challenge whether the information really can't be shared and see if the organization can shift its approach to one of greater involvement and openness.
- *Change the reaction to the situation*: Another approach is to help them be honest about the fact that not everything can be shared. Whether this is effective or not will depend on the degree to which the manager has previously built trusting relationships with team members: if the team trusts their manager, they will find it easier to accept that there are things that he/she can't share, trusting that he/she will share them when it becomes possible.
- *Manage the impact of the reaction*: A third approach is to ensure that the manager has support in dealing with this difficult situation. Managers may find it easier to handle being the holder of sensitive information if they can talk it through with others in the same situation.

Wider level barriers

Wider level barriers were mentioned by many of our research participants, though they differed in type between sectors. Particularly reported by participants in public sector organizations were barriers relating to Governmental targets or shifts in Government policy that changed the objectives or context of managers' work. For example, participants from the National Health Service reported that Government targets could create problems at local levels when the achievement of a national target, such as reducing waiting lists or waiting times, put pressure on departments and could conflict with other aims or objective such as quality of patient care. In private sector organizations, these wider level barriers were more likely to include changes in market conditions, for example pressures caused by the economic downturn or changes in global demand for products or services.

In these situations, it is unlikely that managers can change the situation in terms of altering Government policy or the economic environment. Instead, managers will need to change how they handle the situation. For example: it may be appropriate to work with others who are

Table 9.4. Solutions identified in our research – Organizational and wider level barriers

Barriers to displaying Positive Manager Behaviour	Suggestions for how this barrier might be overcome
Organizational barriers (such as processes and bureaucracy)	o Challenge the processes and make suggestions for improvements o Create a steering group to focus on issues o Speak to others o Find ways round the processes o Develop creative approaches o Find a way to work within the system
IT issues, particularly excessive use of email	o Make senior managers aware of the issue o Challenge those who excessively use email o Ignore/delete 'round-robin' emails o Use 'out of office' or other messages o IT training o Work from home o Use a blackberry to deal with emails on journey to and from work
Not being able to share some information with the team that you would like to	o Build team trust so that they don't need proof o Avoid favouritism o Gain clarity about when to be consultative and when to be directive o Be honest that there are things you can't share o Increase team understanding of your role o Refuse to give false information o Take responsibility for your position o Use your own support structures
Impact of legislation, policy and government targets	o Share ownership and responsibility where appropriate o Consult specialists o Admit when you don't know o Training and development o Recognize the things that 'have to happen'

Source: Adapted from Donaldson-Feilder, Lewis and Yarker (2009)

also dealing with the same issues to find group approaches and ways of handling the difficulties. As mentioned earlier, research suggests that those who have high levels of peer support are less likely to suffer poor well-being (which, in this case, would allow the manager to show greater levels of Positive Manager Behaviour) and that this is particularly the case when the peers involved are dealing with the same stressors.

As a trainer, coach or consultant working with managers in these kinds of situations, it may be appropriate to provide structured opportunities for peer support. For example, facilitated action learning sets or peer networks can be an excellent way of linking managers with one another and giving them the time and space to discuss the kind of barriers and obstacles they are all facing. Where these initiatives are put in place, it is often also the case that the individuals not only benefit from the sessions when they get together as a group, but also that the networking and support becomes more available at other times as well: they feel comfortable contacting other members of the group when they have a specific issue to discuss or want advice between sessions or after the formal facilitated initiative has finished.

The points discussed in this section are summarized in Table 9.4, which can be used to help prompt your memory.

Reference

Donaldson-Feilder, E., Lewis, R. and Yarker, J., (2009). *Preventing Stress: Promoting Positive Manager Behaviour. CIPD Insight Report.* CIPD Publications: London. Available on the CIPD website: www.cipd.co.uk/subjects/health/stress/_preventing_ stress.

10

Supporting managers to change their behaviour

So, the competency framework is clear, managers know the positive management behaviours they need to show, all they have to do is change their management approach to include the relevant behaviours – simple! Or maybe not so simple ... changing behaviour is actually very hard, especially if the individual concerned has been behaving in particular ways for many years.

This chapter is designed to help you explore what you, as a practitioner, can do to support managers in a behaviour change process. It aims to:

- explain why we believe behaviour change is possible;
- take a brief look at some theoretical approaches that can help understand the process of behaviour change; and
- explore a series of factors likely to be important when implementing interventions to help managers make changes in order to behave in more positive ways.

Preventing Stress in Organizations: How to Develop Positive Managers,
Emma Donaldson-Feilder, Joanna Yarker and Rachel Lewis.
© 2011 John Wiley & Sons, Ltd. Published 2011 by John Wiley & Sons, Ltd.

Behaviour Change *Is* Possible

A person's behaviour is shaped by a huge range of factors, including individual determinants, such as personality and attitudes, and environmental determinants, such as social norms and organizational culture. In many cases, particular ways of behaving have become so habitual, that a manager is not even conscious that they are behaving that way or that there are other ways they might behave.

One conclusion from this is that the ideal is to get managers to adopt positive management behaviour really early on in their management careers – at induction, perhaps, when they are just taking on line management responsibility and haven't yet established particular management habits. If they can establish Positive Manager Behaviour as a key part of their repertoire from the start, then they are more likely to show those behaviours for the duration of their management careers. Another conclusion is that, if you want managers who have been in management positions for a while to change their behaviour and behave in more positive ways, you will need to give them considerable support, including training/coaching, and look at how the organizational environment can facilitate adoption of positive management approaches.

In our research, we found that it *is* possible to help managers change their management behaviour, particularly if they have development needs in the areas under consideration. As outlined in Chapter 4, we provided managers with a learning and development intervention based on our Positive Manager Behaviour research findings that included three elements:

- upward feedback, providing managers with a feedback report showing how their manager behaviour was perceived by those they managed;
- face-to-face workshop, providing managers with time to explore their feedback report, understand the behaviours that are important for preventing and reduce stress at work, and look at how to show the relevant behaviours; and
- follow-up upward feedback, providing managers with a second report on how their manager behaviour was perceived by those they managed at a point three months after the workshop (i.e., when they had hopefully had a chance to implement the changes they wanted to make).

We found that the vast majority of managers who attended the workshop felt afterwards that they would be able to apply what they learnt. Three-quarters of managers who participated in the intervention and responded to a follow-up questionnaire felt they had managed to make changes to their management approach during the three months following the workshop. And analysis of the data on manager behaviour suggested that those managers who were perceived not to show the behaviours set out in the Positive Manager Behaviour framework before the intervention were generally perceived both by themselves and by their staff to show these behaviours to a significantly greater extent three months after the workshop.

Thus evidence suggests that, while behaviour change is hard, it is possible. The key is to understand what support and input managers require in order to make appropriate behavioural changes. Of course, what is needed will depend on the individual managers involved and we must not forget that many managers will already show some of the behaviours set out in the competency framework, so will only need to change their behaviour in a few areas. However, some general principles on behaviour change and on implementing interventions to support manager behaviour change can be used to guide your action in this area.

Theories of Behaviour Change

Much of the literature on behaviour change originates in the public health domain and is formulated with the aim of helping people behave in ways that are beneficial to their health, such as stopping smoking, overcoming addiction, avoiding injury and Aids risk reduction. One of the most widely used models is the stages of change theory, developed by Prochaska and Di Clemente in the context of smoking cessation. While the adoption of Positive Manager Behaviour is more about adopting behaviour beneficial to others' well-being than improving the manager's own health, the model of behaviour change is still pertinent. The five stages of change set out in this model are shown in the following text box.

Prochaska and DiClemente's Five Stages of Change

1. *Pre-contemplation*: the person is not even considering changing their behaviour; they may not realize that change is needed, possible or of interest to them.
2. *Contemplation*: the person starts to think about change; something prompts them to realise it is an option.
3. *Preparation*: the person prepares to make changes to their behaviour; they may gather information, find out about the options for change and get things in place to make changes.
4. *Action*: the person makes changes, acting on their decision to change, they use new skills and motivations to shift their behaviour.
5. *Maintenance (or relapse)*: the person maintains the new behaviour consistently over time, incorporating it into their repertoire of behaviour on a permanent basis (alternatively, the person relapses into old patterns of behaviour and has to loop back to the earlier stages to change again).

(Prochaska and DiClemente, 1986, 1992)

Research suggests that behaviour change interventions are most likely to work if they are tailored to the stage of change of the individuals being helped to change their behaviour. Thus, when looking to help managers adopt Positive Manager Behaviour, we need to consider whether they are already contemplating change or even preparing for it or whether we are starting from a point of getting them even to consider behaving in new, more positive ways. We must also recognize that, in many cases, an individual manager will already be showing some or all of the behaviours set out in the Positive Manager Behaviour framework; in this case, they need to maintain these positive behaviours and explore whether there are any gaps in their repertoire where behaviour change is needed. Upward feedback can help with identifying the extent of change needed.

Another model that may be helpful to bear in mind is the eight-factor model that brings together a range of theories of behaviour change. At a meeting of key theorists in the field, a consensus was reached that identified eight variables that appear to account for most of the variation in behaviour change, as shown in the following text box.

Eight variables to account for the variation in behaviour change

1. *The individual's intention*: does the individual have a strong positive intention to show the behaviour?
2. *Environmental barriers or constraints*: are there environmental factors that make the behaviour impossible?
3. *Skills or ability*: does the person have the necessary skills?
4. *Attitude or anticipated outcomes*: does the person believe the benefits of behaving in this way outweigh the disadvantages?
5. *Social norms*: is there social pressure to perform the behaviour or not to perform the behaviour?
6. *Self-standards*: is the behaviour consistent with the person's self-image?
7. *Emotional reactions*: how does the person feel about the behaviour?
8. *Self-efficacy*: does the person believe that they have the capabilities to perform the behaviour under a number of different circumstances?

(Fishbein, 1995; Fishbein *et al.*, 2001)

Again, this model was developed in a health context, but it can be useful to explore which of the factors are present and absent in terms of helping a manager adopt Positive Manager Behaviour. As a practitioner, you can consider how to increase the supportive factors and remove barriers or constraints where possible. Providing learning and development interventions that increase managers' skills and their self-efficacy can be a key part of this, but may well need to be accompanied by activities to gain buy-in and to set a conducive organizational environment.

Implementing Behaviour Change Interventions

So, armed with an understanding of some of the theoretical basis to behaviour change, we hope you are inspired to support managers to behave in more positive ways. This section looks at some of the factors that will help you succeed in this endeavour: based on our research findings, it explores the following areas:

- gaining manager buy-in to a development intervention;
- organizational factors that affect success;
- the importance of upward feedback; and
- ongoing support for behaviour change.

Gaining manager buy-in to a development intervention

In the modern workplace, most managers are under enormous pressure: they have deadlines to hit, workloads to juggle, demands to meet . . . and finding time to develop their people management skills can seem a long way down the priority list. How do you, as a practitioner, persuade managers to invest their time and energy in developing their ability to behave in ways that prevent and reduce stress in their staff? From a 'stages of change' perspective, many of them are at 'pre-contemplation' or 'contemplation': how do you get them through the stages of change to 'preparation' and 'action'? From the 'eight factor model' perspective, how do you influence the range of variables that will determine whether managers are motivated, willing and ready to change their behaviour?

Making the case
This initial shift, or gaining buy-in, may be partly about 'anticipated outcomes' and showing managers that the benefits outweigh the disadvantages. It may help to emphasize the benefits of preventing and reducing stress in staff. Showing the link between Positive Manager Behaviour and relevant outcomes, such as increased performance, reduced absence and lower staff turnover may help. Making the 'business case', or sometimes the legal and/or moral case, can be important, so that managers see what is in it for them – what benefits they may gain from behaving in more positive ways. We have provided information to support you with this in Chapters 2 and 3.

Barriers to participation

As well as making the case for the intervention, this initial stage may also be about removing some of the managers' concerns about the intervention or barriers to participation. In addition to finding that managers were too stressed themselves or too busy and didn't see Positive Manager Behaviour interventions as a priority, practitioners involved in our research identified a range of factors that got in the way of manager participation in the intervention we were running in their organizations. Issues mentioned included finding that managers:

- had concerns about the confidentiality of feedback data;
- were concerned about what participation implied about them;
- found the inclusion of the word 'stress' in the title off-putting and/or lacked a knowledge base about stress;
- were, in some cases, complacent and believed 'we haven't got a problem with stress';
- said they would participate but did not show up on the day;
- resented being instructed to attend compulsory courses; and
- struggled to get sufficient direct report responses to provide upward feedback.

In addition, practitioners felt that senior management who were not engaged/bought-in and difficulties communicating with managers were also issues.

Before planning any kind of intervention in the organization with which you are working, it would be worth considering which of these barriers are likely to be relevant and how you can overcome them: use the framework set out in Table 10.1 to reflect on the situation in the organization.

Overcoming barriers to participation

As you reflect on the barriers, you will see that some issues can be solved relatively easily through effective communication and clear messages. For example:

- clarity about confidentiality and transparency about how feedback will be handled can help allay managers' fears about confidentiality; and
- clarity up front about response rates and asking managers for a sufficient number of team member names can help ensure managers get enough responses to provide upward feedback.

Resolving other issues may be about the decisions taken in setting up and recruiting managers onto the intervention. For example:

- Do you make the intervention compulsory (in which case you may need to find ways of avoiding participants being resentful about being

Table 10.1   Factors to overcome in the organization with which you are working

Factors that may get in the way of manager participation	Relevant? (tick)	Overcoming relevant factors in the organization with which you are working/ client (note ideas)
Managers are too stressed themselves or too busy and don't see it as a priority		
Difficulties communicating with managers to get them interested in participating		
Managers are concerned about the confidentiality of their feedback data		
Managers are concerned about what participation implies about them		
Managers are put off by the inclusion of the word 'stress' in the title and lack a knowledge base about stress		
Managers are complacent and believe 'we haven't got a problem with stress'		
Senior management are not engaged/bought-in		
Managers say they will participate but don't show up on the day		
Managers resent being instructed to attend compulsory courses		
Managers struggle to get sufficient direct report responses to provide upward feedback		
Other issue not mentioned above...		

Note: Use the table to help you consider the factors that might get in the way of managers participating in an intervention in the organization with which you are working and how you might overcome those that are relevant forced to attend) or voluntary (in which case you may need to find ways of drawing in all managers to ensure you are not 'preaching to the converted')? There is some debate about the effectiveness of compulsory training, with a strong feeling expressed by some that people who feel forced to attend are unlikely to learn as they do not have the motivation to do so. Research suggests that training is most effective when it is matched to the 'stage of change' of the trainees, so you may need to adjust the content of the training according to where your managers are in terms of changing to show Positive Manager Behaviour. It is also worth considering the degree to which the 'eight factors' are present for the managers concerned.

- Do you select managers to attend because stress risk assessment or other initiatives suggest there are high levels of stress in their team (in which case you may need to take steps to make sure that they don't feel victimized or embarrassed about attending) or do you roll it out to all (in which case you may need to find ways to ensure that managers in relevant 'hotspot' areas recognize it as a way to solve problems they need to address, rather than believing it doesn't apply to them)?
- Do you use 'stress' in the title of the intervention because you want to raise awareness of the area (which may then require additional education and information) or do you choose another title, such as 'well-being' or 'managing pressure' (but ensure that stress-related problems are acknowledged if necessary)? How will you brand the initiative to get the best response in the organization with which you are working?

Organizational factors, such as gaining buy-in from the top of the organization and embedding the intervention in existing programmes and practices are also highly relevant and are considered in more depth later.

In terms of getting the messages to managers, using a range of communication mechanisms and knowing which ones are most likely to reach the managers you want to target can make a difference. For example, it may be that informal communications and networks are the most effective mechanisms, so it would be worth thinking about how you can access these. Having a steering group and/or taking a multi-disciplinary approach can also be helpful: if HR, Learning and Development, Health and Safety, Occupational Health and Organizational Development professionals are pulling together to achieve a successful initiative, this can help get messages across and managers on board.

In general, our research suggests that considerable planning and preparation, together with consultation, communication and building relationships/trust is required to gain good manager buy-in to and participation in these kinds of interventions. It is natural to want to get on with organizing the mechanics of the intervention, but it may be more beneficial to invest time up front to ensure that the intervention has the take-up, impact and success you want.

Organizational factors that affect success

As the models of change outlined earlier suggest, achieving behaviour change is likely to require more than just getting managers to participate in a learning and development intervention: success will depend to a certain extent on the organizational context in which the managers are working. For individuals to be motivated to show Positive Manager Behaviour, the organizational context needs to be one in which social norms and the environment support this kind of behaviour – and where Positive Manager Behaviour is emphasized through consistent messages from a range of initiatives.

Senior manager role modelling and support
Feedback from managers who participated in our research suggests that one of the things that gets in the way of them showing Positive Manager Behaviour is when they are not being treated in positive ways by their own managers. It follows that managers in an organization are unlikely to change their behaviour if the messages from senior managers and the way senior managers behave does not reinforce this. Thus, as a practitioner aiming to help managers behave in more positive ways, one of the things likely to be most helpful to you is to have senior management buy-in and to get those at the top of the management hierarchy to role model Positive Manager Behaviour. In some organizations, the most senior executives will see the value of this and be willing to take it on board. In other organizations, achieving buy-in can be challenging as some of the quotes in the box show!

Senior management buy-in – not as easy as it sounds

Quotes from practitioners in our research talking about how hard it is to get senior managers to role model Positive Manager Behaviour:

There is a belief [amongst senior managers] that empathic management styles don't work: a feeling that it is a luxury we can't afford...

Senior managers are a self-selecting group – they got there because they are hard-hitting

[Senior managers'] focus is on business goals and maybe then they forget/miss things like people management...

Senior managers show verbal support for these initiatives, but don't follow that through in their behaviour.

Whether challenging or not in the particular organization with which you are working, getting senior management buy-in is well worth doing and may even be critical to the success of initiatives aimed at achieving Positive Manager Behaviour. Some would argue that it is not even ethical/ worthwhile asking first line and middle managers to behave in these ways if senior managers aren't doing so. One possible, perhaps ideal, approach would be to cascade any intervention from the very top of the organization, that is, to start with the Chief Executive or Managing Director and cascade the development intervention from the most senior manager downwards. If you use upward feedback as part of the intervention, this cascade approach has the added value that everyone except the most senior person will have been involved in giving feedback to their manager before receiving feedback from those they manage.

Other ideas for gaining senior manager buy-in include the following:

- *Make a clear business case*: Showing how Positive Manager Behaviour and associated improvements in staff well-being can benefit the organization can be persuasive. Talking in terms of business issues such as reduced insurance premiums, reduced sickness absence, reduced staff turnover and/or improved performance/service delivery may help senior managers buy in. See Chapter 2 for further information on this.
- *Clarify legal responsibilities and risks*: In some organizations, responsibilities under health and safety legislation, linked to the risk of HSE enforcement action, may be considered compelling. Alternatively, talking about the risk of civil litigation and all the potential negative publicity likely to ensue, including showing details of specific cases, might be more attention grabbing. See Chapter 2 for further information on this.
- *Link initiatives to national goals*: Some sectors may have useful national goals or initiatives that can be linked to Positive Manager Behaviour and staff well-being. For example, the public sector may be interested in the link to Dame Carol Black's report on the health and well-being of working age people and the Government's intention to make the public sector an exemplar employer; NHS organizations may value it as a way of implementing the recommendations of the Boorman review of NHS staff well-being; Healthy Schools campaigns may be relevant in the education sector; or assessment for Investors in People status might be another hook.
- *Have a champion within the senior management team*: If one of the top managers is bought-in, they can be a persuasive voice to get others in the senior management team on board. Participants in our research suggested that, if a member of the senior management team chairs the steering group for health and well-being or health and safety, this gives it higher profile and greater significance at all levels of the organization.

- *Take a multi-disciplinary/united approach*: If relevant professionals throughout the organization, such as HR, Learning and Development, Health and Safety, Occupational Health and Organizational Development, are all supportive of the Positive Manager Behaviour initiative, then it is more likely that senior managers and others in the organization will be persuaded of its value.

Integration with other initiatives

Another organizational factor that can contribute to the success of an initiative to increase Positive Manager Behaviour is if it fits with and can be embedded in and/or linked to other initiatives. For example, it may be possible to integrate a learning and development intervention on Positive Manager Behaviour into existing management or leadership development programmes. If it is seen as part of a programme in which managers are already participating, then there is less likely to be resistance; and buy-in generated for the programme as a whole will apply to the Positive Manager Behaviour element in particular. Another possibility might be to make increasing Positive Manager Behaviour a part of a broader stress management or well-being initiative. For example, if the organization has conducted a stress risk assessment, particularly if it has highlighted poor people management as a stress risk, an intervention to increase Positive Manager Behaviour could be part of the actions taken to tackle the problems identified. See Chapter 11 for more on this.

Importance of upward feedback

So, you have gained manager buy-in to a development intervention and set the organizational context through senior management buy-in/role modelling and embedding the intervention in other organizational initiatives... What is it about the intervention itself that is going to make a difference? When looking at what were the 'active ingredients' of the intervention we used in the research, it seemed that upward feedback was an important element. We provided this by getting managers to ask their staff to complete a questionnaire about their manager's behaviour and generating an upward feedback report for each manager.

Helping managers understand how they are currently (perceived to be) behaving seems intuitively likely to be an important way of helping them adopt Positive Manager Behaviour, as it will highlight relevant behaviours that they are not currently showing. It also fits with the models of change, for example:

- Helping managers recognize the behaviours that are not part of their management repertoire, which they may not have realized previously to be the case, can move them from 'pre-contemplation' to 'contemplation' (in terms of 'stages of change'); and it can be a way of showing managers that they are not behaving in ways consistent with their self-image (one of the variables in the 'eight factor model').

* Helping managers understand what they are doing well and clarify what they might do differently can increase their self-efficacy and generate a positive intention to make appropriate changes (two further variables in the 'eight factor model').

Our research findings suggest that this intuitive and theoretical reasoning is borne out in practice:

* Over half of the managers who participated in our research intervention and received an upward feedback report said that receiving upward feedback and/or understanding the views of their staff was the most useful element.
* While there was a strong improvement for all managers in the degree to which they felt they understood their own management behaviour, this improvement was much more marked among those who had received an upward feedback report.

For practitioners working with managers to help them show Positive Manager Behaviour, we would, therefore, suggest that you provide them with a chance to receive feedback on their management behaviour – either upward or 360 degree feedback. Since the managers' direct reports are the ones on the receiving end of their manager behaviour, it is probably their perceptions that are most important, but the manager may find it useful to get their own manager and peers to give their views as well.

Resource

There is a 'management competencies indicator tool' questionnaire that measures the relevant behaviours; it was developed through our research. Self-report, self plus other and 360 degree feedback versions are all available for free download from the HSE website. We also know of at least one commercial provider that offers the questionnaire as an online 360 degree feedback tool.

There are many important considerations when it comes to providing individuals with upward or 360 degree feedback. The most important is probably the issue of confidentiality. For more on this, see the following text box.

Confidentiality in upward feedback

- *Confidentiality for those providing feedback*: Individuals may feel vulnerable when giving feedback on their manager's behaviour, worried that it might affect the employee–manager relationship. For this reason, we strongly recommend that upward feedback results should not be revealed to the manager unless a minimum of three direct reports respond to the feedback questionnaire and that only an average response, combining all direct report questionnaire answers, be given to the manager (perhaps with a range, i.e., minimum and maximum responses, indicated). The same may be true for peers providing feedback. In the case of feedback from the manager's own manager, it may be that they only have one manager, in which case it is important that that manager is aware that their responses will be revealed; however, many organizations now have multiple reporting lines, so it may be advisable/desirable for several managers to provide feedback.
- *Confidentiality of the feedback report*: Managers receiving feedback may be concerned about who will see their report. Some may fear that it will in some way affect how their performance is judged at work. We recommend that this feedback be used in a developmental and supportive way, not as a part of appraisal or judgements about performance. This allows for the report to be entirely confidential to the managers themselves and they can choose to whom they show it. It may be helpful for them to share it with their manager (and others, for example in HR or Learning and Development departments) to support discussions about seeking coaching, training and other development, but it is probably preferable that they have control over whether and to what extent they do this.
- *Confidentiality of the process*: Allied to this, it is important that all participants in the feedback process feel confident that their questionnaire responses will be treated in confidence. This means that anyone seeing the individual completed questionnaires needs to treat them, and be trusted to treat them, with complete confidentiality. Using a web-enabled questionnaire is one way of getting around this as it allows the respondent to answer the questions online and thereby feed them directly into the database without the responses being seen by anyone. Another consideration is whether it would be helpful to make a third party, someone from outside the organization, responsible for the process, so that all responses (whether supplied online, paper-based or by email) are handled off-site.

Another key consideration is how to support the manager receiving feedback in understanding and accepting the information provided. We have found that if a manager is just provided with a written report, it is hard for them to get to grips with the data on their own. Providing either a workshop or one-to-one feedback sessions can be invaluable to help managers understand the contents and meaning of their feedback reports. A more difficult issue is how to get managers to accept feedback that they don't like. We have seen a range of responses to unexpectedly negative feedback, including the following:

Who said that? I bet it was X . . . he has a particular gripe about me at the moment because. . .

This isn't about me. They are unhappy about the workload.

Well they would say that, wouldn't they – anything to get at the boss.

I haven't been managing this team for long; they don't really know me yet.

Their responses have been slanted by the current change programme.

That's just the way I am, I can't do anything different.

Of course, there may be some truth in some of these responses and the manager's view needs to be respected, but it is important to help the manager see that their team members' responses are a useful source of data and may indicate a need for change. The point is that employees' perceptions are relevant and valid, however accurate they are in terms of the way the manager actually behaves, as these perceptions influence the impact the manager has on staff well-being. In a one-to-one feedback session, it may be helpful to allow the manager to vent these feelings and feel understood: then, after they have had time to do this, you can explore why employees may have said these things and what the manager might do to change the team's perceptions. In a workshop or group setting, you may find that other managers in the group help with this process, but it may also be helpful to find time to talk to particularly resistant managers one-to-one away from the group.

In some situations, managers receive unexpectedly positive feedback, having been more negative about themselves than their team/others. In these situations, it is helpful to allow time for the manager really to absorb the positive messages and to think about how they can take advantage of the 'hidden strengths' revealed. It may be a chance to build a manager's confidence in their own management skills and take a strengths-based approach to development: in other words, really to focus on the individual's strengths and how best to use them to achieve their goals. The risk, if you don't do this, is that a self-critical individual uses the feedback only to identify the areas where they score lowest and use these to dwell on the negative implications.

Ongoing support for behaviour change

One of the challenges in any learning and development intervention, particularly those that are about interpersonal skill acquisition, is how to ensure that the new skills or behaviours are actually transferred from the learning environment (coaching session, training course, workshop etc.) into the workplace setting. From a 'stages of change' perspective, this will depend at least partly on whether the intervention has been effective at getting the participants to 'action' and 'maintenance' stage. Or, looking at the 'eight-factor model', has the intervention:

- motivated the manager to use the new behaviour in the workplace setting?
- allowed the new behaviour to be thoroughly/well learnt?
- enabled the manager to believe that Positive Manager Behaviour will be beneficial to themselves, those they manage and the team/ organization?
- generated high levels of confidence/self-efficacy about the new behaviour?

If not, then further intervention or learning and development input may be required to continue the change process. The individual may need further support to change their behaviour through ongoing coaching, action learning and/or further training input.

There will also be factors relating to the context into which the manager returns from the learning setting, particularly:

- whether the new behaviour is welcomed or resisted by others in the workplace environment, be they manager, peers, or direct reports; and
- whether the behaviour, in this case Positive Manager Behaviour, is seen as being part of the social norm.

While some of these contextual issues can be prepared up-front by tackling the organizational factors that affect success, ongoing support may be required to help managers overcome the remaining environmental barriers and resistance. Coaching, action-learning sets, reviews, refresher workshops and so on may be helpful at this point. Action learning sets and peer networking can have the additional benefit of helping to create peer-support for social norms that emphasize Positive Manager Behaviour.

It may also be helpful to consider how the organization with which you are working can provide managers with more time to focus on people management, rather than expect them to do it in addition to their 'day job'. Does the organization's culture emphasize the importance of people management and of developing people management skills? If not, what is needed to raise these things up the agenda? Yet again, the importance of senior management buy-in is reemphasized.

More support recommended – practitioner view

Practitioners whose organizations participated in our research were clear that, to improve the intervention in future, they would aim to provide greater support to manager participants throughout the process and at follow-up. They recognized that for some of them there was a tendency to invest all their effort at the start of the project to get it up and running, but to let their input drop off over time. This was exacerbated by practitioners having high workloads and by changes in personnel or organizational structure/context that diverted energy and attention away from the initiative and took the focus off achieving Positive Manager Behaviour.

Some highly motivated and receptive managers were able to take the learning and apply it just through having upward feedback together with the workshop provided, particularly if their own managers were supportive. However, many of the participants actually needed more support from the in-house specialist practitioners involved (HR, Learning and Development, Health and Safety, Occupational Health etc).

More support recommended – manager view

When we asked managers who participated in the learning and development intervention in our research what further support they would need in order to develop their Positive Manager Behaviour skills, their responses included the following:
- further training input: particularly on leadership and conflict management;
- more time in their schedule to focus on developing their people management skills and for people management activities;
- additional and/or continuing feedback and appraisal; and

(continued)

- input from senior managers: in addition to wanting feedback and appraisal, participants suggested that general buy-in and support from those higher up the hierarchy would be important and that supervision, coaching and mentoring from their seniors would be helpful.

This shows that for some managers, the learning and development intervention led to a greater awareness of their skill gaps without fully meeting their development needs. Thus it had moved them through initial stages of change to recognize the need for change and possibly even prepare for it; to take advantage of this shift, the managers needed further development input to build their skills and self-efficacy.

References

Fishbein M. (1995). Developing effective behavior change interventions: Some lessons learned from behavioral research. In T.E. Backer, S.L. David and G. Soucy (eds), *Reviewing the Behavioral Science Knowledge Base on Technology Transfer*. (NIDA research monograph no. 155). National Institute on Drug Abuse, Bethesda, MD.

Fishbein, M., Triandis, H.C., Kanfer, F.H., Becker, M., Middlestadt, S.E. and Eichler, A. (2001). Factors influencing behavior and behavior change. In A. Baum, T.A. Tevenson and J.E. Singer (eds), *Handbook of Health Psychology*. Lawrence Erlbaum, Mahwah, NJ.

Prochaska, J.O. and Di Clemente, C.C. (1986). Towards a comprehensive model of change. In W.R. Miller and N. Heather (eds), *Treating Addictive Behaviours: Processes of Change*. Plenum Press, NewYork.

Prochaska, J.O. and Di Clemente, C.C. (1992). *Stages of change and the modification of problem behaviours*. In M. Hersen, R.M. Eisler and P.M. Miller (eds), *Progress in Behaviour Modification*. Sycamore Press, Sycamore, IL.

11

Is stress management just good management?

It is often said that 'stress management is just good management' and the reverse is also true – poor management is stressful for those being managed:

> 'bad managers tend to cause stress. It is not necessarily that they are bad at managing stress, but that they are bad at *managing* and that makes life quite stressful for people below them.' (Research participant)

When we set out to explore and identify Positive Manager Behaviour, we wanted to understand *which parts* of good management were important for staff well-being. We expected that there would be considerable overlap between general good management frameworks and the Positive Manager Behaviour framework emerging from our research. However, because most management frameworks are developed from the perspective of managing performance, we thought that there might be some behaviours that are important for stress management/staff well-being that weren't included in general management frameworks; we also foresaw that there would be some elements of general good management that were not

Preventing Stress in Organizations: How to Develop Positive Managers,
Emma Donaldson-Feilder, Joanna Yarker and Rachel Lewis.
© 2011 John Wiley & Sons, Ltd. Published 2011 by John Wiley & Sons, Ltd.

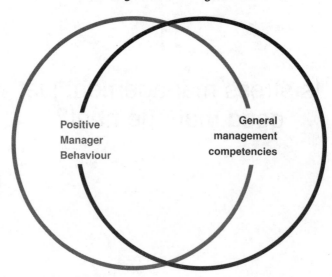

Figure 11.1   Venn diagram representing the expected relationship between Positive Manager Behaviour and general good management frameworks

important for staff stress/well-being. So our hypothesis was something along the lines of the Venn diagram in Figure 11.1.

When we actually did the comparison (or 'mapping'), one of the noticeable things was that there is a huge diversity of general management frameworks and they are all slightly different from one another. This suggests that there is no universal definition of good management, so what constitutes good management will depend on which model or framework you happen to use in the organization with which you are working or work. In terms of overlap with the Positive Manager Behaviour framework, this variability in what constitutes general good management translates into different degrees and areas of overlap, depending on which of the general management models you look at. This means that which parts of the Positive Manager Behaviour framework are included within the general good management framework are different for each model. So the picture looks more like Figure 11.2.

This chapter explores how the Positive Manager Behaviour framework compares with general management/leadership frameworks and the implications for practice. It aims to help you make your own comparison between any framework of management/leadership behaviour being used in the organization with which you are working and the Positive Manager Behaviour framework and explore how any missing behaviours might be identified and integrated into organizational practices. It also explores how organizations can move towards

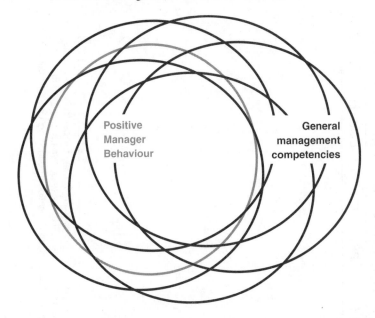

Figure 11.2   Venn diagram representing relationship actually found between Positive Manager Behaviour and general good management frameworks

valuing people management more than is often currently the case. The chapter is divided into the following sections:

- Comparing Positive Manager Behaviour with general management/ leadership competency frameworks
- Implications for practice
- How to do your own mapping
- How to identify missing Positive Manager Behaviour elements
- How to integrate missing Positive Manager Behaviour elements into:
    1. appraisal systems;
    2. management and leadership development programmes; and
    3. assessment and selection processes
- Valuing people management skills

Comparing Positive Manager Behaviour with General Management/Leadership Competency Frameworks

During our Positive Manager Behaviour research, we conducted mapping exercises to explore the similarities and differences between the framework that emerged from our research and measures that relate to the management models most often cited in the research literature. Tables 11.1 and 11.2

Table 11.1. Mapping the Positive Manager Behaviour (PMB) framework onto transformational leadership frameworks/metrics

PMB competency	PMB cluster	MLQ 5X	LBS	GTL	TLQ (Pub)	TLQ (Priv)
Respectful and Responsible: Managing emotions and having integrity	Integrity	✓	✓	✓	✓	✓
	Managing Emotions	✗	✗	✗	✓	✓
	Considerate Approach	✓	✓	✓	✓	✓
Managing and Communicating existing and future work	Proactive work management	✓	✓	✓	✓	✓
	Problem Solving	✓	✗	✗	✓	✓
	Participative/empowering	✓	✓	✓	✓	✓
Reasoning/Managing difficult situations	Managing Conflict	✗	✗	✗	✗	✗
	Use of organizational resources	✗	✗	✗	✓	✓
	Taking responsibility for resolving issues	✗	✗	✗	✗	✗
Managing the individual within the team	Personally accessible	✓	✗	✗	✓	✓
	Sociable	✗	✗	✗	✗	✗
	Empathetic engagement	✓	✓	✓	✓	✓

Notes: Showing the mapping against: the Multifactor Leadership Questionnaire (MLQ-5X, Avolio, Bass and Jung, 1999); the Leader Behaviour Scale (LBS, Podsakoff, Mackenzie, Moorman, and Fetter, 1990); the Global Transformational Leadership Scale (GTL, Carless, Wearing and Mann, 2000); the Transformational Leadership Questionnaire (Public, Alimo-Metcalfe and Alban-Metcalfe, 2001); and the Transformational Leadership Questionnaire (Private, Alimo-Metcalfe and Alban-Metcalfe, 2001)

Adapted from Yarker, Donaldson-Feilder and Lewis (2008)

© Crown Copyright 2008

Table 11.2. Mapping the Positive Manager Behaviour (PMB) framework onto other management frameworks/metrics

PMB competency	PMB cluster	LBDQ	Great 8	SMP	ELS	ILS
Respectful and Responsible:						
Managing emotions and having integrity	Integrity	✓	✓	✓	✓	✓
	Managing Emotions	✗	✓	✗	✗	✗
	Considerate Approach	✓	✓	✓	✓	✗
Managing and Communicating existing and future work	Proactive work management	✓	✓	✓	✓	✓
	Problem Solving	✓	✓	✗	✗	✓
	Participative/empowering	✓	✓	✓	✓	✓
Reasoning/Managing difficult situations	Managing Conflict	✗	✗	✗	✗	✗
	Use of organizational resources	✗	✓	✗	✗	✗
	Taking responsibility for resolving issues	✗	✓	✗	✗	✗
Managing the individual within the team	Personally accessible	✓	✓	✓	✗	✓
	Sociable	✓	✓	✓	✗	✓
	Empathetic engagement	✓	✗	✓	✓	✓

Notes: Showing the mapping against: the Leader Behaviour Description Questionnaire (LBDQ, Stogdill, 1963); the Great 8 competency framework (Bartram, 2002); the Survey of Management Practices (SMP, Wilson and Wilson, 1991); the Ethical Leadership Scale (ELS, Brown, Trevino, and Harrison, 2005); and the Inspirational Leadership Scale developed by the DTI (ILS, Garrett and Frank, 2005)

Source: Adapted from Yarker, Donaldson-Feilder & Lewis (2008)
© Crown Copyright 2008

provide a summary of the findings of these mapping exercises, showing a ✓ where the Positive Manager Behaviour cluster is included in that particular framework and a × where it isn't.

Tables 11.1 and 11.2 show considerable variation between different models of management/leadership: what constitutes good management – and which bits of the Positive Manager Behaviour framework are included – depends on which model you adopt. Even the models of transformational leadership, which apparently measure the same overall construct, are different from one another and include different parts of the Positive Manager Behaviour framework. It becomes clear that all of the Positive Manager Behaviour clusters are covered by at least one of the other models of general good management/leadership. However, no one model includes all the Positive Manager Behaviour clusters.

Implications for Practice

Since any framework setting out 'good management' includes only a subset of the behaviours covered by the Positive Manager Behaviour framework, whichever framework the organization with which you are working is using (explicitly or implicitly), there will almost certainly be some elements of Positive Manager Behaviour that are not included. This in turn means that the organization, and its managers, will be missing out on some behaviours that are important for staff well-being. Thus, if an organization uses a particular general management competency framework to structure its appraisal and performance management, there will be elements of Positive Manager Behaviour that are not being recognized and valued; if an organization is using a particular general management competency framework to guide its management or leadership development programme, managers won't be receiving support or training to develop some elements of Positive Manager Behaviour.

The specific Positive Manager Behaviour behaviours that are missing from the organization with which you are working's framework will depend on which model of management is being used. As a practitioner, you can help the organization identify how any frameworks it is using compare with the Positive Manager Behaviour framework. Once you have identified which of the Positive Manager Behaviour elements are and are not currently included in the framework the organization is using, you can then help them integrate any behaviours that are missing. The following sections show you how to conduct a mapping exercise to do this kind of comparison and how to use the results to ensure that all the behaviours from the Positive Manager Behaviour framework are integrated.

How to Do Your Own Mapping

'Mapping' one behavioural model against another is simply a matter of comparing the behaviours covered by each framework with one another and seeing where the similarities and differences lie. To provide an example of a mapping, we will use the National Occupational Standards for management and leadership (NOSML) as the comparator framework and show how a mapping against the Positive Manager Behaviour framework looks.

The NOSML are 'statements of best practice which outline the performance criteria, related skills, knowledge and understanding required to effectively carry out various management and leadership functions'. They were developed by the Management Standards Centre, the UK's Government-recognized national standards setting body in management and leadership. They are designed to be applicable to managers and leaders in all sizes of organizations in all sectors and were updated in 2008. The mapping below uses the latest version.

Tables 11.3a, 11.3b, 11.3c and 11.3d show the results of mapping the NOSML against the Positive Manager Behaviour framework: in other words, they show which behaviours from the NOSML are similar to behaviours in the Positive Manager Behaviour framework. To generate this, we have taken all the 'behaviours which underpin effective performance' listed in the NOSML framework (which can be downloaded from www.management-standards.org) and, where we have identified that an NOSML behaviour is similar to a Positive Manager Behaviour indicator, we have listed the NOSML behaviour in the right hand column of the table.

The tables provided in the Appendix provide you with the Positive Manager Behaviour framework in a format that you can use to do your own mapping: just fill in the blank right-hand column with the behavioural descriptors from the organization with which you are working's framework that are similar or equivalent to the Positive Manager Behaviour indicators listed on the left.

An alternative approach would be to start with the organization with which you are working's management framework and identify which of the Positive Manager Behaviour indicators are similar or equivalent to the behaviours it contains. This way, the organization with which you are working's management behaviours would be on the left and the Positive Manager Behaviour indicators on the right.

Table 11.3a.　Positive Manager Behaviour mapped against the National Occupational Standards for Management and Leadership

		Competency: Respectful and responsible – Managing emotions and having integrity	
Cluster	Do (✓)/ Don't (✗)	Examples of manager behaviour	Relevant behaviours from the NOSML
Integrity	✓	■ Is a good role model ■ Treats team members with respect ■ Is honest	o You show integrity, fairness and consistency in decision-making. o You model behaviour that shows respect, helpfulness and co-operation. o You treat individuals with respect and act to uphold their rights. o You keep promises and honour commitments. o You keep confidential information secure. o Keep your commitments made to others. o You show an awareness of your own values, motivations and emotions.
	✗	■ Says one thing, then does something different ■ Speaks about team members behind their backs	
Managing emotions	✓	■ Acts calmly in pressured situations ■ Takes a consistent approach to managing	o You give a consistent and reliable performance.
	✗	■ Is unpredictable in mood ■ Passes on stress to employees ■ Panics about deadlines ■ Takes suggestions for improvement as a personal criticism	

Competency: Respectful and responsible – Managing emotions and having integrity

Cluster	Do (✓)/ Don't (×)	Examples of manager behaviour	Relevant behaviours from the NOSML
Considerate approach	×	■ Makes short term demands rather than allowing planning ■ Creates unrealistic deadlines ■ Gives more negative than positive feedback ■ Relies on others to deal with problems ■ Imposes 'my way is the only way' ■ Shows a lack of consideration for work–life balance	o You set demanding but achievable objectives for yourself and others. o You consider the impact of your own actions on others. o You show sensitivity to stakeholders' needs and interests and manage these effectively. o You recognize the achievements and the success of others. o You show respect for the views and actions of others. o You give feedback to others to help them develop their performance.

Source: Yarker, Donaldson-Feilder and Lewis (2008)
© Crown Copyright 2008

Table 11.3b. Positive Manager Behaviour mapped against the National Occupational Standards for Management and Leadership

Competency: Managing and communicating existing and future work

Cluster	Do (✓)/ Don't (×)	Examples of manager behaviour	Relevant behaviours from the NOSML
Proactive work management	✓	■ Clearly communicates employee job objectives ■ Develops action plans ■ Monitors team workload on an ongoing basis ■ Encourages team to review how they organize their work ■ Stops additional work being taken on when necessary ■ Works proactively ■ Sees projects/tasks through to delivery ■ Reviews processes to see if work can be improved ■ Prioritizes future workloads	o You recognize changes in circumstances promptly and adjust plans and activities accordingly. o You prioritize objectives and plan work to make best use of time and resources. o You clearly agree what is expected of others and hold them to account. o You anticipate likely future scenarios based on realistic analysis of trends and developments. o You constructively challenge the status quo and seek better alternatives. o You say no to unreasonable requests. o You work to turn unexpected events into opportunities rather than threats. o You try out new ways of working. o You identify systemic issues and trends and recognize their effect on current and future work. o You work towards a clearly defined vision of the future. o You identify the implications or consequences of a situation. o You protect your own and others' work against negative impacts. o You address multiple demands without losing focus or energy.

Competency: Managing and communicating existing and future work

Cluster	Do (✓)/ Don't (×)	Examples of manager behaviour	Relevant behaviours from the NOSML
			o You reflect regularly on your own and others' experiences, and use these to inform future action. o You constantly seek to improve performance. o You identify the range of elements in a situation and how they relate to each other. o You identify the implications or consequences of a situation. o You demonstrate an understanding of the objectives and priorities of the teams you support. o You make best use of available resources and proactively seek new sources of support when necessary. o You monitor the quality of work and progress against plans and take appropriate corrective action, where necessary. o You agree achievable objectives for yourself o You develop systems to gather and manage information and knowledge effectively, efficiently and ethically o You identify strengths, weaknesses, opportunities and threats to future and current work o You state own opinions, views and requirements clearly.

(continued)

Table 11.3b. *(Continued)*

		Competency: Managing and communicating existing and future work	
Cluster	Do (✓)/ Don't (×)	Examples of manager behaviour	Relevant behaviours from the NOSML
Problem solving	✓	■ Deals rationally with problems ■ Follows up problems on team's behalf ■ Deals with problems as soon as they arise	○ You find practical ways to overcome barriers. ○ You respond positively and creatively to setbacks. ○ You take and implement difficult and/or unpopular decisions, if necessary.
	×	■ Is indecisive at decision making	○ You take timely decisions that are realistic for the situation. ○ You respond quickly to crises and problems with a proposed course of action. ○ You find practical ways to overcome barriers. ○ You monitor the quality of work and progress against plans and take appropriate corrective action, where necessary. ○ You take repeated or different actions to overcome obstacles and respond positively and creatively to setbacks. ○ Identify problems with systems and procedures before they begin to affect your customers. ○ Identify the options for resolving a customer service problem. ○ You recognize recurring problems and promote changes to structures, systems and processes to resolve these.

Competency: Managing and communicating existing and future work			
Cluster	Do (✓)/ Don't (×)	Examples of manager behaviour	Relevant behaviours from the NOSML
Participative/ empowering	✓	■ Gives employees the right level of responsibility ■ Correctly judges when to consult and when to make a decision ■ Keeps employees informed of what is happening in the organization ■ Acts as a mentor ■ Provides regular team meetings ■ Delegates work equally ■ Helps team members develop in their role ■ Encourages team participation	○ You encourage and support others to take decisions autonomously. ○ You encourage and support others to make the best use of their abilities. ○ You identify people's information needs. ○ You keep people informed of plans and developments. ○ You make best use of existing sources of information. ○ You give feedback to others to help them develop their performance.
	×	■ Gives too little direction to employees	○ You encourage others to share information efficiently, within the constraints of confidentiality. ○ You create a common sense of purpose. ○ You make appropriate information and knowledge available promptly to those who need it and have a right to it. ○ You empower staff to solve customer problems within clear limits of authority. ○ You give people opportunities to provide feedback and you respond appropriately

Source: Yarker, Donaldson-Feilder and Lewis (2008)
© Crown Copyright 2008

Table 11.3c. Positive Manager Behaviour mapped against the National Occupational Standards for Management and Leadership

Competency: Managing the individual within the team

Cluster	Do (✓)/ Don't (×)	Examples of manager behaviour	Relevant behaviours from the NOSML
Personally accessible	✓	■ Speaks personally rather than uses email ■ Provides regular opportunities to speak one to one ■ Returns calls/emails promptly ■ Is available to talk to when needed	○ You make time available to support others.
Sociable	✓	■ Brings in treats ■ Socializes with the team ■ Is willing to have a laugh at work	
Empathetic engagement	✓	■ Encourages employee input in discussions ■ Listens when employees ask for help ■ Makes an effort to find out what motivates employees at work ■ Tries to see team members' point of view ■ Takes an interest in team's life outside work ■ Regularly asks 'how are you?' ■ Treats all team members with equal importance	○ You seek to understand people's needs and motivations. ○ You show empathy with others' needs, feelings and motivations and take an active interest in their concerns. ○ You use communication styles that are appropriate to different people and situations. ○ You identify people's preferred communication media and styles and adopt media and styles appropriate to different people and situations. ○ You use a range of leadership styles appropriate to different people and situations. ○ You seek to understand individuals' needs, feelings and motivations and take an active interest in their concerns. ○ You listen actively, ask questions, clarify points and rephrase others' statements to check mutual understanding. ○ You are alert to verbal and non-verbal communication signals and respond to them appropriately.
	×	■ Assumes rather than checks employees are OK	

Source: Yarker, Donaldson-Feilder and Lewis (2008)

© Crown Copyright 2008

Table 11.3d. Positive Manager Behaviour mapped against the National Occupational Standards for Management and Leadership

Cluster	Do (✓)/ Don't (×)	Examples of manager behaviour	Relevant behaviours from the NOSML
		Competency: Reasoning/Managing difficult situations	
Managing conflict	✓	▪ Acts as mediator in conflict situations ▪ Deals with squabbles before they become arguments ▪ Deals objectively with conflicts ▪ Deals with conflicts head on	○ You state your own position and views clearly and confidently in conflict situations. ○ You confront performance issues and sort them out directly with the people involved. ○ You recognize when there are conflicts, acknowledge the feelings and views of all parties, and redirect people's energy towards a common goal. ○ You act to uphold individuals' rights.
	×	▪ Acts to keep the peace rather than resolve issues	
Use of organizational resources	✓	▪ Seeks advice from other managers when necessary ▪ Uses HR as a resource to help deal with problems ▪ Seeks help from occupational health when necessary	○ You identify and work with people and organizations that can provide support for your work. ○ You consult with internal and/or external experts when necessary. ○ You make best use of available resources and proactively seek new sources of support when necessary.
Taking responsibility for resolving issues	✓	▪ Follows up conflicts after resolution ▪ Supports employees through incidents of abuse ▪ Makes it clear they will take ultimate responsibility if things go wrong	○ You take personal responsibility for making things happen.
	×	▪ Doesn't address bullying	

Source: Yarker, Donaldson-Feilder and Lewis (2008)
© Crown Copyright 2008

How to Identify Missing Positive Manager Behaviour Elements

Whichever way round you do the mapping, the key aim from a practical perspective is to identify which of the Positive Manager Behaviour elements are not included in the organization with which you are working's framework – i.e. the missing behaviours. If you have the Positive Manager Behaviour framework on the left, the missing behaviours will be identified by blank spaces in the right hand column. For example, in the sample mapping against the NOSML shown in Tables 11.3a, 11.3b, 11.3c and 11.3d, you can see that:

- The behaviours relating to the Positive Manager Behaviour cluster 'Sociable' are completely missing – they are not included in the NOSML framework at all.
- The Positive Manager Behaviour clusters 'Managing emotions', 'Personally accessible' and 'Taking responsibility for resolving issues' have only one similar behaviour from the NOSML behavioural lists, suggesting that they are not fully included in the model – they are at least partially missing from the NOSML framework.
- The Positive Manager Behaviour competency 'Managing and communicating existing and future work' is much better covered in the NOSML framework than the other three Positive Manager Behaviour competencies.

The missing behaviours identified in the mapping show which parts of the Positive Manager Behaviour framework are not currently covered by the interventions for which the management framework is being used. An organization might be using the NOSML framework to:

- guide its appraisal system for assessing manager performance;
- structure of its management and leadership development programme; or
- design its selection and promotion processes for recruiting people into management positions.

If so, the NOSML mapping in Tables 11.3a, 11.3b, 11.3c and 11.3d show that the cluster 'Sociable' would not be being covered at all and the clusters 'Managing emotions', 'Personally accessible' and 'Taking responsibility for resolving issues' would only partially/barely be being covered. Thus, if the organization wants to instil Positive Manager Behaviour into its workplaces, these clusters would need to be integrated or added back in.

How to Integrate Missing Positive Manager Behaviour Elements

In order to ensure that the full complement of behaviours that are important for staff stress/well-being are covered by the organization with which you are working's relevant policies and practices, you will need to find ways of adding in the missing behaviours. How this is done will, of course, depend on the intervention concerned, which behaviours are missing and the organizational context. Some ideas follow.

Appraisal systems

If the organization with which you are working uses a behavioural framework as part of its appraisal process, the missing behaviours can be added into the framework either by creating an additional assessment criterion or by adding the relevant behaviours as part of the specification of existing, relevant criteria. For example, if the existing appraisal forms don't include the cluster 'Integrity', an additional criterion could be added rating the manager on whether they do what they say they will do, are a good role model, treat team members with respect etc.

If the organization uses upward feedback or 360 degree feedback as part of its appraisal process, the questionnaire could be adapted to include additional questions relating to the missing behaviours. If the organization does not include upward or 360 degree feedback as part of its appraisal process, this could be an opportunity to consider doing so. (NB A questionnaire designed to measure whether a manager shows Positive Manager Behaviour is available on the HSE website and can be used in self-report, upward feedback and 360 degree feedback formats.)

Management and leadership development programmes

Our research suggests that this is one of the areas in which the findings of the Positive Manager Behaviour research are most likely to be used. Where the organization with which you are working has an existing management and leadership development programme and a mapping process has identified which Positive Manager Behaviour elements are covered and which are not, the missing behaviours can be integrated into the programme:

- either by adding additional modules that provide learning and development input (exercises, case studies, discussions etc.) specifically

on the missing areas: for example, adding a whole module on conflict management, covering all elements of that cluster;
- or by integrating the missing behaviours into existing modules, perhaps adding additional exercises to the module or broadening discussions to pick up the missing behaviours: for example, expanding a module on interpersonal skills so that it covers the behaviours in the cluster 'Empathic engagement'.

In addition, there is a range of ways in which the Positive Manager Behaviour framework could inform the design of management and leadership development programmes:

- Using the questionnaire developed during the Positive Manager Behaviour research to provide managers with upward (or 360 degree) feedback on the extent to which they are perceived by their employees (and others) to show the relevant behaviours. The results of the feedback can then be a basis from which the managers decide what learning and development input they need. For example, if the feedback identifies that a manager is not showing behaviours relating to conflict management, they can attend training targeted at that; or if the feedback reveals that a manager is not behaving in empathetic ways towards their employees, they can receive training or coaching to help them develop greater empathy. (A questionnaire is available on the HSE website that can be used to gather upward or 360 degree feedback about a particular manager.)
- Adding a workshop based on the Positive Manager Behaviour research as a module within an overall management and leadership development programme or providing a workshop as a standalone learning and development offering (materials are available on the HSE website to support practitioners in running such a workshop).
- Providing coaching for managers based on the Positive Manager Behaviour research – perhaps starting with an upward (or 360 degree) feedback process and then supporting the manager to develop in areas that the feedback shows to be development needs for them. (In addition to the questionnaire mentioned above, guidance is available on the HSE website on designing a coaching programme based on the Positive Manager Behaviour research.)
- Using the Positive Manager Behaviour framework as a check-list in the design of management and leadership development programmes or when designing training on related areas (such as communication, conflict management and workload planning).

Our research suggests that it could be particularly useful to integrate the Positive Manager Behaviour framework into induction training for managers. By setting expectations that managers will behave in the ways set out in the Positive Manager Behaviour framework from the start of their management careers, this can help them develop a management style that is good for staff well-being. It seems likely that it would be easier to adopt Positive Manager Behaviour from the start than to try and change behaviour later in one's management career.

Assessment and selection processes

When a mapping process has identified missing behaviours in an assessment and selection process, they can be added in by:

- generating specific behaviourally-based interview questions to add to an interview schedule;
- creating exercises based on the particular behaviours to include in an assessment or development centre;
- adding the behaviours to the criteria on which candidates are assessed during relevant exercises, interviews or discussions.

For more on how Positive Manager Behaviour can guide policies, practices and interventions in organisations, see Chapter 12.

Valuing People Management Skills

Including the Positive Manager Behaviour competencies in your management framework, management development etc, helps to put the emphasis on people management skills as compared with other aspects of management. Our research suggests that there is a need to help organizations make this shift in emphasis. We found that there is a tendency in some organizations to value 'technical' management skills rather than people management. In these situations, the emphasis is on managers achieving the task – hitting government targets, for example, or producing particular outputs in sales or delivery – and the way they treat their team is not given much attention.

In some cases, this emphasis on task at the expense of people is a result of the way people become managers and is a systemic issue built into the culture and practices of the organization; see Figure 11.3 for an example of this.

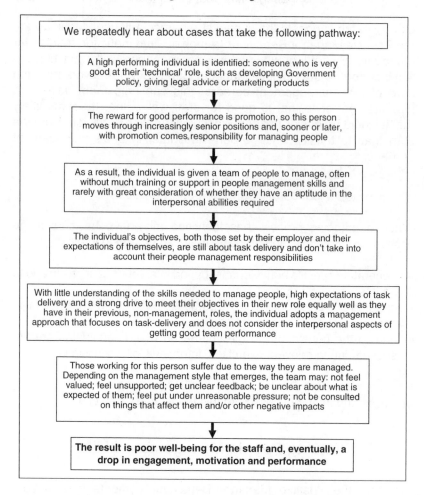

Figure 11.3   The promotion path to poor people management

It doesn't have to be this way. If employers put more emphasis on good people management, including providing managers with development opportunities that emphasize managing people, and assessing managers' performance on the interpersonal aspects of their role, then it can become embedded in the culture and expectations of the organization. The chain of events shown in Figure 11.3 can be changed at each of the stages to ensure a different outcome, as shown in Figure 11.4.

As can be seen from Figure 11.4, establishing a culture of good people management is partly about effective learning and development interventions at induction and throughout a manager's career. It could also include talent management practices – using appropriate promotion routes for those with the potential to manage people and those who would be better staying in 'technical' roles. And it involves ongoing support and feedback to ensure that managers' people management skills are maintained, encouraged and valued.

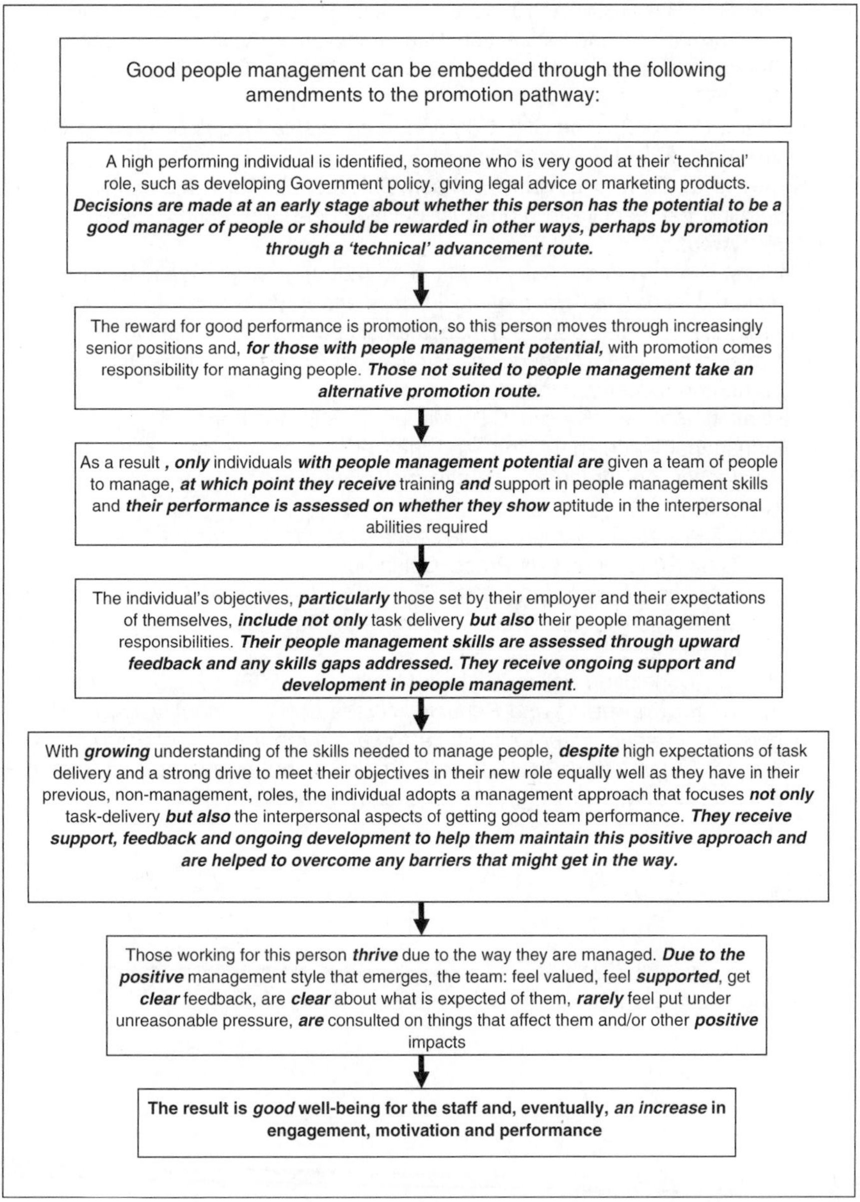

Good people management can be embedded through the following amendments to the promotion pathway:

A high performing individual is identified, someone who is very good at their 'technical' role, such as developing Government policy, giving legal advice or marketing products. *Decisions are made at an early stage about whether this person has the potential to be a good manager of people or should be rewarded in other ways, perhaps by promotion through a 'technical' advancement route.*

The reward for good performance is promotion, so this person moves through increasingly senior positions and, *for those with people management potential,* with promotion comes responsibility for managing people. *Those not suited to people management take an alternative promotion route.*

As a result *, only* individuals *with people management potential are* given a team of people to manage, *at which point they receive* training *and* support in people management skills and *their performance is assessed on whether they show* aptitude in the interpersonal abilities required

The individual's objectives, *particularly* those set by their employer and their expectations of themselves, *include not only* task delivery *but also* their people management responsibilities. *Their people management skills are assessed through upward feedback and any skills gaps addressed. They receive ongoing support and development in people management.*

With *growing* understanding of the skills needed to manage people, *despite* high expectations of task delivery and a strong drive to meet their objectives in their new role equally well as they have in their previous, non-management, roles, the individual adopts a management approach that focuses *not only* task-delivery *but also* the interpersonal aspects of getting good team performance. *They receive support, feedback and ongoing development to help them maintain this positive approach and are helped to overcome any barriers that might get in the way.*

Those working for this person *thrive* due to the way they are managed. *Due to the positive* management style that emerges, the team: feel valued, feel *supported*, get *clear* feedback, are *clear* about what is expected of them, *rarely* feel put under unreasonable pressure, *are* consulted on things that affect them and/or other *positive* impacts

The result is *good* well-being for the staff and, eventually, *an increase* in engagement, motivation and performance

Figure 11.4 Alternative promotion path to good people management

References

Alimo-Metcalfe, B. and Alban-Metcalfe, R.J. (2001). The development of a transformational leadership questionnaire. *Journal of Occupational and Organizational Psychology*, 74, 1–27.

Avolio, B.J., Bass, B.M. and Jung, D.L. (1999). Re-examining the components of transformational and transactional leadership using the Multifactor Leadership Questionnaire. *Journal of Occupational and Organisational Psychology*, 72 (4), 441–463.

Bartram, D. (2002). *The SHL Corporate Leadership Model.* SHL White Paper. Version 1.1.9. SHL Group Plc.

Brown, M.E., Treviño, L.K. and Harrison, D.A. (2005). Ethical leadership: A socio learning perspective for construct development and testing. *Organisational Behaviour*, 97, 117–134.

Carless, S.A., Wearing, A.J. and Mann, L. (2000). A short measure of transformational leadership. *Journal of Business and Psychology*, 14, 389–405.

Garrett, J. and Frank, J. (2005) *Inspirational Leadership – Insight to Action. The Development of the Inspired Leadership Tool.* Caret Consulting, Department of Trade and Industry, London.

Podsakoff, P.M., MacKenzie, S.B., Moorman, R.H. and Fetter, R. (1990). Transformational leader behaviors and their effects on followers' trust in leader, satisfaction, and organizational citizenship behaviors. *Leadership Quarterly*, 1, 107–142.

Stogdill, R.M. (1963). *Manual for the Leader Behavior Description Questionnaire.* The Ohio State University Press, Columbus.

Wilson, C.L. and Wilson, J.L. (1991). *Teams and Leaders: A Manual for the Clark Wilson Publishing Company Training and Development Programs*, Clark Wilson Group, Silver Spring, MD.

Yarker, J., Donaldson-Feilder, E.J. and Lewis, R. (2008) *Management Competencies for Preventing and Reducing Stress at Work: Identifying and Developing the Management Behaviours Necessary to Implement the HSE Management Standards: Phase 2.* HSE Books, Norwich, available on the HSE website: http://www.hse.gov.uk/research/rrhtm/rr633.htm.

12

The way forward

The aim of this book has been to give you an understanding of Positive Manager Behaviour, as derived from our research, and how it might be applied in organizations. This final chapter aims to orientate you in terms of where you are now and how you might use the Positive Manager Behaviour framework in your own organization/practice. It takes a step-by-step approach as follows:

- Working out where you are now
- Starting out – understanding Positive Manager Behaviour and how it might be useful
- Deciding how to use Positive Manager Behaviour
- Gaining buy-in
- Applying Positive Manager Behaviour
- Achieving sustainable impact

Where are you Now?

Figure 12.1 sets out the step-by-step approach we suggest, providing a process that you may want to follow in order to apply Positive Manager

Preventing Stress in Organizations: How to Develop Positive Managers,
Emma Donaldson-Feilder, Joanna Yarker and Rachel Lewis.
© 2011 John Wiley & Sons, Ltd. Published 2011 by John Wiley & Sons, Ltd.

Behaviour in an organization. You may be some way through the process already, in which case the flow chart may help you situate yourself at a point along the journey and clarify your next steps. It also provides some key questions for each stage.

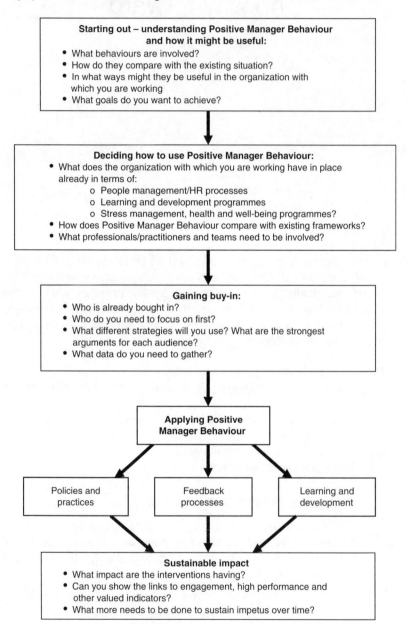

Starting out – understanding Positive Manager Behaviour and how it might be useful:
- What behaviours are involved?
- How do they compare with the existing situation?
- In what ways might they be useful in the organization with which you are working
- What goals do you want to achieve?

Deciding how to use Positive Manager Behaviour:
- What does the organization with which you are working have in place already in terms of:
  - o People management/HR processes
  - o Learning and development programmes
  - o Stress management, health and well-being programmes?
- How does Positive Manager Behaviour compare with existing frameworks?
- What professionals/practitioners and teams need to be involved?

Gaining buy-in:
- Who is already bought in?
- Who do you need to focus on first?
- What different strategies will you use? What are the strongest arguments for each audience?
- What data do you need to gather?

Applying Positive Manager Behaviour

Policies and practices

Feedback processes

Learning and development

Sustainable impact
- What impact are the interventions having?
- Can you show the links to engagement, high performance and other valued indicators?
- What more needs to be done to sustain impetus over time?

Figure 12.1 Where are you now?

Starting Out – Understanding Positive Manager Behaviour and How It Might Be Useful

The fact that you are reading this book means that you are at least in the first box of Figure 12.1: you have started to explore Positive Manager Behaviour and perhaps considered its usefulness. Hopefully, Chapters 5, 6, 7 and 8 have given you a good feel for the behaviours involved in each of the four competencies of the Positive Manager Behaviour framework.

As you read through the behavioural descriptors within the Positive Manager Behaviour framework and the various case studies, you will have had a chance to think about how they compare with the management behaviour you experience in your day-to-day work. Perhaps you thought about the way your own manager behaves. If you are an external consultant, perhaps you reflected on the different management styles you have seen in different client organizations. In some organizations, where a 'command and control' or 'laissez faire' management approach is the norm, introducing Positive Manager Behaviour might constitute a complete culture change. In other organizations, managers have the intention to behave in positive ways, but barriers get in the way and stop them from doing so – or perhaps some managers show Positive Manager Behaviour and others don't.

In what ways might Positive Manager Behaviour be useful?

Reflecting on the extent to which managers in the organization(s) with which you are working already show Positive Manager Behaviour will give you an initial sense of whether and how the competency framework could be useful.

- If you work *in-house* in HR, Occupational health/well-being, Health and Safety or other relevant department, you may feel that you want to find ways of integrating Positive Manager Behaviour into organizational policies, practices or interventions. You may decide that specific interventions to introduce Positive Manager Behaviour would be useful.
- If you work as an *external* consultant, you may feel that Positive Manager Behaviour could be integrated into your existing client offerings or you may see it as an opportunity to add new services to your portfolio.

The following sections are taken from the perspective of working with a particular organization to introduce and/or integrate the competencies. However, they will hopefully also spark ideas and support external consultants in terms of how they might use the Positive Manager Behaviour framework and research findings in their practice.

What goals do you want to achieve?

In order to set the context for your activities relating to Positive Manager Behaviour, it would probably be helpful to think at an early stage about what you want to achieve. You may be clear about your goals right from the start or you may prefer to set goals once you have decided how to use the competencies in the next step.

Setting clear goals can help you focus on why you are doing what you are doing, what outcomes you are seeking and how you will know whether you have achieved these outcomes. Your goals may be:

- ambitious (e.g., achieve culture change to establish Positive Manager Behaviour as the norm in this organization) or more limited (e.g., work with at least two teams to improve managers' Positive Manager Behaviour skills);
- about immediate outcomes (e.g., improved scores on the management competencies indicator tool questionnaire) or more distal measures (e.g., improved staff well-being);
- about the process (e.g., achieve multi-disciplinary working to implement a Positive Manager Behaviour initiative) or the outcome (e.g., behaviour change, well-being).

Whatever goals you set, it is important to ensure they are SMART:

- *Specific* – be clear and precise about what you want to achieve;
- *Measurable* – clarify how you will know whether you achieve them;
- *Agreed* – get agreement from those whose support will be instrumental in achieving the goals, be they other professionals, senior management or the part of the organization with which you are working;
- *Realistic* – don't set yourself up for failure; and
- *Timed* – have specific timescales and milestones.

Deciding How to Use Positive Manager Behaviour

Exactly what will be the best way to use Positive Manager Behaviour in a particular organization will depend on the current situation in that organization. Our research suggests that initiatives to help managers show Positive Manager Behaviour are most likely to be effective if they are linked to, or integrated with, existing activities within the organization. We have also found that Positive Manager Behaviour is relevant to a number of different areas and can be a bridge between, for example, well-being initiatives and people management, so it may have relevance beyond what you initially envisage. Thus, in order to decide how best to use Positive Manager Behaviour, it would be advisable to spend some time exploring and reflecting on what the organization has in place already and how the Positive Manager Behaviour framework compares with any existing frameworks.

What does the organization have in place already?

Since Positive Manager Behaviour is relevant to a range of domains, it would be useful to review what the organization with which you are working has in place in all of the following areas:

1. *HR/People management processes*: In order to make Positive Manager Behaviour the norm for all those in management positions in the organization, it may be helpful to integrate the framework into the range of HR processes that give managers an indication of what is expected of them. For example, performance management and appraisal, selection and assessment, and talent management may all be relevant. This means that, before deciding how to use the competencies in the organization with which you are working, it would be helpful to understand what is in place in these areas. Organizations vary enormously in the degree of structure underpinning their HR practices. In the organization with which you are working:
   - Are these practices underpinned by an explicit model of management/leadership that sets out the behaviours managers are expected to show?
   - Or are the underpinning expectations of management behaviour more implicit and/or unstructured?
   - Or are manager behaviours not really considered at all in these practices?

2. *Learning and development programmes*: Many managers will need support and development to help them show Positive Manager Behaviour. As mentioned in previous chapters, helping managers understand and adopt Positive Manager Behaviour right from the start of their management career is probably the best way of getting them to show these behaviours on a long-term basis – simpler than having to change behaviour once they have been in management positions for a while. However, managers may need support throughout their management careers. Reviewing the learning and development that is provided for managers, ask yourself:
   - How do the organization's induction processes, particularly those for new managers, set behavioural expectations?
   - What is included in management and/or leadership development programmes and how are they delivered?
   - What is included in other interpersonal skills courses, such as conflict management and coaching skills?

- Where might Positive Manager Behaviour fit into any or all of these learning and development programmes, where is already be covered and where does it need reinforcing?

3. *Stress management and well-being programmes*: Our research shows that looking at Positive Manager Behaviour can be a way to establish a bridge between people management/management development on the one hand and staff well-being/stress management on the other. It can be an excellent way of integrating diverse initiatives. Therefore, it would be useful to understand how getting managers to show Positive Manager Behaviour might fit with any well-being or stress management activities in the organization with which you are working, including policies, stress risk assessment, stress management training and other well-being initiatives. Even if stress management activities are limited to training to help individuals manage their own stress, this may be relevant as managers being able to manage their own emotions and handle pressure effectively for themselves is a vital part of Positive Manager Behaviour.

The check list in Table 12.1 may be helpful as you review all the different facets of what the organization already has in place.

How does Positive Manager Behaviour compare with existing frameworks?

As mentioned earlier, some or all of the relevant practices may be underpinned by an explicit model of management/leadership that sets out the behaviours managers are expected to show: alternatively, the way manager behaviours are specified may be more implicit and/or unstructured. For example, a management development programme may be designed based on a particular management or leadership model; an appraisal process may use a management framework to define the manager behaviours expected of line managers – it may even include upward or 360 degree feedback using a questionnaire covering specific management behaviours. The management or leadership model/framework used in these cases may either be taken from a broadly used approach to management/leadership (such as transformational leadership or one of the commercially available frameworks) or it may be a tailored framework developed specifically for the organization involved.

If the organization uses a particular model of management behaviour, the likelihood is that a proportion of the behaviours set out in the Positive Manager Behaviour framework will be covered. As shown in Chapter 11, there is a high degree of overlap between the Positive Manager Behaviour framework and general good management: however, we have found no other management model that covers all the behaviours set out in the

Table 12.1. Checklist for reviewing what the organization already has in place

Practice or process	In place? (Y/N)	Description of existing situation – including who is responsible	Ways in which Positive Manager Behaviour could be integrated
HR/People management			
Appraisal/performance management processes (Do these specify manager behaviours? What framework do they use? How are development needs picked up and addressed? Do managers get upward or 360 degree feedback? If so, what does it cover and how is it fed back and followed up?)			
Manager selection and assessment processes (Do these assess people management behaviours and, if so, how? What framework do they use? How much weight is given to people management?)			
Talent management practices (Are internal promotions and succession planning considered in a systematic and strategic manner? Is people management potential considered when considering promotions and identifying those with 'high potential'? Is there a non-people management promotion path for those unlikely to be good at managing people? Do 'high potential' individuals get development input on people management and, if so, what?)			

(continued)

Table 12.1 (*Continued*)

Practice or process	In place? (Y/N)	Description of existing situation – including who is responsible	Ways in which Positive Manager Behaviour could be integrated
Learning and development			
Induction programmes (Are there induction programmes specifically for managers? Do they set behavioural expectations relating to people management and, if so, how?)			
Management and/or leadership development programmes (What do these cover? To what extent are people management and interpersonal skills emphasized? How are programmes delivered? Do they involve a development centre? Coaching? Upward or 360 degree feedback? Modules spread over time or intensive course? Internal or external provider?)			
Interpersonal and personal skills training (What training is provided in areas such as conflict management, coaching skills, delegation, handling difficult conversations, team building, negotiation etc? What is the content of these courses and how are they delivered? Are managers expected to attend? Internal or external provider?)			

Stress management/well-being

Stress management or well-being policy or other relevant policies (Do any policies set out responsibilities for managers? Do they specify how managers should behave and, if so, how? How are policies rolled out? How is delivery of policies monitored?)				
Stress risk assessment (At what level is risk to health and well-being assessed – organization, department, team, individual? How are the results used to minimize risks? What is the role of line managers? Are local diagnostics used to link stress risk to manager behaviour and, if so, how?)				
Stress management/well-being training for managers (Does any training include input on how managers prevent stress? Are relevant manager behaviours covered? Is the training compulsory? Is it part of a broader programme – either of management development or stress management/well-being initiatives?)				
Stress management training for individuals (Does any training help individuals manage their own emotions? Is it provided to managers?)				
Other stress management/well-being activities (What else is the organization doing to improve staff well-being/reduce stress? Is the role of line managers explicitly covered?)				

Positive Manager Behaviour framework. This means that there are likely to be manager behaviours that are important for the well-being of those being managed that are not currently assessed/developed in the organization with which you are working.

In order to establish which manager behaviours are and are not included in the organization with which you are working's existing framework, we recommend conducting a 'mapping' exercise between the two frameworks. Chapter 11 provides information on how to do this, together with a table you can complete to conduct your own mapping; it also helps explore how to identify missing behaviours and how they might be integrated into the organization with which you are working's framework/practices.

What professionals/practitioners and teams need to be involved?

Conducting the reviews outlined will help show you all the different activities in the organization with which you are working that are relevant to Positive Manager Behaviour. It will hopefully also have identified who is responsible for each activity. For example, the appraisal process may be the responsibility of the HR team, while learning and development is managed by a separate Training team, and stress management/staff well-being may be part of the Health and Safety or Occupational Health team's remit. This will show you which other professionals, practitioners and teams are or should be, directly or indirectly, involved in enabling managers in the organization with which you are working to show Positive Manager Behaviour.

Our research suggests that initiatives to help managers show Positive Manager Behaviour are most likely to be successful if you take a multi-disciplinary approach. When the range of professionals (HR, L&D, H&S, OH etc) is working together, they are more likely to:

- achieve buy-in from the organization;
- ensure that Positive Manager Behaviour is linked into the relevant existing activities;
- ensure that appropriate support is provided to managers; and
- maintain continuity over time.

Getting the relevant individuals and teams on board may therefore be an important first step to an effective Positive Manager Behaviour programme.

Gaining Buy-In

In order to implement successful Positive Manager Behaviour initiatives, it is essential to get buy-in from the key individuals. Without the support and engagement of the main players and decision-makers, the likelihood is that, even if you get the initiative started, you will find it hits the buffers, stalls or requires inordinate amounts of effort to drive through. So, an analysis of who these key individuals are and how to get their buy-in is a vital next step in the process of implementation.

Who are the key players?

The answer to this question will depend on the situation in the organization with which you are working. However, some groups to consider are:

- *Other professionals/practitioners*: As mentioned earlier, taking a multi-disciplinary approach is likely to boost effectiveness, so your gaining buy-in campaign may need to start with the range of professionals on whose work the initiatives touch. This may include HR, Learning and Development, Health and Safety, Occupational Health and others.
- *Senior management*: Without the support of those at the top of the organization, it is hard to get the resources and impetus needed to secure this kind of initiative. This is particularly true if implementing Positive Manager Behaviour initiatives requires a shift in management style or culture. Getting those in senior positions to role model Positive Manager Behaviour and cascading the approach from the top of the organization throughout all levels in the management hierarchy is the ideal way to embed the approach. At the very least, having some senior management champions, together with backing in the form of resources and statements of support, will be important.
- *Line managers*: As described in Chapter 10, if you are helping managers change their behaviour, they will need to be persuaded that it is worth their while doing so. This is particularly true if you are planning to undertake an upward or 360 degree feedback process and/or learning and development activities.
- *Employees and their representatives*: If you are planning to run an upward or 360 degree feedback process for managers, you will need their employees to complete questionnaires about them. Individuals may need persuading that it is worth their while to do this.

What messages can you use to gain buy-in?

It will be important to use messages about the initiative that are persuasive to those whose buy-in you are seeking. This may vary depending on the audience you are targeting. Some ideas might be:

- For organizations that like to take an evidence-based, scientific or structured approach it might be helpful to emphasize the credibility of the research underpinning the Positive Manager Behaviour framework. The research reports available on the HSE and CIPD websites give full details and we have found that some people feel that the rigorous research process that led to the development of the frame-work is important for credibility.

- Professionals/practitioners may be keen to participate if they see the initiative as a way of enhancing the content and/or success of their programmes or practices through linking them to or adding in Positive Manager Behaviour – see 'What does the organization already have in place'.
- Senior managers may be most interested in the business case or benefits in terms of performance/service delivery that the initiative can generate or the legal responsibility to ensure staff well-being – see Chapter 2 for information on the business and legal cases and Chapter 10 for more on gaining senior manager buy-in.
- Line managers may be more likely to be persuaded by the team-level benefits of the initiative – Chapter 10 looks at some of the potential barriers to manager buy-in and how they might be overcome.
- Individual employees may be most interested in the effect of Positive Manager Behaviour on their well-being and job satisfaction. They may have concerns about confidentiality of any feedback they provide – see Chapter 10 for more on feedback confidentiality.

In some cases, you may need to gather data to prepare persuasive arguments, for example, to be able to cite the cost of stress-related sickness absence to the organization or team, the impact on productivity etc.

How can you best get messages across?

Of course, the best way to get across the key messages will depend on the particular circumstances and audiences involved. It is worth considering how to reach different people most effectively. For example, senior managers may need to be talked to one-to-one or at an executive team meeting; whereas individual staff members may best be reached through email, team meetings or in-house communication mechanisms (notice boards, newsletters, intranet sites).

Putting together a multi-disciplinary steering group or implementation team may be a helpful way of getting the relevant professionals around the table and involving them in decisions. In some cases, it may be appropriate to include a broad range of people in a steering group, from senior management to front-line staff and across the range of departments within the organization. This can help not only ensure that the activities planned are shaped by those who will be involved, but also that the messages about what is happening are disseminated at a local level by individuals drawn from all parts of the organization.

The checklist in Table 12.2 is designed to help you think through who are your audiences and how you gain their buy-in.

Table 12.2. Checklist for gaining buy-in

Part of the organization	Priority ranking/ order	Who are the key players and who is already bought in?	What messages will gain these people's buy-in?	How can you best get the messages across?	What do you need to do to prepare for and then communicate with these people?
Other practitioners (e.g., HR, Health & Safety, Occupational Health, Learning & Development)					
Senior management					
Line managers					
Employees and their representatives (unions, consultative committees etc)					
Other					

Applying Positive Manager Behaviour

As you will have gathered from this chapter so far and from Chapter 11, there is a multitude of ways in which the Positive Manager Behaviour framework and related findings from our research can be applied. It may be integrated into existing activities, used to enhance and add to existing activities, or be the basis for a new initiative. For simplicity, we will look at application in terms of three approaches:

- policy and practice;
- diagnostic/feedback; and
- learning and development.

These three areas are by no means mutually exclusive: you may choose to apply the Positive Manager Behaviour framework in any or all of them. See also Chapter 11 for ideas on integrating Positive Manager Behaviour elements found to be missing from the organization's existing framework.

Policy and practice

One way of applying Positive Manager Behaviour in organizations is to embed the competencies into relevant policies and practices. Since Positive Manager Behaviour is relevant to a range of practices relating to people management, HR, learning and development, and staff well-being, it may even be a way of linking and integrating these different areas. For example:

1. *HR/people management*: the Positive Manager Behaviour framework and associated behavioural indicators can be used to revise existing policy/practice or to develop new policy/practice in areas such as: appraisal and performance management; manager assessment and selection; and talent management. Where these are already based on a behavioural/competency framework, conducting a mapping exercise (see details of how to do this in Chapter 11) can identify any behaviours from the Positive Manager Behaviour framework that are missing. Decisions can then be taken about whether and how the missing behaviours can be added in. Where these policies/practices are not currently based on a specific behavioural/competency framework, the Positive Manager Behaviour framework can be integrated as a basis or to guide activities. Examples might include:
   - *Appraisal and performance management*: the Positive Manager Behaviour framework could be added to appraisal forms to ensure that managers' appraisals take into account the degree to which they show Positive Manager Behaviour.

- *Assessment and selection*: the behavioural indicators from the Positive Manager Behaviour framework could be used to design behaviour/competency-based interview questions or exercises for an assessment centre.
- *Talent management*: the Positive Manager Behaviour framework could be used as a basis for considering whether 'high potential' individuals have the capacity to show Positive Manager Behaviour, which could help determine the promotion routes they take. This might be assessed through appraisal, assessment/development centre or, when they have people management responsibility, through upward or 360 degree feedback.

2. *Learning and development*: the Positive Manager Behaviour framework may be relevant to a range of different learning and development policies, including: induction; management and leadership development; and interpersonal and personal skills training. It might provide a guiding framework, setting out what behavioural areas need to be covered in these different learning and development activities. Alternatively, it might be a source of information and inspiration for the design of particular parts of a training programme (see section on learning and development interventions). Another option is that the management competencies indicator tool, used as an upward or 360 degree feedback questionnaire might be introduced as a way of helping managers understand their learning and development needs (see section on diagnostic/feedback).

3. *Stress management/health and well-being*: here the Positive Manager Behaviour framework may inform policies and/or be part of intervention practices. For example:
   - *Stress management/well-being policy*: where this kind of policy sets out responsibilities and expectations, the Positive Manager Behaviour framework can be used to help indicate what is expected of managers in terms of how their people management approach prevents and reduces stress/improves staff well-being.
   - *Stress risk assessment*: where an organization-wide stress risk assessment is conducted, perhaps including use of a staff survey, Positive Manager Behaviour can be used to inform local level follow-up diagnosis and/or intervention. For example, if a risk assessment identifies management behaviour as a source of stress, the management competencies indicator tool questionnaire can be used to identify exactly what manager behaviours are the problem and where (see section on diagnostic/feedback) and/or learning and development interventions based on the framework can be used as a risk-reduction intervention (see section on learning and development interventions). Alternatively, if the risk assessment identifies particular hotspot departments or

teams with high stress risk levels, the management competencies indicator tool can be used to help managers in these areas understand how their behaviour may be contributing to the problem and what they might need to change to reduce stress risks.

- *Stress management/well-being interventions*: where an organization has a programme of stress management/well-being interventions – perhaps training or team-based interventions – the Positive Manager Behaviour framework can help integrate manager behaviour into it. This may be through integration into training programmes or as a team level diagnostic.

Diagnostic/feedback

A second way of applying Positive Manager Behaviour is to use it in a diagnostic or feedback process. During our research, we developed a questionnaire to measure the extent to which a particular manager shows the behaviours set out in the Positive Manager Behaviour framework. This questionnaire is called the 'management competencies indicator tool' and consists of 66 questions covering the four competencies/12 clusters. It can be used as:

- a self-report measure, for managers to rate their own behaviour;
- an upward feedback measure, in which the manager's direct reports provide feedback on the manager's behaviour (which can be compared with the manager's own perspective); or
- a 360 degree feedback measure, where a range of people, including direct reports, manager(s) and peers provide feedback, which is again compared with the manager's self-rating.

Our research suggests that upward feedback is an important factor in helping managers change their behaviour (see more in Chapter 10). While completing a self-report questionnaire can help managers reflect on their behaviour and may motivate some change, it cannot tell the manager how their behaviour is perceived by others. Research and experience suggest that managers are not always terribly accurate at judging how they come across to others or the impact they are having on their staff. We have probably all had experiences of managers who seemed very out of touch with their effect on (us) their employees! In our research, we found that there were often differences between the manager's self-score and the score given by their staff:

- Sometimes the manager had a more positive view of their people management approach. In these cases, 'blind spots' and new areas of development could be identified.

- Other managers actually had a more negative view of their skills and were pleasantly surprised by the positive feedback they received. For these individuals, the feedback on their 'hidden strengths' provided reassurance and a chance to look at how they could better use their management strengths.

Of course, this kind of feedback process also generates understanding of known strengths and weaknesses, where both the manager and their staff give high or low scores. These can be used to emphasize strengths that the manager can build upon and/or development needs that can be addressed through learning and development. Table 12.3 provides a representation of the different permutations of self vs. employee feedback.

Table 12.3. The different permutations of self vs. employee feedback

		Manager rating of own behaviour	
		High	*Low*
Employee rating of manager behaviour	*High*	*Known strength* Feedback confirms that this is an area of strength on which the manager can build	*Hidden strength* Feedback provides new insights on a strength on which the manager can build
	Low	*Blind spot* Feedback uncovers a development need the manager did not recognize before	*Known development need* Feedback confirms a development need that the manager knew they needed to work on

As highlighted in Chapter 10, receiving feedback of this kind can act as a motivator for the manager to change their behaviour and address the development needs identified. It can, therefore, be a powerful first step in a learning and development intervention. This might form part of either a management development programme or a stress management/well-being programme:

- *In management development*: the feedback process might be used at an early stage or before the start of the development intervention to ensure that development activities are focused on the behavioural areas identified as development needs. This might be part of a development centre or an appraisal process that identifies development needs or could be a stand-alone activity.

- *In stress management/well-being*: the feedback might form the next step after a stress risk assessment has identified that management skills are a stress risk and/or particular departments or teams have high levels of stress risk. Our research suggests that using the questionnaire to provide feedback to individual managers can be a way of getting their buy-in and helping them understand the issues at the local, behavioural level.

Resource

Self-report, self plus other and 360 degree feedback versions of the management competencies indicator tool are all available for free download from the HSE website at: http://www.hse.gov.uk/ and http://preventingstress.hse.gov.uk/. We also know of at least one commercial provider that offers the questionnaire as an online 360 degree feedback tool.

Learning and development interventions

The third way the Positive Manager Behaviour framework can be used is as a basis for learning and development interventions to help managers show the behaviours identified. In these situations, the intervention is about achieving behaviour change where Positive Manager Behaviour is not being shown and reinforcing Positive Manager Behaviour where it is already being shown. Such interventions can be guided by the results of a diagnostic process using the management competencies indicator tool as outlined in the previous section. See Chapter 10 for more on supporting behaviour change in this context.

In terms of the positioning and roll-out of this kind of learning and development intervention, there are a number of issues to consider:

1. *Integration into management development or stress management/well-being training*: As discussed earlier, Positive Manager Behaviour is relevant to both management development and stress management/well-being agendas. Overall, our research suggests that it will enhance effectiveness to integrate any learning and development relating to Positive Manager Behaviour into existing initiatives (see Chapter 10). Often, where it sits in a particular organization will depend on the background of the practitioner driving the initiative: the ideal is to take a multi-disciplinary approach. If possible, Positive Manager Behaviour could provide the means to bridge or integrate the relevant programmes, showing the relevance of good people management to staff well-being and vice versa.

2. *Stand-alone intervention or module(s) for integration*: During our research, we designed a stand-alone learning and development intervention based on the Positive Manager Behaviour framework. This consisted of an upward feedback process, followed by a workshop and then a further upward feedback process three months later to look at whether managers had changed their behaviour. The workshop aimed to:

- help managers understand the importance of Positive Manager Behaviour;
- increase awareness of their own behaviour (in particular, by understanding their feedback report); and
- equip them with the tools to further enhance or develop their skills (by understanding the key management behaviours, identifying their development needs, and planning the changes they wanted to make, together with the support they would need to seek).

We established that behaviour change is possible: those who were not showing Positive Manager Behaviour before the intervention increased the degree to which they were showing these behaviours by the three month follow-up point. So, it is possible to deliver a stand-alone intervention in this way. However, it would also be possible to use the Positive Manager Behaviour framework to generate a module or a series of modules addressing the relevant behaviours in order to fit in with a broader learning and development programme.

3. *Coaching vs group workshop/training*: So far, most of our implementation of learning and development interventions to help managers show Positive Manager Behaviour has been in the form of group workshops and training. The advantage of this is that you can address a number of managers in a short period of time and there are opportunities for managers to learn from and support one another. However, there are limitations to this format as it cannot provide individually tailored input or ongoing support over time to ensure that managers continue to address their development needs and change their behaviour. For some managers, providing a programme of coaching may be an effective way of supporting them over time and helping them achieve sustainable behaviour change. Coaching can allow the manager to try out new ways of behaviour in the workplace, reflect on it with their coach and make further changes as appropriate; it can support them in overcoming barriers that they meet that might otherwise stop them showing Positive Manager Behaviours; and it can give them space to reflect on the progress they make and what more they need to do. Another possibility might be to provide managers with action learning sets so that a group of individuals support one another in the process of behaviour change over time.

Resource

If you are planning to design a learning and development intervention to help managers show Positive Manager Behaviour, we hope that the contents of this book will give you much of the information, materials, case studies and exercises you need.

In addition, we have developed a range of online materials, based on our research, that aim to support learning and development interventions addressing the behaviours covered by the Positive Manager Behaviour framework. These are free to access/download from the HSE website at http://www.hse.gov.uk/ and http://preventingstress.hse.gov.uk/. In addition to the questionnaires already mentioned, they include:

- *Materials for line managers to access and use directly*: these are e-learning materials such as case studies, podcasts, video clips and reflection exercises designed to help managers understand the key behaviours and support them in changing their behaviour. They could be used by organizations for e-learning or as part of a blended learning programme (research suggests it may be more effective to combine e-learning with other mechanisms to give a fuller learning and development experience).
- *Materials for practitioners to use in their work supporting managers*: these are designed for use by consultants, trainers, coaches, learning and development professionals and other practitioners to help them implement learning and development interventions based on the Positive Manager Behaviour research. They include a range of materials such as case studies, exercises, videos, a workshop timetable, work-book and presentation, ideas for a coaching programme and advice on how to enhance the effectiveness of interventions based on these materials.

Sustainable Impact

Whatever you do relating to Positive Manager Behaviour, if you are looking to achieve a sustainable and long-term impact, it is important both to measure the impact you are having and also to find ways of sustaining the impetus and maintaining the benefits achieved.

Evaluating outcomes

Assuming you set SMART goals at the start, you will have had in mind throughout the process the outcomes you were aiming to achieve and how you would measure them. Depending on your aims, you may need to instigate a specific activity to measure your outcomes, or you may be able to use statistics that are gathered as a matter of course anyway. For example:

- If your goal was to achieve manager behaviour change, you will need to measure managers' behaviour at the start and then again at a follow-up point after your intervention, so that you can compare scores to see if there has been a change. You can use the management competencies indicator tool questionnaire to do this, preferably using upward or 360 degree feedback.
- If your goal was to achieve improved staff well-being as measured by your stress risk assessment survey tool, you will need to have run the survey before the intervention and to run it again after the intervention to see if there has been a change.
- If your goal was to achieve improved staff well-being as measured by reduced (stress-related) sickness absence, then it will be a matter of ensuring that sickness absence recording is happening and is accurate, then monitoring it over time. It may be helpful to talk to the team/person that collects absence data to work out over what timescales you should make your comparisons.
- If your goal was to achieve reduced staff turnover, fewer grievances, fewer employment tribunal cases or other management indicators, again the key is to ensure that the relevant statistics are being recorded effectively and to monitor changes over time. Again, it may be helpful to talk to the team/person that collects this data to work out over what timescales you should make your comparisons.

As well as measuring these desired outcomes, it may also be useful to look at whether the activity or intervention has yielded additional, unexpected benefits and how the process itself has been perceived.

- *Additional, unexpected benefits*: At evaluation time, it is worth thinking broadly about the impact your activities have had. For example, you may find that what you have done has improved communication between internal practitioners such as HR, Health & Safety, Occupational Health and Learning & Development: this may lead to better multi-disciplinary working on other projects or in other areas. Another unexpected benefit might be that the establishment of a steering group may have led to new ideas on other initiatives related to management or well-being. Perhaps running the process has given you new skills and insights. What other positive outcomes can you spot?
- *Process evaluation*: As well as looking at the outcomes achieved, it can be helpful to understand how the process itself has worked. This

can help provide learning for future interventions, about what worked well and not so well, what contextual issues facilitated or impeded the process. It can also indicate what more needs to be done to ensure successful outcomes or maintain impetus. There is a range of ways to evaluate an intervention process, from informal mechanisms, such as noting down your own observations and ad hoc feedback, to more formal processes, such as specifically seeking feedback through interviews, focus groups or questionnaires.

Seeing the links – employee engagement, performance...

Throughout this chapter, we have emphasized that Positive Manager Behaviour is relevant to and offers a potential bridge between people management, management development and staff well-being/stress management. It is possible that its relevance goes broader still.

As covered in Chapter 2, organizations that are well-managed and have high staff well-being, are likely to have higher performance. We would argue that healthy workplaces are essential for *sustained* high performance, as opposed to short-term high performance that is only achieved through excessive pressure and risk of burnout. In addition, Positive Manager Behaviour and good staff well-being may be important for employee engagement. The evidence currently accumulating on what drives employee engagement suggests that the way people are managed is one of the key factors. The UK Government's review of employee engagement (MacLeod and Clarke, 2009) specifically mentions 'engaging managers' as one of the four broad enablers/drivers of high engagement. Much of what the report says about engaging managers fits with the Positive Manager Behaviour framework set out in this book. It may be that, over time, you can show benefits in terms of increased employee engagement and performance from increased Positive Manager Behaviour.

In addition to benefits around engagement and performance, implementing Positive Manager Behaviour initiatives may link to other agendas in which the organization with which you are working is interested. For example, enhancing management skills may link to the skills and education agenda; improving the way staff are treated may be relevant to Corporate Social Responsibility (on the basis that this responsibility starts 'at home'); and showing that the organization emphasizes Positive Manager Behaviour may be a way of enhancing employer brand. Either at the start of the process or at evaluation time, it may be worth reflecting on whether these or similar agendas are pertinent to the organization and how what you are doing to enhance Positive Manager Behaviour might contribute. This may even be one of the ways you achieve buy-in from relevant players too.

Sustaining impetus over time – what more needs to be done?

So, you have completed a Positive Manager Behaviour intervention and conducted an evaluation, what next? How do you maintain your own and others' motivation to keep the activities going? How do you make it sustainable?

The answers to these questions will depend on a range of things. If your evaluation shows that the intervention has achieved a range of beneficial outcomes and has been positively perceived, this will help motivate those driving it and engage others in the organization to continue the success. For example, if you started small, perhaps with one team or department, this may give you the evidence you need to gain buy-in and resources to roll it out more widely. If you have rolled something out fairly broadly already, it may be more about setting up follow-up activities to ensure that managers maintain their positive behaviour. For example, you might want to set up action learning sets for managers to meet and learn from one another, support each other in overcoming barriers etc; or you might want to run refresher days, advanced skills workshops or other events.

Process evaluation can give you some clear guidance on how to improve things and what follow-up might be useful. Our research suggests that it is important to maintain ongoing support to ensure managers are able to develop their skills and overcome the barriers to Positive Manager Behaviour.

In terms of long-term sustainability, the ideal is that Positive Manager Behaviour becomes part of the organizational culture: it is how managers at all levels in the organization expect and are expected to behave. For this to happen effectively there needs to be visible leadership from the top: senior managers need to role-model the behaviours and hold those in the next rank of the management hierarchy accountable for behaving positively as well. Achieving this can be challenging and, if the organization is not already close to it, will not happen overnight. If the organization has stated values and/or specifically looks at the culture it wants to achieve, it may be possible to make Positive Manager Behaviour an explicit part of the picture.

References

MacLeod, D. and Clarke, N. (2009). *Engaging for Success: Enhancing Performance Through Employee Engagement.* A report to the UK Government, available at www.berr.gov.uk/whatwedo/employment/employee-engagement/index.html.

Appendix

Preventing Stress in Organizations: How to Develop Positive Managers,
Emma Donaldson-Feilder, Joanna Yarker and Rachel Lewis.
© 2011 John Wiley & Sons, Ltd. Published 2011 by John Wiley & Sons, Ltd.

Table A1. Blank Positive Manager Behaviour table for use in mapping against the organization with which you are working's management/leadership framework

Cluster	Do (✓)/ Don't (✕)	Competency: Respectful and responsible – Managing emotions and having integrity	
		Examples of manager behaviour	Relevant behaviours from framework
Integrity	✓	▪ Is a good role model ▪ Treats team members with respect ▪ Is honest	
	✕	▪ Says one thing, then does something different ▪ Speaks about team members behind their backs	
Managing emotions	✓	▪ Acts calmly in pressured situations ▪ Takes a consistent approach to managing	
	✕	▪ Is unpredictable in mood ▪ Passes on stress to employees ▪ Panics about deadlines ▪ Takes suggestions for improvement as a personal criticism	
Considerate approach	✕	▪ Makes short term demands rather than allowing planning ▪ Creates unrealistic deadlines ▪ Gives more negative than positive feedback ▪ Relies on others to deal with problems ▪ Imposes 'my way is the only way' ▪ Shows a lack of consideration for work–life balance	

Source: Yarker, Donaldson-Feilder and Lewis (2008)
© Crown Copyright 2008

Table A2. Blank Positive Manager Behaviour table for use in mapping against the organization with which you are working's management/leadership framework

Cluster	Do (✓)/Don't (×)	Examples of manager behaviour	Relevant behaviours from framework
		Competency: Managing and communicating existing and future work	
Proactive work management	✓	■ Clearly communicates employee job objectives ■ Develops action plans ■ Monitors team workload on an ongoing basis ■ Encourages team to review how they organize their work ■ Stops additional work being taken on when necessary ■ Works proactively ■ Sees projects/tasks through to delivery ■ Reviews processes to see if work can be improved ■ Prioritises future workloads	
Problem solving	✓	■ Deals rationally with problems ■ Follows up problems on team's behalf ■ Deals with problems as soon as they arise	
	×	■ Is indecisive at decision making	
Participative/ empowering	✓	■ Gives employees the right level of responsibility ■ Correctly judges when to consult and when to make a decision ■ Keeps employees informed of what is happening in the organization ■ Acts as a mentor ■ Delegates work equally ■ Helps team members develop in their role ■ Encourages team participation ■ Provides regular team meetings	
	×	■ Gives too little direction to employees	

Source: Yarker, Donaldson-Feilder and Lewis (2008)
© Crown Copyright 2008

Table A3. Blank Positive Manager Behaviour table for use in mapping against the organization with which you are working's management/leadership framework

Cluster	Do (✓)/Don't (×)	Examples of manager behaviour	Relevant behaviours from framework
		Competency: Managing the individual within the team	
Personally accessible	✓	▪ Speaks personally rather than uses email ▪ Provides regular opportunities to speak one to one ▪ Returns calls/emails promptly ▪ Is available to talk to when needed	
Sociable	✓	▪ Brings in treats ▪ Socializes with the team ▪ Is willing to have a laugh at work	
Empathetic engagement	✓	▪ Encourages employee input in discussions ▪ Listens when employees ask for help ▪ Makes an effort to find out what motivates employees at work ▪ Tries to see team member's point of view ▪ Takes an interest in team's life outside work ▪ Regularly asks 'how are you?' ▪ Treats all team members with equal importance	
	×	▪ Assumes rather than checks employees are OK	

Source: Yarker, Donaldson-Feilder and Lewis (2008)
© Crown Copyright 2008

Table A4. Blank Positive Manager Behaviour table for use in mapping against the organization with which you are working's management/leadership framework

	Competency: Reasoning/Managing difficult situations		
Cluster	Do (✓)/ Don't (×)	Examples of manager behaviour	Relevant behaviours from framework
Managing conflict	✓	■ Acts as mediator in conflict situations ■ Deals with squabbles before they become arguments ■ Deals objectively with conflicts ■ Deals with conflicts head on	
	×	■ Acts to keep the peace rather than resolve issues	
Use of organizational resources	✓	■ Seeks advice from other managers when necessary ■ Uses HR as a resource to help deal with problems ■ Seeks help from occupational health when necessary	
Taking responsibility for resolving issues	✓	■ Follows up conflicts after resolution ■ Supports employees through incidents of abuse ■ Makes it clear they will take ultimate responsibility if things go wrong	
	×	■ Doesn't address bullying	

Source: Yarker, Donaldson-Feilder and Lewis (2008)
© Crown Copyright 2008

Index

Note: Page numbers in italics refer to tables and figures. Aberrations used: PMB for Positive Manager Behaviour

Preventing Stress in Organizations: How to Develop Positive Managers,
Emma Donaldson-Feilder, Joanna Yarker and Rachel Lewis.
© 2011 John Wiley & Sons, Ltd. Published 2011 by John Wiley & Sons, Ltd.